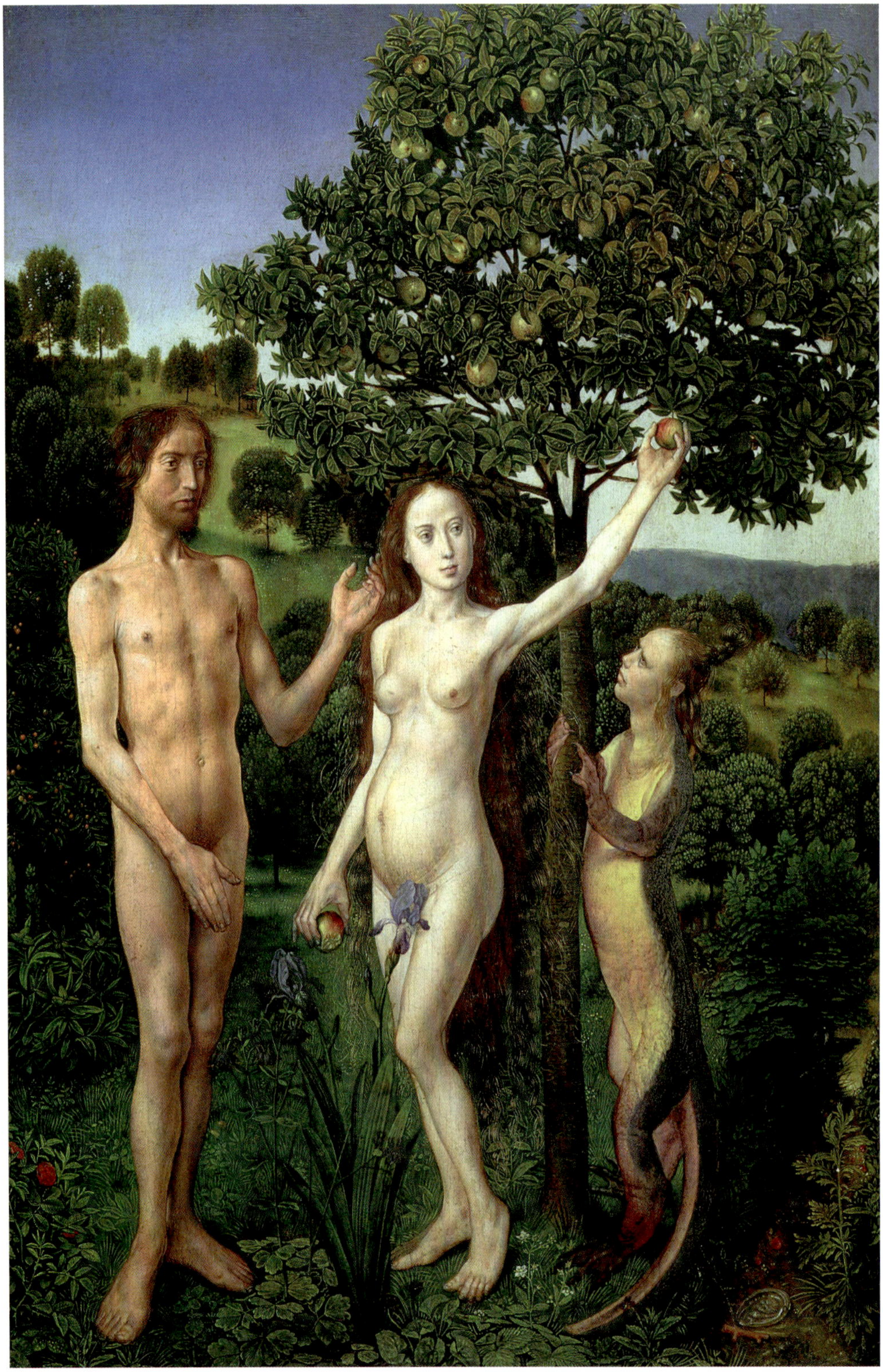

The QUEST for PARADISE

Gardens, past, present and future

Saba Risaluddin

NIYOGI
BOOKS

Published by
NIYOGI BOOKS
D-78, Okhla Industrial Area, Phase-I
New Delhi-110 020, INDIA
Tel: 91-11-26816301, 49327000
Fax: 91-11-26810483, 26813830
email: niyogibooks@gmail.com
website: www.niyogibooksindia.com

Editor and design: Malini Saigal

ISBN: 978-93-81523-78-0
Publication: 2013

Printed at: Niyogi Offset Pvt. Ltd., New Delhi, India

For Risal, who loved this book,
but did not live to see it in print

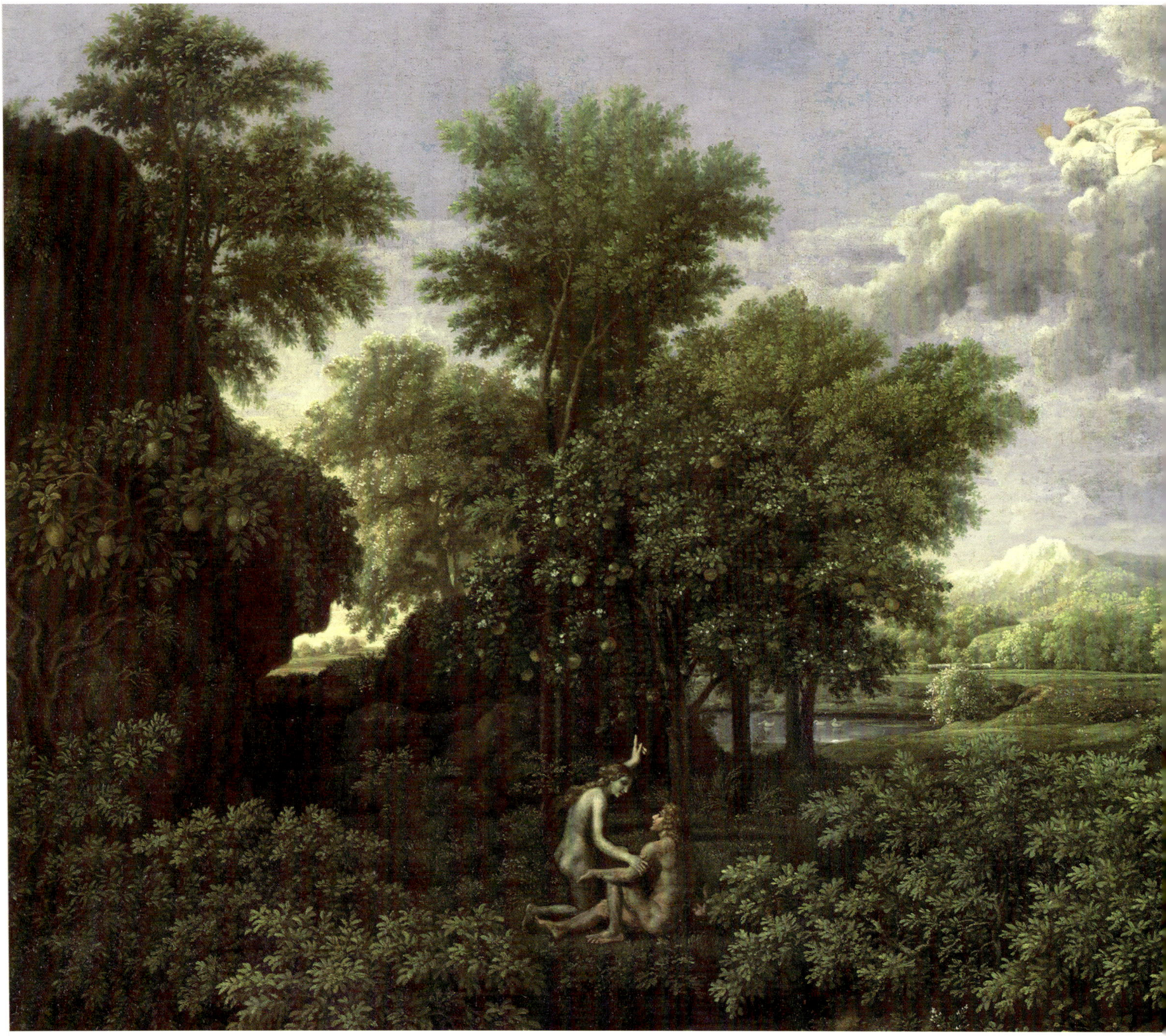

Above: *Nicolas Poussin (1594–1665), Spring, from the Four Seasons, painted for the Duc de Richelieu in Rome between 1660 and 1664.* Illus. 2 and Title page: *Hugo van der Goes (d.1482), The Fall of Man. Kunsthistorisches Museum, Vienna. "Now the serpent was more subtil than any beast of the field which the Lord God had made. . . And the woman said, The serpent beguiled me, and I did eat." (Genesis 3,1 and 13).*

Introduction

All of us live, knowingly or unknowingly, enmeshed in myth. Myths are a way of making sense of this disordered world, in which hardship and adversity are the common experience. One of the most fundamental and compelling myths is the myth of the lost paradise – of a place where, in contrast to hostile and threatening nature, all is ordered, beautiful and fruitful. In the paradise myth, more than any other, the sense of loss and disconnection is assuaged by beauty. It is not only nostalgic for lost perfection, but also consolatory, looking forward to a reward after death; time as we know it in this world ceases to have meaning, as we dream of an elusive moment in a place which is no place, when all was, or shall be, perfect.

For millennia, mankind saw the march of time as a steady decline from the age when there was a golden race of men, living in an Eden where all was perfect. But the golden race gave way to baser metal, and Eden was lost through mankind's fault. Mythological time is a way of escaping from the inexorability of this degeneration. It is measured differently from linear time: it is recurrent, cyclical, circular, and events which occur within mythological time may, if certain rituals are properly performed, be recreated. We know that bodily we are born, live and die within linear time, but the myth of a perfect origin which we have lost and to which we shall return was universal, at least in pre-modern times. One of the questions this book poses – without presuming to have an answer – is whether the myth still retains its potency; and if not, what can we set in its place. And it does so through the metaphor of the garden, the *locus amoenus*, an idealized place where all is well.

I have tried throughout this book to set the wider context for the garden as the expression of the quest for paradise. Directly or indirectly, many religious, spiritual, intellectual and artistic movements have influenced the making of gardens, both real and imaginary, as an expression of the paradise impulse, however little it may have been consciously recognized. It is a single, frail strand in the history of human thought in which myth, as an attempt to interpret the ancient perplexities of mankind, slowly develops into philosophical, hermetic and scientific speculation, but never entirely renounces its hold on our hearts and minds.

The twin concepts which merged to create the idea of Paradise – the dream of a flawless garden, attainable only by heroes or the blessed, and the nostalgia for a golden age, long past – are already present in the ancient classical civilizations, inheritors of the great myth-makers and myth-sayers. In certain spiritual traditions, the lost paradise is explicitly imagined as a garden – indeed, the very word derives from the Old Persian *pairidaeza*, meaning simply an enclosed garden. Later, however, it gave rise to the Greek *paradeisos* and Latin *paradisus*, as well as the Hebrew *pardes* and Arabic *firdaus*, leading us into the world of the spirit. It seems that there is a direct, if subtle, connection between gardens and the life of the spirit, in its striving to attain knowledge and wisdom. Here, perhaps, is where myth, gnosis and reason meet. The emergence of philosophy is associated with gardens; the Academy was no arid, dusty hall of learning, but was set in the grove where Athena's sacred olive trees grew. Later, as the monastic tradition developed in Christianity, the cloister garden came to provide peaceful security conducive to contemplative thought.

As the Hellenic and Judaeo-Christian traditions develop and influence one another, the word paradise

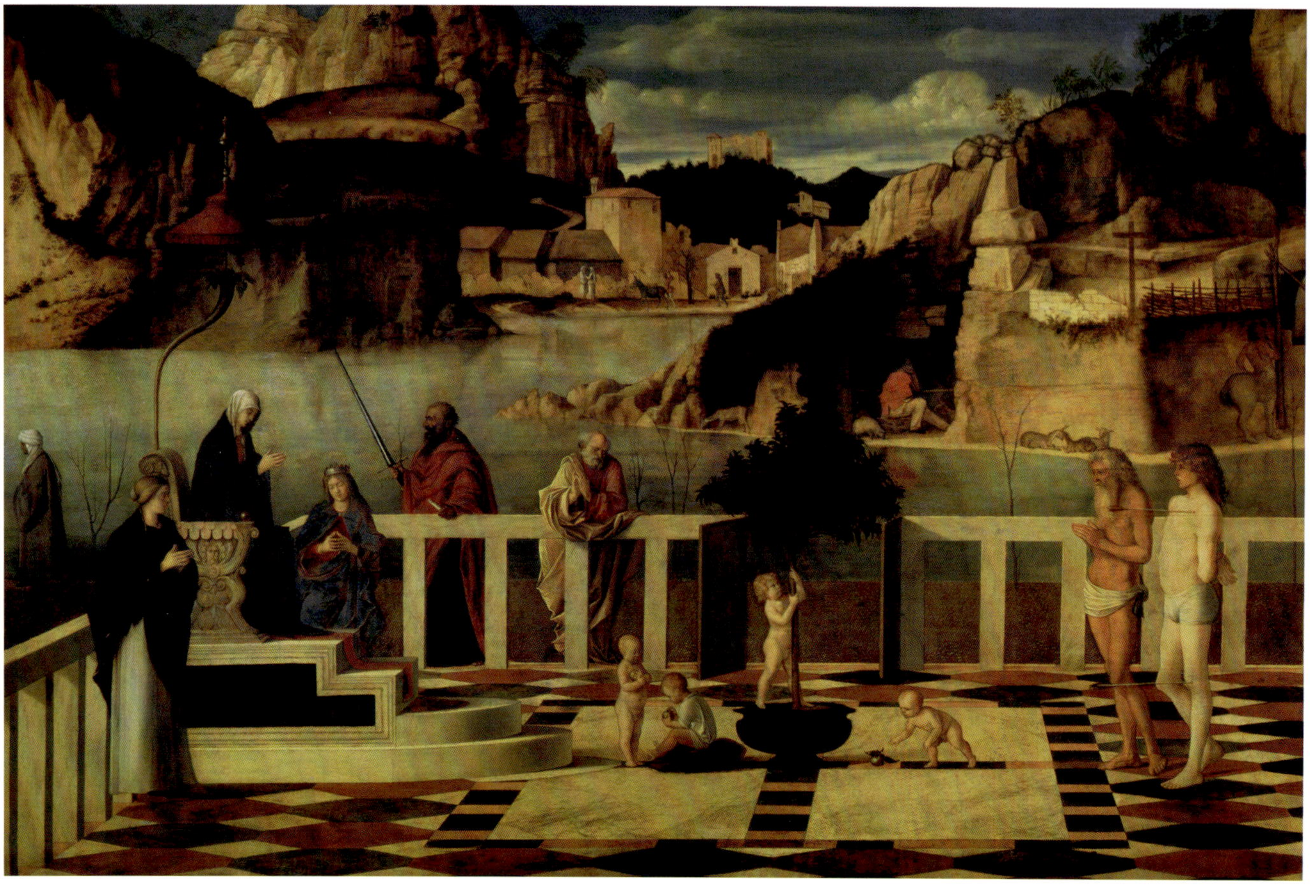

Illus. 1 *Giovanni Bellini (1430–1516), Allegory of the Progress of the Soul. Uffizi Gallery, Florence. In this painting, the twin concepts of Paradise meet in images of the Golden Age and of the Christian paradise mingled: saints stand and cupids play in a marble-paved court with a cosmic cross design and the tree of life in the centre, while beyond lies one of the most beautiful natural landscapes of the Quattrocentro, with a centaur lurking near the Cross.*

acquires a multiple freight of meaning: the royal garden of the Persians, the Hebrew Bible's earthly paradise or Garden of Eden and the enclosed garden of the Song of Songs, and the heavenly paradise of the New Testament.

In the Judaeo-Christian traditions the lost paradise came to be identified with the Garden of Eden, no longer seen only as a terrestrial paradise but also as the heavenly abode of the blessed. The Qur'an, the culmination of the Abrahamic revelation, repeatedly describes the reward of the righteous as a beautiful garden, shaded with trees, refreshed with rivers of pure water, milk, honey, and wine that does not intoxicate, and endowed with abundant fruits. This is the Qur'anic *jannah*, which is of course the Arabized form of *Gan Eden*, the Garden of Eden of Genesis. *"And the Lord God planted a garden eastward in Eden"* is transformed, over the centuries, into the often-repeated Qur'anic *"Surely the God-wary shall be in a station secure among gardens and fountains."*

The Qur'anic paradise also promises sinless sexuality to the faithful – to the outrage of Christian polemicists, who characterized Islam as a licentious faith, while themselves remaining inattentive to the *Song of Songs*, a supreme example of the fusion of the erotic and the spiritual, pervaded by images of the beloved as a garden. Religions often seek to control sexuality, yet, as Hindus know well, eroticism may itself be one of the faces of religion. The elaborate language of symbolism in later mystical poetry, in which flowers, trees, gardens are ever-present, above all in the Islamic tradition, is capable of interpretation equally as the expression of romantic love or of mystical yearning for union with God.

Perhaps the Christian polemicists were subconsciously unable to accept that *jannah*, unlike many other paradises, is apparently otherwise flawless. For dangerous powers lurk in paradise, almost always in the form of a serpent or dragon, the guardian of the sacred. Hercules slays the guardian dragon Ladon who lies coiled about the sacred tree, to reach the golden apples of the Hesperides in Hera's far-western orchard. In the Indian traditions too, the serpent retains its original role of guardian of a sacred spring or tree, the source of immortality. In the Vedo-Brahmanic cosmology, a Naga, a holy water snake, lies coiled around the roots of the sacred tree that grows on Mount Meru. To the Chinese, dragons – here too, often associated with water – are beneficent creatures. In the Biblical story, Eve is tempted by the serpent, who has become the personification of perfidy, a reflection of the dark side of the human psyche.

The fluidity of antique myth, protean and kaleidoscopic, gives way within and between the great Abrahamic faiths to a struggle between rival fixed interpretations, contesting dogmas. The eastern religions, meeting the challenge of human fallibility and mortality with the notion of reincarnation or seeking to circumvent the cycle of death and renewal by attaining nirvana, are often seen as fundamentally *other* than the Abrahamic faiths. Yet here too, gardens may be the reward of the righteous after their passage through life on this earth. In ancient Chinese belief there were three Mystic Isles located off the coast of Shantung, steeply mountainous, where trees bore pearl and gemstone blossoms and fruit that brought immortality to those who ate them. These beliefs blended later with Buddhist notions of the heavens above a world of mountain ranges and seas. The dwelling place of the immortals is a fabled mountain topped by a jade palace and surrounded by magnificent gardens; the souls of the just find eternity in the Land of Extreme Felicity in the west, where the trees have branches of precious stones, and lakes floored with golden sand are filled with lotuses.

The lotus is invested with powerful symbolism in the eastern tradition, for on earth it grows not from golden sand but from slime, emerging unsullied through the life-giving water – as the soul escapes, ultimately pure, from the trammels of earthly existence. Symbolism is an integral part – one might even say, the very essence – of every religion. For long before religions became a way of controlling human behaviour, and thereby laid themselves open to cooption by temporal powers, the spiritual life of mankind was expressed above all in symbols, myths and images.

Even as the mediaeval mindset began to yield to the modern, the quest for the perfect origin continued. The Renaissance prince Cosimo de Medici (1389-1464), who revived the Platonic tradition of the Academy in a garden, believed – wrongly – that the *Corpus hermeticum* which we shall meet in Chapter II represented the primordial revelation, preceding that of Moses and inspiring Pythagoras, Plato and the Persian Magi. Perhaps it is the very power of symbolism and myth that has led mankind to build a counter-myth of the supremacy of the rational mind. The counter-myth struggles for dominance again and again: with the Greek philosophers, with Descartes (1596-1650), with the Enlightenment.

Another creation of the Renaissance and the Reformation was the idea of utopia. By now, the idea of paradise had evolved from myth to religious belief and doctrine, but as simple belief came under assault from new ideas, the myth resurfaced

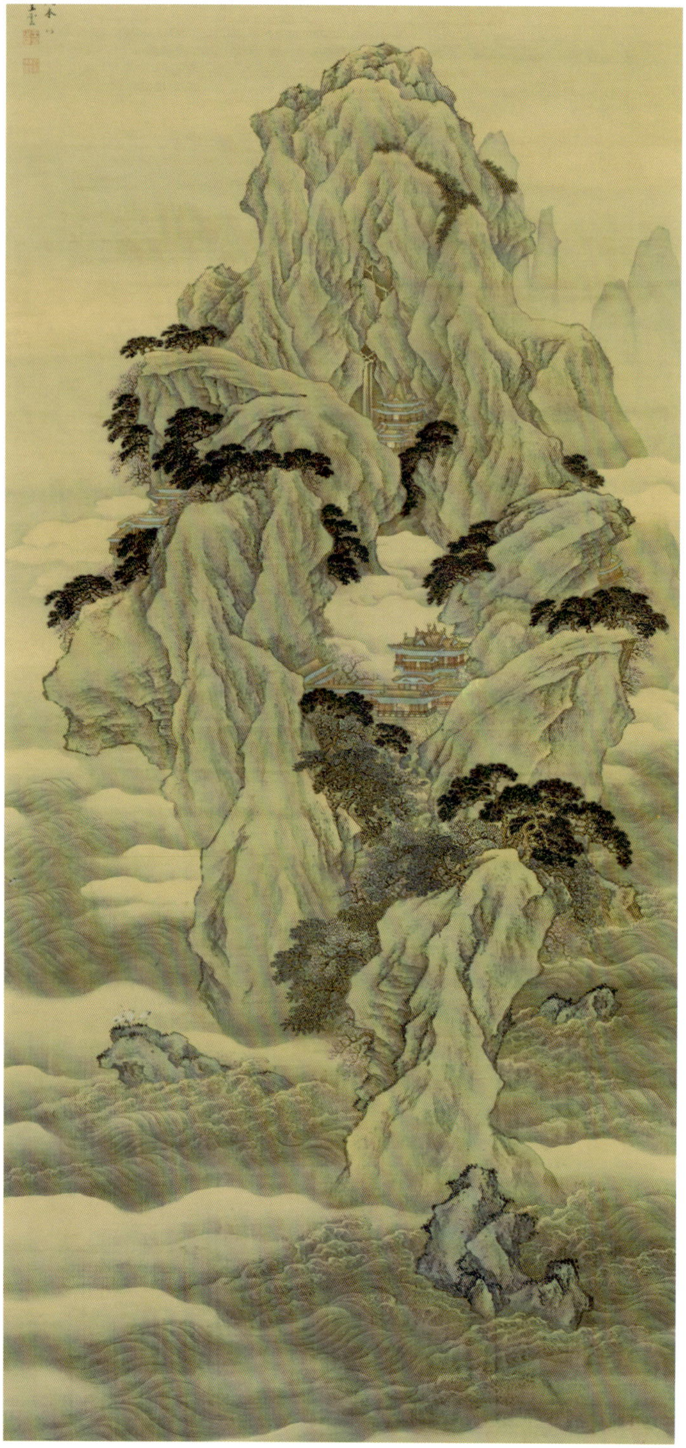

Illus. 3 *Wang Yun (1652-1735 or later), The Fanghu Isle of the Immortals, 1699, Qing dynasty.*

in a different form. Ever since Sir Thomas More wrote his *Utopia* (1516), an allegory of a fictional, seemingly perfect island society, for which he drew both on Plato's *Republic* and the Judaeo-Christian paradise, it has been a constant presence in the Western psyche. This was also the time of the great navigators, seeking new routes for the spice trade but also hoping to discover Eden on earth – Columbus even thought he had found it – or the means of recreating it.

Civilization was becoming firmly identified with the city. As belief in the earthly existence of the lost paradise waned, the power of its artificial image, the enchanted garden, to lure men away from their duty also faded; instead, all that was both alluring and dangerous came to be identified with the city. Here were not only great achievements of the human spirit, but also both the illicit pleasures of the flesh and a dehumanizing environment of grinding poverty, illness and toil. Escape lay, for the privileged few, in the villa garden or the idealized cottage plot, or in a rejection of the very notion of the lost paradise as desirable. Among those who held a jaundiced view of the Garden of Eden was the essayist Charles Lamb (1775-1834), who wrote in a letter to Wordsworth that "A garden was the primitive prison till man with Promethean felicity and boldness luckily sinned himself out of it." And the Swedenborgian visionary Henry James, father of William and Henry, put it thus: "The first and highest service which Eve renders Adam is to throw him out of Paradise."

In the nineteenth century, the new science of comparative religion was the matrix for a continued search for the origins of mind and spirit, even as scientists were seeking to identify other origins: Charles Darwin (1809-1882) published the *Origin of Species*, Herbert Spencer (1820-1903) his *First Principles*. Scientists learned from fossil evidence and stone tools that life for the first hominids, and for early *Homo sapiens* himself, was by no means paradisal. The life of the hunter-gatherer in the

African savannah or the cave-dweller of the ice-ages was a continual struggle for survival, far removed from the dream of nature as a garden where ripe fruit dropped unasked into the hand. By the mid twentieth century, anthropology had furthered our understanding of human development, with Claude Levi-Strauss's (1908-2009) concept of lost innocence: man has not so much progressed, as become shaped by and imprisoned in deep structures, pre-eminently those of myth. Yet, though scientific advances often depend on an intuitive leap of the mind, the new insistence on trusting only those intuitions which could subsequently be proven by empirical evidence left myth discredited as a means of explaining the world.

The paradise myth, no less than others, has become cruelly distorted by these changing habits of mind and heart. The shift from a frame of mind which sees everything as a symbol of the sacred to the Enlightenment insistence on rationality, and the concomitant erosion of faith, deprives many of both the hope of heaven and the fear of hell. We are left with hell on earth, and a terminally enfeebled paradise myth. It is part of our spiritual and intellectual heritage; but we no longer know what to make of it.

The shift from the sacred to the rational is superficial and frail, though; and rationality has not triumphed. There have always been other voices, other images; poets and artists keep the memory alive, reminding us of a reality that the rational is impotent to describe. Yet, our innocence irrevocably lost, can the myth regain its power over our minds and hearts? And if not, what shall we set in its place, to help us through the dark, oppressive places of our lives?

The unusually fortunate may find paradise on earth; a poor substitute, perhaps, for the inexpressible glories of the mythical paradise, but what use is a paradise in which one cannot believe? In writing this book, I have come to realize that my decision to settle in post-war Sarajevo was an existential choice that had very little to do with the rational; that if paradise on earth is to be found anywhere, for me at least it is in Sarajevo. I found myself, on my first visit to the city, seized by an inexpressible sense of belonging; I understood without knowing it what the old wisdom means when it speaks of sacred places.

My earthly paradise has turned out to be a city – and why not, for the old Germanic and Romanic words that have given us *garden* and *yard* are related to the Old Slavic word *gradu*, which meant both town and garden. We shall meet the same ambiguity in the Christian tradition, where the story begins with the Garden of Eden and ends with the City of God. The intimation of artifice is inescapable: both city and garden imply the human endeavour to impose an external will upon the environment. The expression may differ – ranging from the geometric symmetry of an imagined ideal in contrast with the imperfections of disorderly nature, to the idealized imitation of nature's own impenitently wild beauty; from an enclosed, flower-spangled place of refuge, to the self-assertive modern domination of the countryside and the social order or the new loss of self-confidence of post-modernism. But whatever form it takes, the idea of the garden as perfection is deeply embedded in the human psyche, the locus of our yearnings for that which is beyond our human reach, an expression of refusal to accept that life is incurable and death no more than an ending. We know that it is a dream, and cannot be attained on this earth; that the gardens we make in its image are earned by toil and threatened by drought, pests and the implacability of linear time. The promises of prophets and the songs of poets resound in our ears down the centuries, and the dream lives on – only now, faded by excess of "realism" to a vague nostalgia, it has lost the power to move us spiritually, and we do not yet know what to put in its place.

Saba Risaluddin
Sarajevo, November 2011

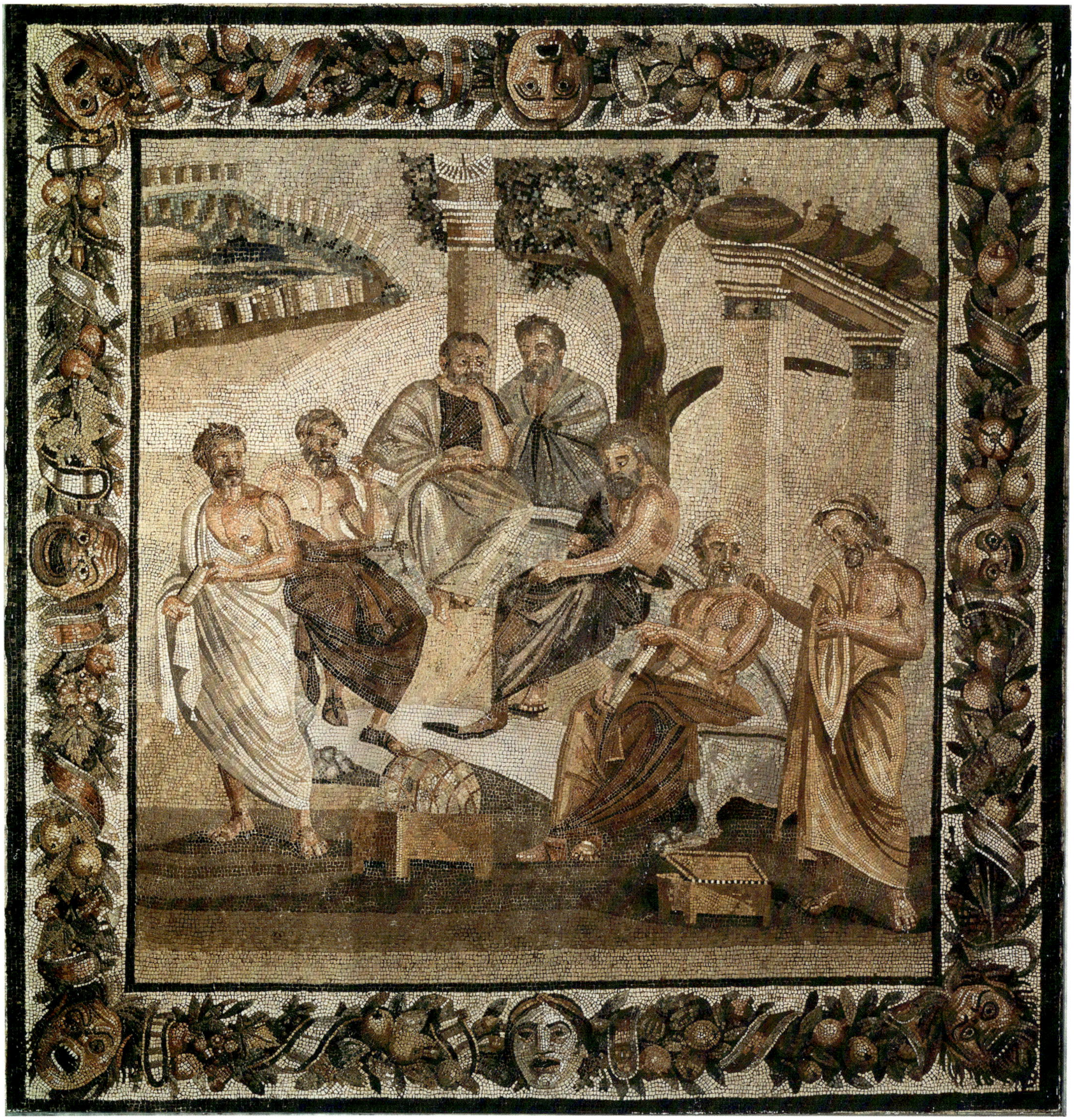

Illus. 7 *Plato's Academy, floor mosaic from the workshops of the bronze sculptor in the Villa of T Siminius Stephanus in Pompeii, late 2nd/early 1st century BCE. Museo Archeologico Nazionale, Naples.*

The Ancient, Pagan World

The first known record of the paradise myth is in cuneiform, the earliest known writing of humankind, on tablets of the Sumerian period (fourth millennium BCE), one of the great civilizations of the dawn of history that arose in the Fertile Crescent. It recounts how the waterless land of Dilmun, where there was no war, disease or old age, was transformed into a true paradise of meadows and fruit trees when Enki, God of Water, ordered the Sun God Utu to water it from beneath the earth. In the garden grew the gesdin tree, standing beside a sacred fountain. This is a garden "eastward in Eden,"[1] a Semitic garden of the dawn, in the land between the two rivers, the land we call Mesopotamia. In this region of extreme insecurity, gardens must indeed have seemed a dream, an unattainable paradise; though many centuries after the time of the Sumerians, Sennacherib (705-681 BCE) claimed to have beautified Nineveh with gardens.

Nineveh was destroyed in 612 BCE by the Babylonians, and Assyria's might was no more. The scene was set for another garden: the fabled hanging gardens of Babylon. Nebuchadnezzar (605-562 BCE) set about restoring the old city of Babylon and, as the story has it, built these gardens for his beloved wife, a Median princess from Ecbatana in the cool Zagros hills, who yearned for the shade of trees to refresh her wilting spirit. A Greek writing some five hundred years later described them as terraced roof gardens.[2]

Of Gods, Kings and Gardens

One after another, during millennia of turbulence, great civilizations rose and fell in Mesopotamia. In contrast, Egypt appeared unchanging as dynasty upon dynasty of Pharaohs succeeded each other. This ancient land had its own rich mythology, its own pantheon of gods. Egyptians such as Neferhotep, Chief Scribe of Amun at Thebes (fourteenth century BCE), whose tomb inscription includes the words "The span of our earthly deeds is as a dream; but fair is the welcome that awaits him who has reached the hills of the West," dedicated immense resources to ensuring that their dead were properly provided for in the life to come.

In ancient Egypt, the cult temple was the dwelling-place of the god to whom it was dedicated; it represented heaven, the universe, and the land of Egypt. To honour the god with a cool and pleasant place where he could refresh himself, the temple must be set in a sacred landscape with an orchard and a palm-fringed lake where lotus and papyrus grew. For the god's further delectation, he was offered fragrant flowers, grown in the temple gardens. Queen Hatshepsut (1489-1460 BCE) commissioned an expedition to Punt to bring thirty-one frankincense or myrrh trees "for the majesty of this god Amun, Lord of Thebes."[3] Her journey is illustrated in the temple at Karnak, which she extolled as "the heavens abiding on their four pillars." Her co-monarch Tuthmosis III (c. 1490-1436 BCE) made many expeditions, returning from one of them with plants that he immortalized by having a series of reliefs depicting them carved on the walls of the temple at Karnak. The inscription claims that they were "all plants that grow, all flowers that are in God's land."[4] These words echo the Genesis description of Eden, and anticipate by thousands of years the aims of the men who made the first botanic gardens of Europe. Amenhotep III (1405-1349 BCE) built another temple at Karnak, with "an enclosure. . . made to shine with flowers. . . it is planted with all flowers."[5]

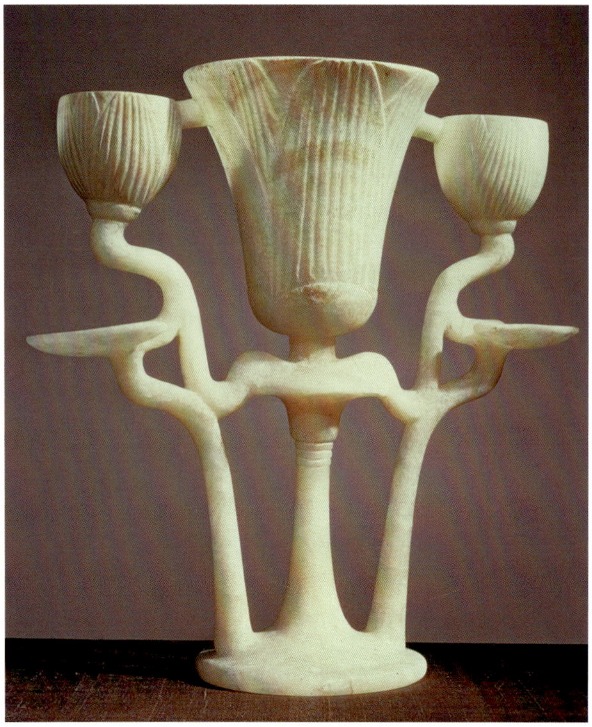

Illus. 4 *Alabaster lamp in the form of three lotus flowers, found in the tomb of the pharaoh Tutankhamun (c. 1341–3123 BCE), Valley of the Kings, Thebes. Egyptian National Museum, Cairo.*

The heretic-king Akhenaten (1379-1336 BCE), who worshipped the one and only sun god Aten, made Amarna into a sun city in his honour. Its fine gardens were echoed in the painted or tiled walls and pavements of the buildings, depicting palm trees, lotus and papyrus and other water plants, olive trees, vines heavy with grapes, and the sycomore fig. These were no mere pleasure gardens, but replete with religious meaning. The northern garden is described as the *maru* of the Aten – the sacred enclosure where the god was "seen" by his priests or by the king. Its lake represented the god Nun, the primeval waters, from which rose the island-mound of creation. Beside the island were offering-pools and a garden, where the offering-flowers grew. The *maru*-Aten represented, then, both the origin of life and the Field of Offerings on the horizon of heaven.

Akhenaten's monotheistic heresy died with him, and his successors again worshipped the traditional gods. The offerings of Ramses III (1198-1166 BCE) to the gods are recorded in the Harris papyrus in the British Museum: flowers in garlands, lotus – most prized of flowers – for the hand, bouquets of papyrus flowers, and blossoms of "garden fragrance." Nor did Ramses have any inhibitions about reminding the gods of his munificence. In the Temple of Ra at Heliopolis he tells the god, "I made for thee groves and arbours containing date trees, lakes supplied with lotus flowers, *isi* flowers, the flowers of every land, *dedmet* flowers, myrrh and sweet and fragrant woods for thy beautiful face."[6]

Osiris, god of the dead, was originally a god of vegetation, who like the Babylonian Tammuz and the Greek Adonis annually died and was resurrected. He was the corn, the vine and the trees, the Nile which rises and falls each year to make fruitful his spouse Isis, the light of the sun which sinks each evening to reappear at dawn. As god of the dead he gave his worshippers the hope of eternal happiness. In the Old and Middle Kingdoms, royal burial grounds were modelled on the tomb of Osiris, in the shape of a chamber covered by a mound, representing creation arising out of the primeval waters. The mound would be shaded by trees, especially the tamarisk, sacred to Osiris; for the king became Osiris when he died, and the god's grove must accompany his tomb. The symbolism persisted into the New Kingdom; Queen Hatshepsut's tomb was also of the Osiris-mound type.

Mere mortals, however influential, did not share the royal fate of dying as Osiris. But they, too, looked forward to an afterlife. A soul that was judged and found to be righteous could expect to be reborn in heaven, in a "garden in the west." The wealthy prepared for the next life, as repeatedly instructed by the Coffin Texts, by building for themselves a "domain in the west," digging pools and planting sycomores. A standard petition inscribed on many

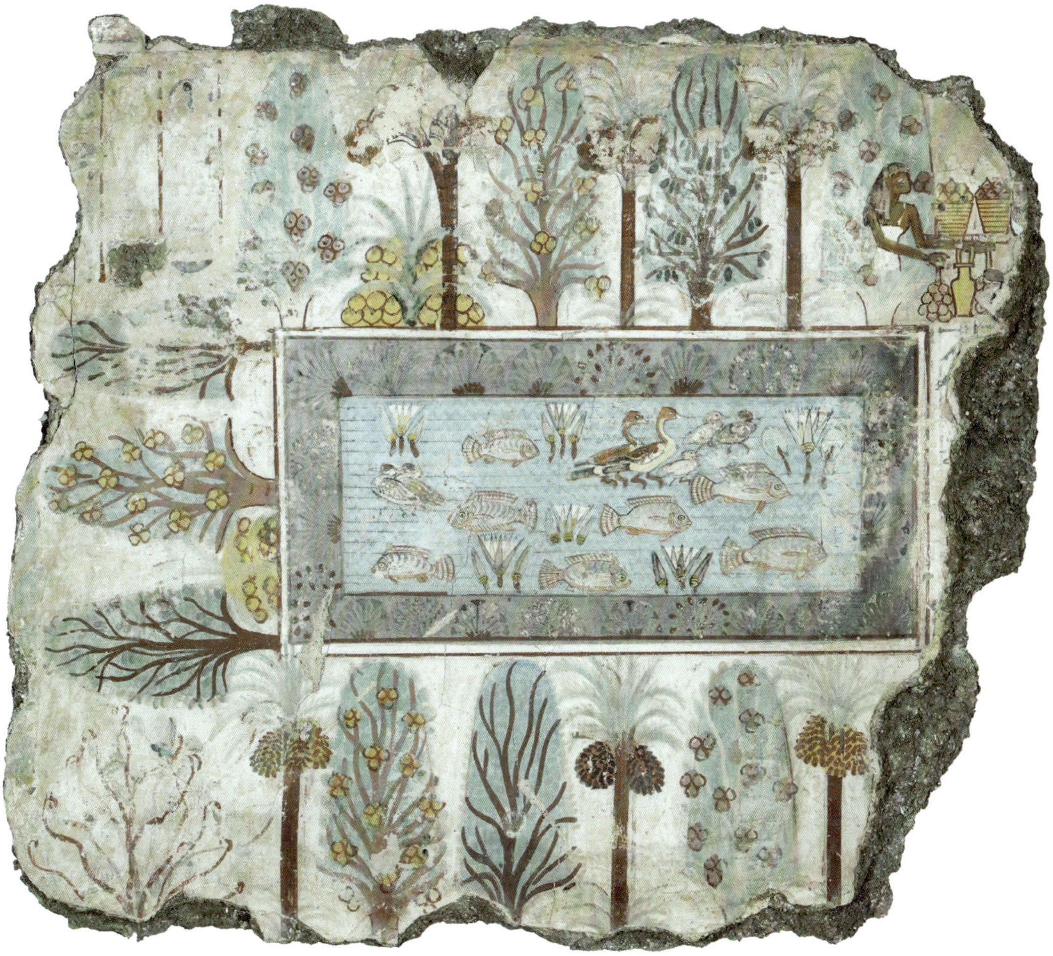

Illus. 5 *A garden pool: fragment of a wall painting from Nebamun's garden at Thebes, c.1400 BCE. British Museum, London.*

tombs of Dynasty XVIII prayed that "I may each day walk unceasingly on the banks of my water, that my soul may repose on the branches of the trees that I have planted, that I may refresh myself under the shade of my sycomore."

Thanks to the tomb paintings of ancient Egypt, we have contemporary impressions of what their gardens – both of this world and of the imagined next – were like. We also have both literary and archaeological evidence of the great royal parks, the original *pairidaeza*, of Persia, which briefly ruled Egypt before itself being conquered by Alexander the Great in 332 BCE.

The Persian *Pairidaeza*

Ancient Persia was a land with its own rich myths, in which the dream of paradise also features. It was the land of the fire-worshipping Magi and of the religious reformer Zoroaster (c. 660-583 BCE). The holy scriptures of the Zoroastrians, the *Avesta*, promise paradise to the faithful; but the *pairidaeza* of Persia was a real garden. The palace and garden of Cyrus II the Great (556-530 BCE), at Pasargadae, formed a single whole, with a geometric layout, stone watercourses, and trees set symmetrically in plots. Much of the layout survives to this day, though largely in ruins. The Greek historian Xenophon describes a later Persian garden in his Socratic Discourse, the *Oeconomicus* of 401 BCE. He relates that the Persian king excelled in the arts of war and of cultivation alike: wherever he lives or travels, "he is concerned that there be gardens, the so-called pleasure gardens, . . . and in these he himself spends most of his time."[7] He also recounts how in 407 BCE the Spartan Lysander, commander of the Peloponnesian Fleet, visited the Persian prince Cyrus the Younger at his palace in Sardis, where he marvelled at the *pairidaeza*:

> *The beauty of the trees all planted at equal intervals. . . in perfect regularity – the rectangular symmetry of the whole and the many sweet scents which hung about them.*

After the death of Cyrus the Great, his tomb, within the precincts of the royal garden, was surrounded by a grove of trees, also planted in a symmetrical design, set in a grassy meadow.

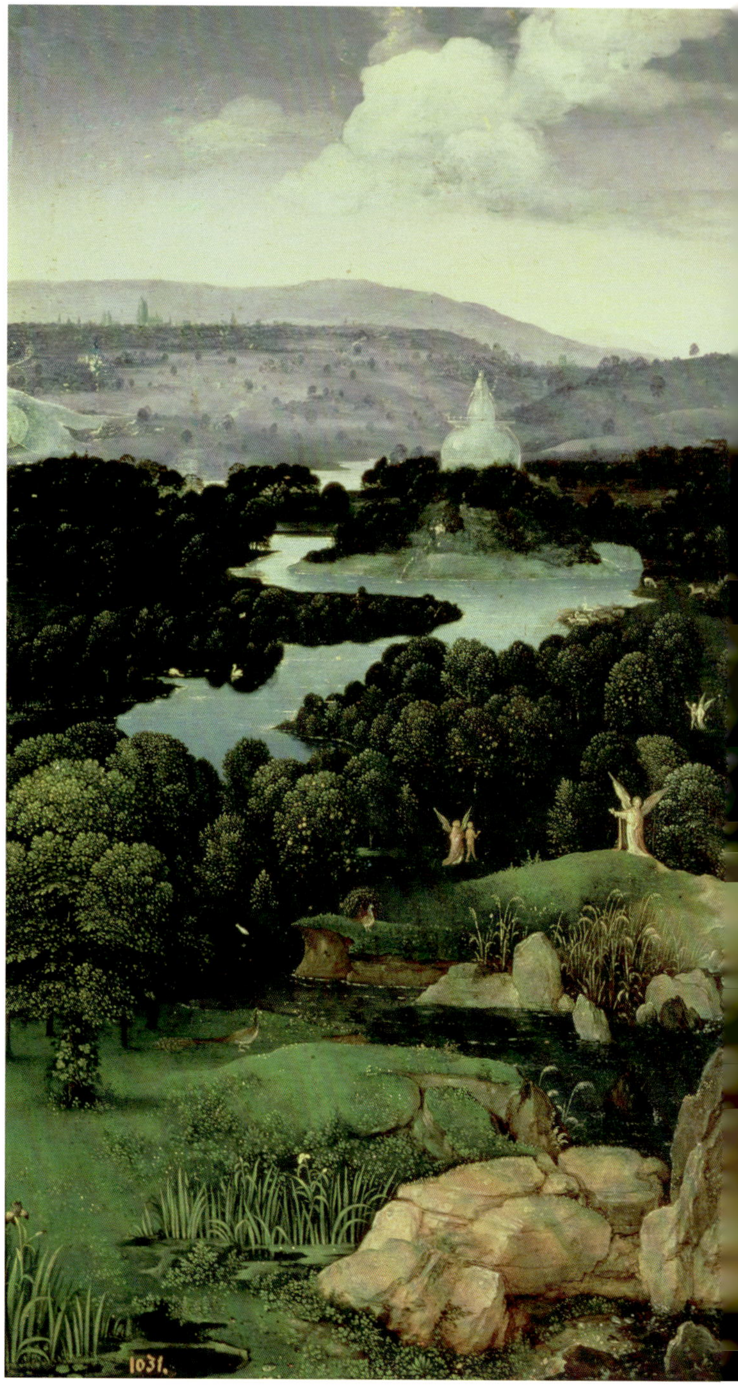

The Paradise Isles

Through the swirl of myths of the ancient Greek world, there emerge the twin ideas of paradise – the nostalgia for a lost Golden Age, and the dream of bliss after death that we hope to earn through virtuous conduct in this life. Hesiod, in his *Works and Days* (mid eighth century BCE), tells us that the first men "lived like gods. . . for the fruitful earth unforced bare them fruit abundantly and without stint."[8] This is a vision of a time when newly-created mankind lived in perfect harmony with nature. The myth was told and re-told by Greeks and Romans, and was still redolent with nostalgia in these words of Ovid (43 BCE – 18 CE), who describes the Golden age when:

> *The teeming Earth, yet guiltless of the plough,*
> *And unprovok'd, did fruitful stores allow:*
> *Content with food, which Nature freely bred,*
> *On wildings and on strawberries they fed;*
> . . .

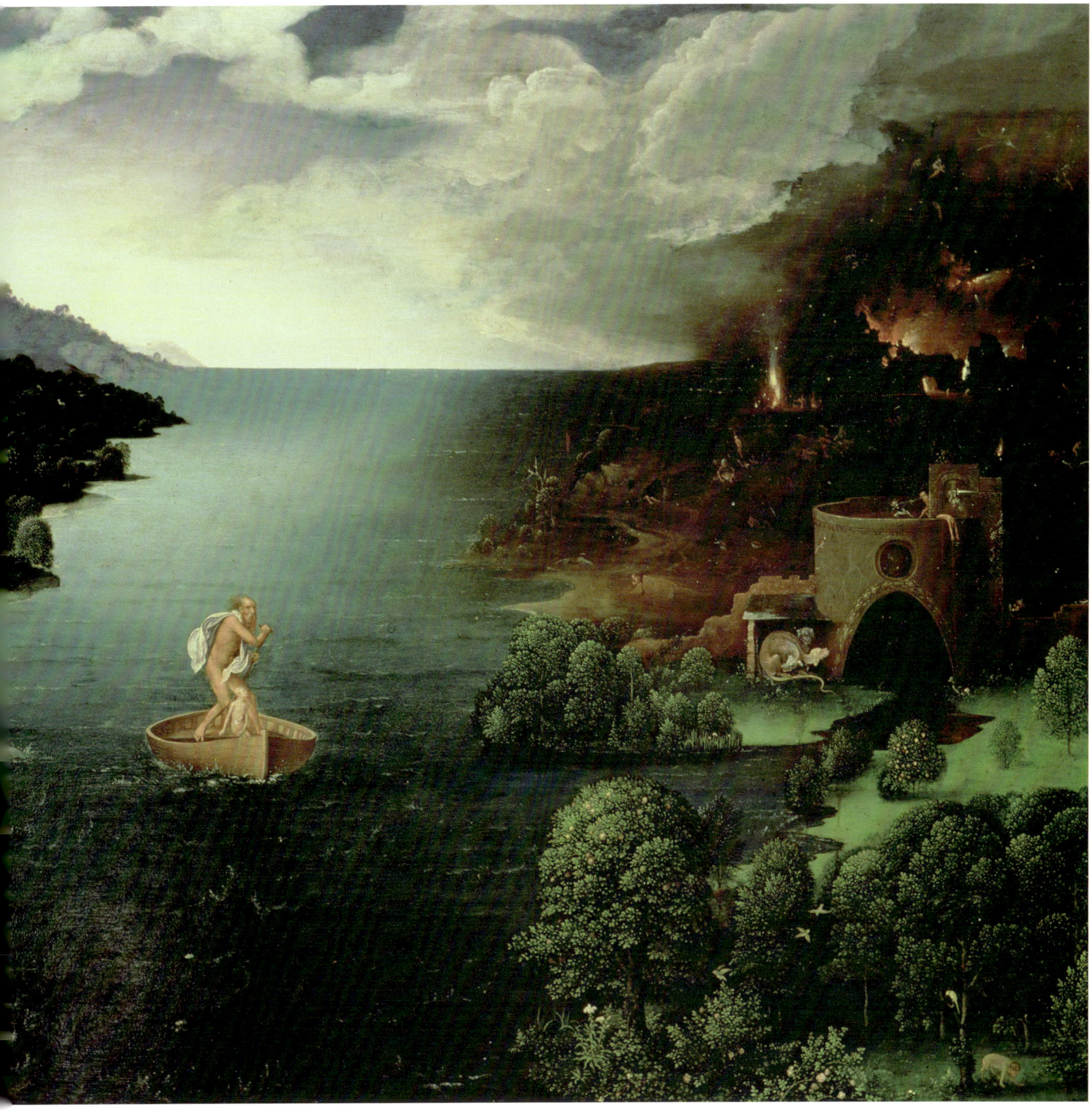

Illus 6 *Joachim Patinir (c. 1480–1524), Charon's Boat. Prado National Museum, Madrid. Charon, official ferryman of the underworld, carries the souls of the dead across the Acheron to hell or to Elysium. The underworld has five rivers: the Acheron, the Cocytus, the Phlegethon, Lethe, and the Styx. Lethe flowed at the edge of the Elysian fields; whoever drank her waters forgot the past.*

The flow'rs unsown, in fields and meadows reign'd:
And Western winds immortal spring maintain'd.
In following years, the bearded corn ensu'd
From Earth unask'd, nor was that Earth renew'd.
From veins of vallies, milk and nectar broke;
And honey sweating through the pores of oak. [9]

But perfection is not for this world, as we all learn in earliest childhood; the idyll could not last. The golden race – which Hesiod associates with the rule of Cronos, father of Zeus – gave way to the silver, and the perpetual vernal climate yielded to a year divided into seasons, bitter winter and blazing summer mocking ephemeral spring. Humankind began to know the hard toil of agriculture.

Death, for those first men, was a mere falling asleep; knowing nothing of hardship in life, they had no need of Paradise after death. But for those who lived after them, it was another matter. By the time of Homer, men seem to have believed in an afterlife that offered neither reward nor punishment, only a bleak existence as effete shades in the underworld, the realm of Hades. The dim Homerian underworld nostalgia for earthly life, in turn, began to give way to a richer and more consoling mythology of the life to come.

Ancient Greek myths are protean, untidy; they offer us many different interpretations of the metaphysical and existential issues which perplex humankind. The myths of the afterlife were no exception. The mythographers Hesiod and Homer, and the many poets of classical Greece and Rome who were inspired by them, tried to reconcile conflicting beliefs. They claimed that the underworld itself held two domains. One was Tartarus, where Hades ruled: an icy, barren land where grew only black poplars, sterile willows and asphodel, that ash-grey funerary flower that blooms even on arid islands. The Homeric *Hymn to Demeter* tells us the story of Persephone, daughter of Demeter the goddess of the ripe corn. Persephone must have loved flowers, for she was picking crocuses, iris and hyacinths, roses and lilies, and was reaching to pluck a fragrant, radiant white narcissus, when Hades snatched her away to his dread kingdom. But even in the frozen wastes of Tartarus there were shadow gardens, with pomegranate trees, and a gardener, Ascalaphus, to tend them, who saw Persephone absently eating a few of the juicy-sharp, cinnabar-red seeds from the fruit that Hades offered her to ensure her return.

The other domain of the underworld described by Homer was Elysium, ruled over by Cronos. This was the dwelling place of the souls of the virtuous, which Homer located at the world's end, a land of perpetual day where snow, storm and tempest were unknown. Here the only wind that fanned the Elysian Fields was Zephyrus, god of the west wind, blowing gentle, refreshing airs from the ocean. Homer's account of the life of bliss in the Elysian Fields, promised to Menelaus, was echoed and amplified by later classical writers such as Virgil and Pindar. Virgil (70-19 BCE) describes the shady woods, soft river-banks and fresh, stream-watered meadows where, in "an ampler air [that] clothes the plains with brilliant light,"[10] the Blest live in the fields of joy of Elysium. And in a threnody of which a fragment survives, Pindar describes the abode of the righteous after death:

the red rose meadows about their city are heavy with the shadowy incense tree and golden fruits.[11]

In the far west, too, in the land of the setting sun, lay the garden of Hera, on the slopes of Mount Atlas, beyond the ocean. Here the Hesperides, the nymphs of the west, guarded the golden apples that had been the wedding gift of the Earth Mother Gaia, the Great Goddess, to her grand-daughter Hera, daughter of Cronos, on her marriage to her brother Zeus. The garden of Hera was, we may surmise, an orchard, where ripe fruit was always to hand. Though the Elysian Fields seem to have been an open meadow, the name Elysium, as Robert Graves suggests,[12] may derive from the pre-Gallic word *alisier*, a sorb-apple, and Elysium would then mean apple-land. The apple is itself a potent symbol, linking the land of the setting sun to Aphrodite, the goddess born of the sea-foam. The setting sun is an apple, golden deepening to crimson, sinking into the western ocean where the Hesperides guard Hera's orchard of golden apples. And when the sun has gone, Hesperus, the evening star, appears in the sky. Hesperus is Aphrodite's star; and an apple, cut in half across, reveals the five-pointed star at its heart.

As time passed, the underworld came to be thought of not merely as the land of the dead, but as a place where souls were judged. Hesiod had already associated the golden race with the Isles of the Blessed on the far shore of the ocean, where the original perfection still exists in perpetuity. Cronos, lord of that blissful, innocent time, was carried off by Zeus to those Isles, where he still rules, and where the heroes live under his rule. Like Homer's Elysium, home of the souls of the virtuous, the Isles are located at the world's end. The poet Pindar introduced the idea of the easeful life on the Isles as a reward for those who lived a righteous and pure life, and for the souls of heroes favoured by the gods. They find rest at the furthermost edge of the world, where, Pindar tells us, "round the islands of the blest the ocean-breezes blow, and golden flowers are glowing, some from the land on trees of splendour."[13]

Sanctuary Gardens in Ancient Greece

Paradise has become no longer merely a wistful dream, a memory of a distant, mythical past; it now has the power to console, for it may be earned, by just conduct in this life.

Greek literature has also bequeathed to us some magnificent descriptions of gardens and idealized landscapes. These were exemplars of ideal harmony and peace; sanctuaries, where mortals could experience an epiphany, could communicate with the gods. They are not paradises in the sense the word now bears, of a place of lost innocence or future reward for a virtuous life; but in contributing to the Judaeo-Christian concept of the earthly paradise, they became, as it were, retrospectively paradisiac. The most famous is Homer's description, in the *Odyssey*, of the gardens of Alcinous, king of Corcyra (Corfu). This very down-to-earth account of the estate, with its orchard, vineyard and vegetable beds surrounded by a hedge, is interwoven with echoes of the golden age of perpetual spring and unfailing harvest. A literary stereotype, perhaps; but stereotypes do not arise in a vacuum, and maybe there had been a royal garden, which survived in folk memory. We know that the Homeric stories drew upon a long oral tradition of praise-singers and poets; why should they not recall a great garden as well as the deeds of heroes? Here is Alexander Pope's translation:

Close to the gates a spacious garden lies,
From storms defended, and inclement skies:
Four acres was th'allotted space of ground,
Fenced with a green enclosure all around.
Tall thriving trees confessed the fruitful mold;
The red'ning apple ripens here to gold,
Here the blue fig with luscious juice o'erflows,
With deeper red the full pomegranate glows,
The branch here bends beneath the weighty pear,
And verdant olives flourish round the year.
The balmy spirit of the western gale
External breathes on fruits untaught to fail:
Each dropping pear a following pear supplies,
On apples apples, figs on figs arise:
The same mild season gives the blooms to blow,
The buds to harden, and the fruits to grow.
Here ordered vines in equal ranks appear
With all th'united labours of the year,

Some to unload the fertile branches run,
Some dry the black'ning clusters in the sun,
Others to tread the liquid harvest join,
The groaning presses foam with floods of wine.
Here are the vines in early flow'r descried,
Here grapes discoloured on the sunny side,
And there in autumn's richest purple dyed.
Beds of all various herbs, for ever green,
In beauteous order terminate the scene.[14]

The lyric poet Ibycus, a contemporary of Sappho from the early sixth century BCE, describes another garden. The sense of a sacred space still echoes in his words, but by now the seasons have taken their normal course, for as he writes:

'Tis but in Spring the quince trees of the Maids' holy garden grow green with the watering rills from the river, and the vine-blossoms wax 'neath the mantling sprays of the vines.[15]

There are many descriptions of gardens and idealized landscapes in the Greek poetry of Theocritus (c. 310 – c. 250 BCE), author of the *Idylls* and creator of bucolic or pastoral poetry, with its sense of ease and fulfilment amid bountiful Nature. He and other early pastoral poets often associated their landscapes with love; and this was to influence the Christian vision of the earthly paradise, as well as poets seeking a setting for Love allegorized or Love profane.

The Philosophers' Garden

As time passed, the myths of the gods and heroes began to fill not only with religious but also with philosophical meaning. For the future of Greek thought lay with the philosophers, not the myth-makers. In the fifth century Athens was beautified by the aristocratic statesman, Cimon of Athens. The Agora was planted with plane trees; trees and shrubs in pots were set to adorn temples such as the Temple of Hephaestus (Theseum) on the west side of the Agora. And the Academy, Plutarch tells us, was converted by Cimon from "a dry and unsightly plat; he brought water to it, and sheltered it with groves, so that it abounded with clean alleys and shady walks."[16] Tradition has it that here too grew twelve olive trees sacred to Athena.

Thus groves of trees became not only the sacred space around a temple or oracle, but also the setting for philosophical discussion. Two generations after Cimon, Socrates' brilliant pupil Plato (c. 429-327 BCE) expounded the philosophy of the immortality of the soul, and the judgment passed after death, at the Academy. The resting place of souls that have yet to become eternally discarnate is described by Plato as the "true earth,"[17] an earthly paradise where the colours of trees and flowers and even common stones are brighter and purer than on this earth. We catch a glimpse of its beauty in the precious metals and stones that are so rare here, gold and silver, cornelian and jasper and emerald, mere chips from the mountains of the true earth. Aristotle (384-322 BCE), like Socrates before him, taught in the Lyceum outside the city walls, "in the shady walks of the divine Hecademus." The idea caught on. Aristotle's pupil Theophrastus (c. 370-285 BCE), to whom Aristotle had entrusted the study of botany, left his garden in his will to his friends "to study literature and philosophy there in common."[18] Epicurus, the Philosopher of the Garden (341-271 or 270 BCE), whose academy was close to Plato's, also left instructions in his will for the maintenance of his garden, on which he spent huge sums.

When they were not philosophizing in the shade of their trees, the Greeks were often at war with neighbouring tribes, or with their powerful enemy the Persians. As we have seen, the Persians had a rich tradition of royal parks and gardens. Some years after his Persian expedition in 401 BCE, the historian Xenophon of Athens – he who described the *pairidaeza* of Cyrus the Younger – laid out his

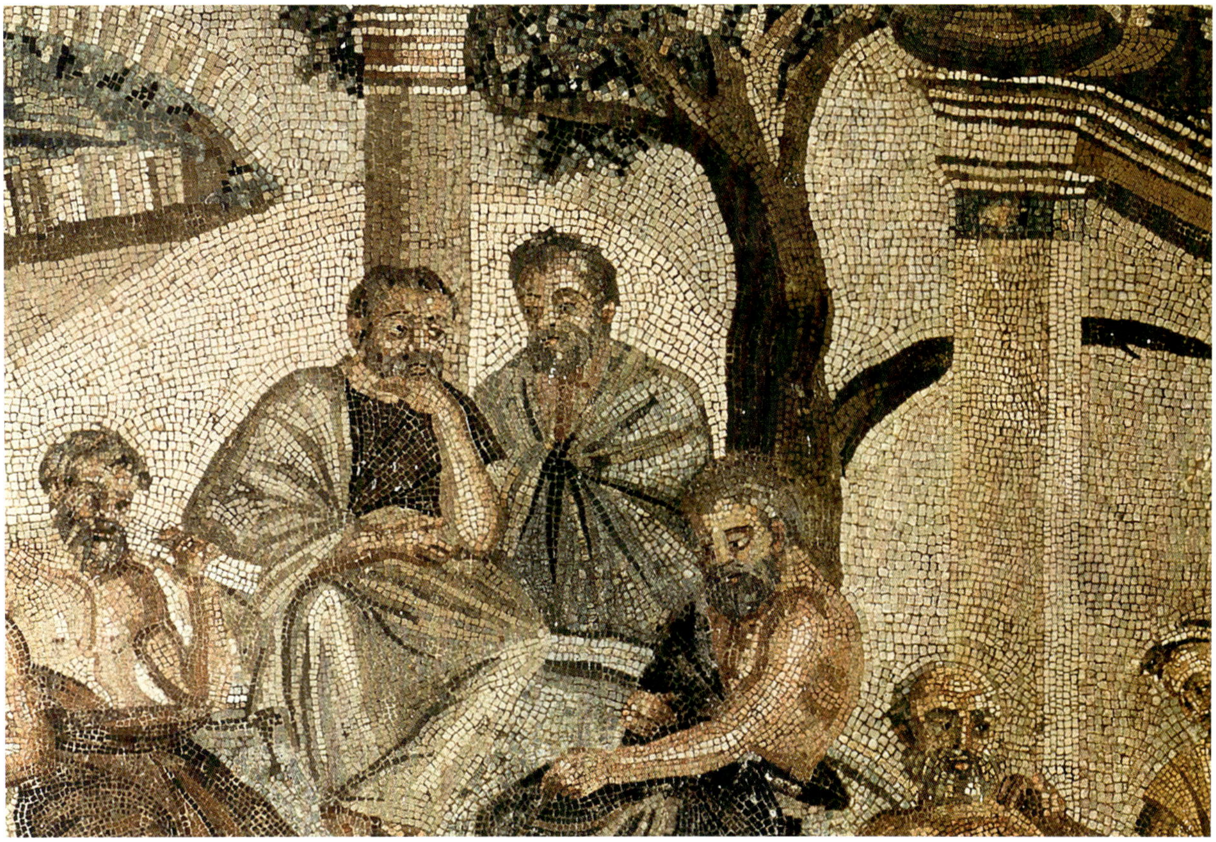

Detail of Illus. 7, Plato's Academy, floor mosaic.

own *pairidaeza* on his estate in Scillus, in imitation of Cyrus'. Both Xenophon's writing and his garden influenced the design of Greek gardens, and later of those of Rome. Virgil, it seems, was inspired by Xenophon to plant a *paradisus* around a temple. Other influences were felt after the conquests of Alexander the Great in 334-323 BCE, which took him and his men as far as the Indus, and to new and more intimate contacts with Persians and Indians. Ptolemy, one of Alexander's Greek commanders, founded a new dynasty in Egypt, where Alexandria became the centre of a Hellenistic culture that was both practically and creatively inventive. Strabo, a traveller of the first century BCE, commented on the beauty of the city's gardens.

In this same century, the gardens of the Greek philosophers would be visited by Romans such as Cicero. For the Greeks and the Romans alike, the groves of Academe may have been more than mere Cimonian amenity; perhaps they were a living memory of the sacred groves of archaic Greece. These words from one of Horace's *Epodes*, *Atque inter silvas Academi quaerere verum* ("And seek for truth in the groves of Academe") may call us also to a deeper, older truth than that of the philosophers. For to the Romans, as to the Greeks, every field and forest had its nymphs and numina, so revered that sacred groves of trees survived in the very heart of Rome even as late as the first century BCE.

The Roman Garden

Both practical and superstitious, the Romans borrowed other cults and other gods. They imported wholesale the Greek pantheon, merely

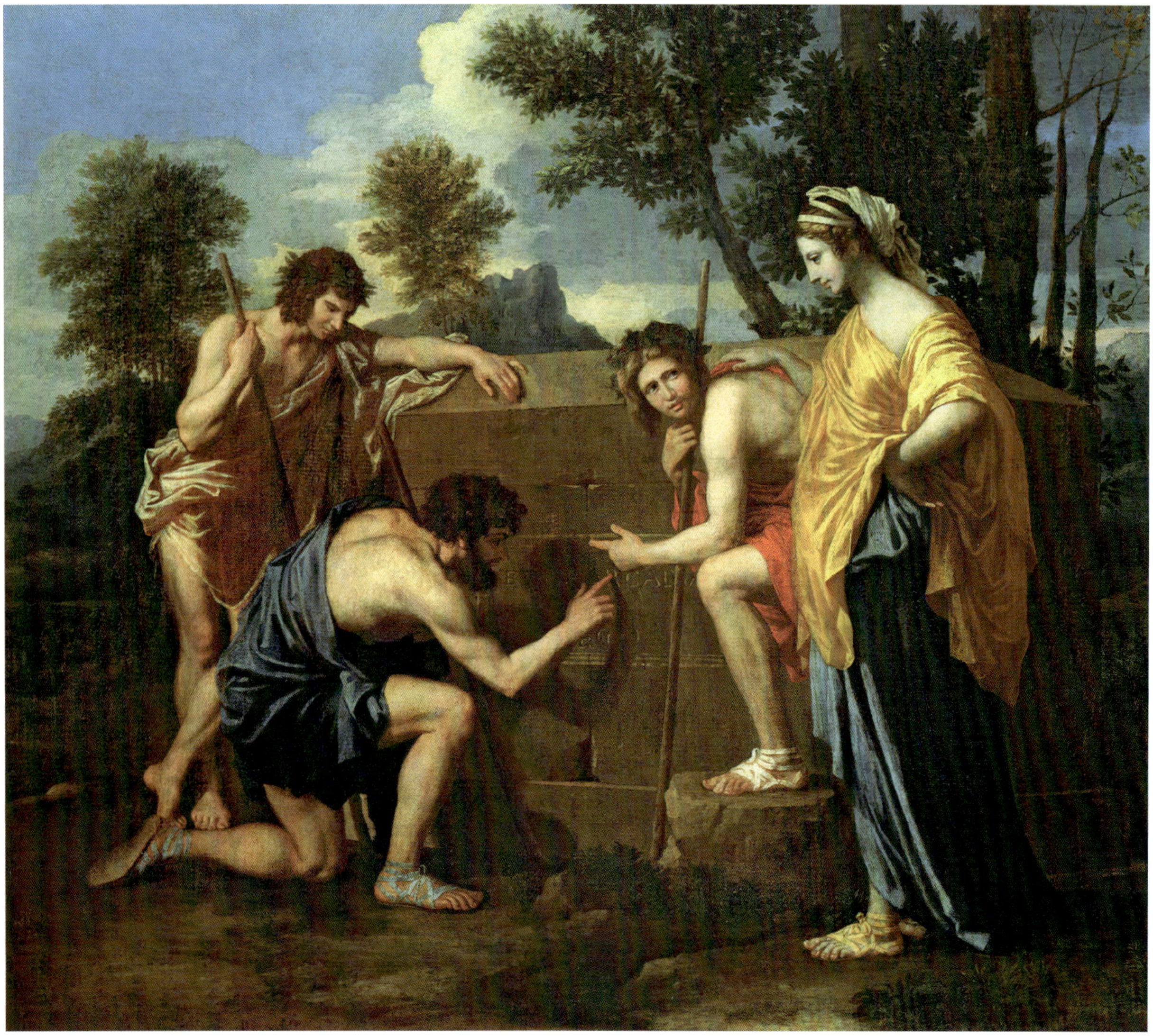

Illus 8 *Nicolas Poussin (1593/4-1665) Et in Arcadia Ego, 1638. Louvre, Paris.*

changing the names: Cronus became Saturn, whose rule remained associated with the Golden Age; Zeus became Jupiter, and his spouse Hera, Juno; Demeter became Ceres and her daughter Persephone, Proserpina. They turned also to other sources to express their mystical feelings for nature. Adopted thus from more primitive peoples of Italy, the goddess Flora watched over budding spring time, the vine and flowers, and shared responsibility for fruit trees with Pomona. Before she became identified with Aphrodite, the goddess of love, Venus too symbolized both spring and fruitfulness. The Etruscan Lares became, for the Romans, the protectors of homes and gardens; and gardens must have been very much in demand in Rome.

For the lawyer Pliny (c 61-114 CE), his garden was not merely formal with box topiary and fragrant with roses, but also shady with plane trees and ivy. It had a vine-shaded room where he could imagine himself in a wood, but sheltered from the elements; a place of escape; a small personal paradise. After the death of his beloved only daughter Tullia in 45 BCE, Cicero – not himself a religious man – wanted to dedicate a garden in Rome as a memorial to her as solace for his grief. But none was available, and his wish seems to have remained unfulfilled. However, Cicero did make a garden of his own. Among his letters is one to his friend Atticus, asking for a description of Atticus' Amaltheum. This was a garden he had made in the style of a sacred landscape inspired by the legend of the nymph Amaltha, brought up by Zeus in a grotto. Cicero imitated this garden beside a stream, shaded by plane trees, in his villa at Arpinum.

The growth of private, household cults brought with it a profusion of small shrines in the private houses of Pompeii, Herculaneum and cities like them, where not only the Roman civic gods were worshipped but also personal gods such as Isis and Serapis, borrowed from the Greek East as Flora and Pomona had been from pre-Roman Italy. Surviving paintings, especially from Pompeii, show us what Atticus' and Cicero's sacred landscape gardens might have been like. They depict small temples set among gnarled trees and rocks, often with statues, and herms garlanded with flowers. The sole survivor in Rome is the Temple of the Sibyl above the waterfalls at Tivoli, dating from the early years of Augustus' reign.

The poets of Rome took up the themes of the pastoral poets of Greece as well as that of the Golden Age. Living in exile on the Black Sea, Ovid looked back in regret at the loss of his Roman garden; and gardens permeate his *Fasti*. Horace (65-8 BCE) prayed for

A piece of land not very large,
Wherein there should a garden be,
A clear spring flowing ceaselessly,
And where, to crown the whole, there should
A patch be found of growing wood[19]

and often extols the simple pleasure of reclining on turf or moss in a landscape of ancient ilex trees, with the sound of bubbling brooks and birdsong.

In a reversal of the nostalgia for the lost Golden Age expressed by Horace and others, Virgil – the site of whose pastoral poetry is Arcadia – voiced his yearning for the lost Golden Age in the prophecy that it might return. He described it as a time when

... slowly will the plains yellow with the waving corn, on wild brambles the purple grape will hang, and the stubborn oak distil dewy honey... every land will bear all fruits. Earth will not suffer the harrow, nor the vine the pruning hook.

The similarities between the Golden Age existence and that of Elysium were later to be of great importance for the Christian concept of the earthly paradise. Classical Greece and Rome, though long since gone, together constitute one of the three great intellectual and spiritual traditions that have formed the culture of the West, along with those upon which the classical tradition was to have such an influence: the monotheistic Judaeo-Christian and Islamic traditions of Semitic origin, and the Enlightenment.

The Semitic and the Hellenic meet in the Mediterranean, the Middle Sea, in the Cretan hymn on the stele of Palaiokastro. Here Zeus is described as *pankrates gánous*, "sovereign of the liquid splendour;" the *Etymologicum Magnum* explains that to the Cypriots, *Gános* means *paradeisos*. The next chapter explores how the monotheistic religions of the Semitic world imagined paradise, and how Islam drew together the strands of the Semitic, the Greek and the Persian spirits to weave a paradise myth that found glorious expression in the gardens of the Islamic world.

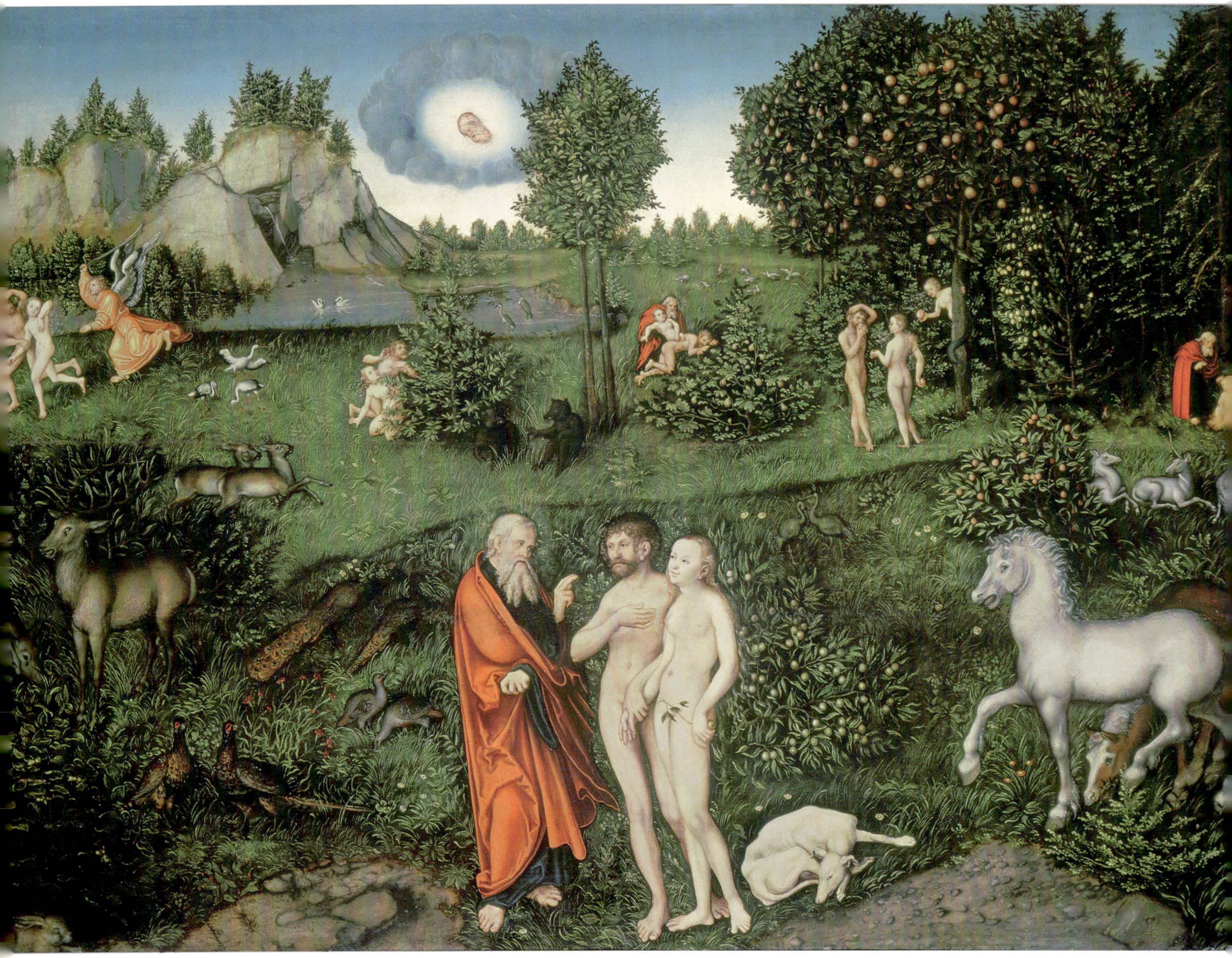

Illus. 9 *Lucas Cranach the Elder (1472–1553), Adam and Eve in the Garden of Eden – depicting Adam and Eve with an admonitory God, together with the story of the creation of Eve from Adam's rib, and the fall: the serpent tempting Eve with the apple, the couple being banished by an angel with a flaming sword. Kunsthistorisches Museum, Vienna.*

Gardens and the Abrahamic Faiths

In the great Christian allegory, the *Commedia* (*Divine Comedy*), composed by the Florentine Dante Alighieri in the early fourteenth century, the poet, guided by Virgil, takes us with him from a dark wood down through the nine circles of Hell, up the terraces and cornices of Mount Purgatory to the Earthly Paradise at its summit. In book III, the *Paradiso*, he advances from sphere to sphere of the heavens finally to see the Divine Splendour. When the poet and his companions enter the Sacred Wood, Dante's Earthly Paradise, they encounter there the lady Matilda, picking flowers by a stream – as Persephone was picking flowers when she was carried off to the Underworld by Hades. Matilda answers the poet's questions about the place they are in, and hints that this is not only a Christian dream, but one that belongs to all mankind, the same that was sung by the pagan poets.

They, whose verse of yore
The golden age recorded and its bliss,
On the Parnassian mountain, of this place
Perhaps had dream'd. Here was man guiltless, here
Perpetual spring and every fruit. . .[20]

There are similarities between Dante's allegorical treatment of the soul's progress towards God and those found in Islam. In this chapter I shall focus specifically on the notion of paradise as a garden – and the garden as paradise – in the Abrahamic faiths, starting with the Genesis story.

The Garden of Eden

The distinction between the earthly paradise and the heavenly paradise that awaits the faithful after death has not always been as clear as it was to Dante. Indeed, the Genesis story has nothing at all to say about the after-life; it is the Semitic equivalent of the Golden Age, a time and place to look back upon with nostalgia and an aching sense of loss.

And the Lord God planted a garden eastward in Eden; and there he put the man whom he had formed. And out of the ground made the Lord God to grow every tree that is pleasant to the sight, and good for food: the tree of life also in the midst of the garden, and the tree of knowledge of good and evil. And a river went out of Eden to water the garden; and from thence it was parted, and became into four heads.[21]

It seems the Lord God himself enjoyed the garden, for after Adam and Eve had eaten the forbidden fruit, "they heard the voice of the Lord God walking in the garden in the cool of the day" and hid themselves among the trees. In the Greek myths the Golden Age gives way to the harsher Silver Age by the apparently arbitrary decision of Zeus, but in the Semitic myth it is mankind's disobedience that brings about the end of Eden and its seasonless bounty.

And the Lord God commanded the man, saying, Of every tree of the garden thou mayest freely eat; But of the tree of the knowledge of good and evil, thou shalt not eat of it.[22]
So he drove out the man; and he placed at the east of the garden of Eden Cherubims, and a flaming sword which turned every way, to keep the way of the tree of life.[23]

The Hebrew Bible tells us that both punishment for transgression of the Lord's commands and reward for obedience will be received in this life. As in the Genesis story, the early great prophets are silent about the after-life of the individual soul. This is not to say that the yearning for paradise, for the coming of the kingdom of God, is absent from the Hebrew Bible. The shift from prophecy of this-worldly events to eschatology takes place with Isaiah around 740 BCE. Inveighing against his "sinful nation, a people laden with iniquity," Isaiah foretold that in the last days, "the Lord's house shall be established in the top of the mountains, and shall be exalted above the hills. . . and he shall judge among the nations, and shall rebuke many people."[24] The centre of the world was the holy mountain of Zion, where the sacred made itself manifest on earth, and all nations would flow to it. And as in the Garden of Eden, all creation would live in harmony: "The wolf also shall dwell with the lamb, and the leopard shall lie down with the kid."[25]

The Israelites in Jerusalem continued to worship other deities until the destruction of the city by Nebuchadnezzar in 586 BCE. Not until during the exile to Babylon (597-539 BCE) did the Israelites finally decide that there was only one God, the same God who had walked in the cool of the evening in the Garden of Eden and spoken to the man and woman he had created to live there. And during the exile Ezekiel had his vision of the return to Jerusalem, and a new creation when the people would say "This land that was desolate is become like the garden of Eden." In this new Eden, "by the river upon the bank thereof, on this side and on that side, shall grow all trees. . , whose leaf shall not fade, neither shall the fruit thereof be consumed: it shall bring forth new fruit according to his months . . . and the leaf thereof for medicine."[26]

Just as in ancient Greek thought the Golden Age, preserved in perpetuity in the Fortunate Isles, was also later seen as the reward of heroes and the just in the afterlife, so in post-exilic times the Garden of Eden, the earthly paradise which men sought for centuries, came to represent heaven, the abode of the righteous. At first the only mortals to find a place there were Enoch and Elijah, who were taken alive up to heaven; but by the first century BCE, when the later parts of the first Book of Enoch were written, it was believed that they had been joined by "the elect who dwell in the garden of life."[27] The location of this heavenly garden was at first as uncertain as that of the earthly Garden of Eden itself. Some said that both God and the righteous lived in paradise, but for others the righteous belonged in one of the seven heavens, above which was paradise where only God was to be found. The second Book of Enoch opts for the third firmament; Enoch's angel guides led him

> *. . . up on to the third heaven, and placed me there; and I looked downwards, and saw . . . all the sweet-flowering trees and beheld their fruits, which were sweet-smelling, and all the foods borne by them bubbling with fragrant exhalation.*
>
> *And in the midst of the trees that of life, in that place whereon the Lord rests, when he goes up into paradise; and this tree is of ineffable goodness and fragrance, and adorned more than every existing thing; . . . and it has produce from all fruits.*[28]

After the Maccabean revolt of 173-164 BCE, its heroes were thought to find eternal rest in heaven, as martyrs. This new sense of an afterlife must have contributed to the belief that the just, too, could look forward, after the Judgment, to their reward in paradise. This heavenly garden closely prefigures the Qur'anic *jannah*; not a metaphor, but a place of physical pleasures, such as they could only dream of on this earth. This was to remain the Jewish concept of the afterlife throughout the rabbinic period. Sacred groves may have been execrated by Isaiah as pagan, but the images of paradise as a garden were too compelling to resist.

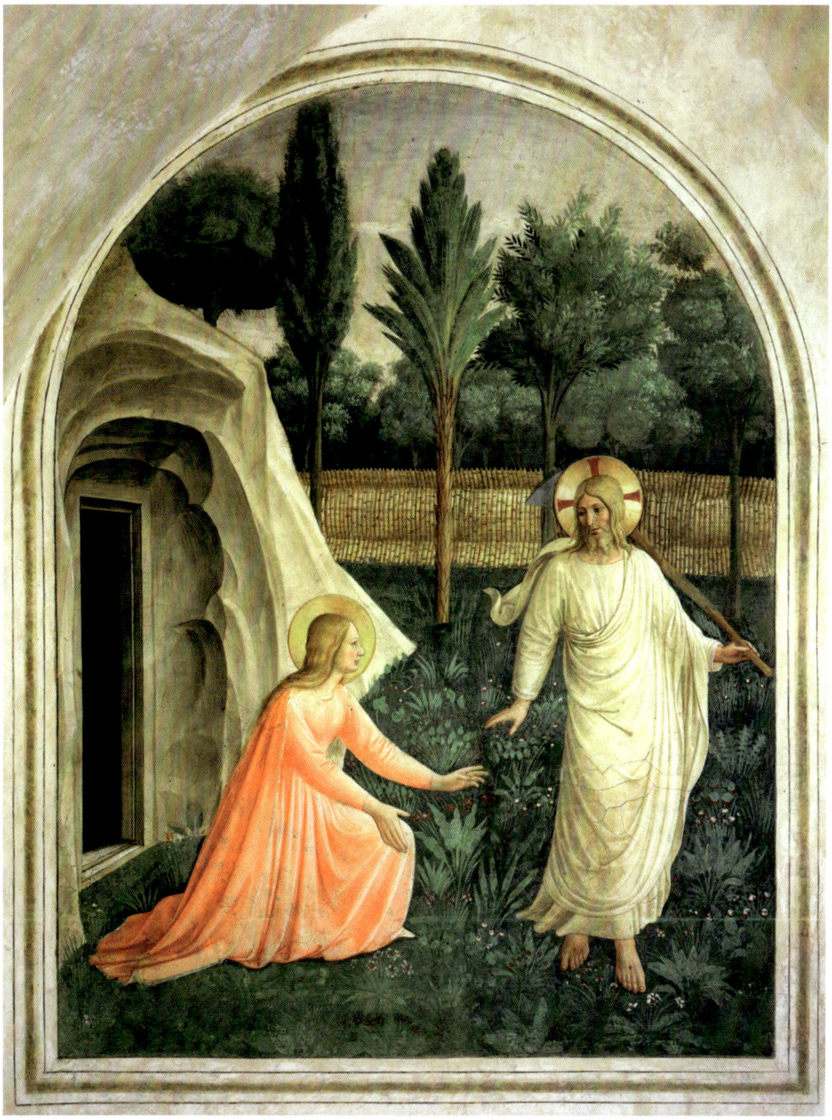

Illus 10 The Risen Christ in a Garden: Fra Angelico (c.first half of 15th century), Noli me tangere. Convent of San Marco, Florence.

Early Christian Ideas of Paradise

The reality of the earthly paradise, the Garden of Eden itself, was not doubted even as it became intertwined with the idea of the heavenly paradise. Inaccessible it might be; mythical it certainly was not, in the minds of most Jews, and later of Christians, whether they interpreted the Genesis stories literally or allegorically. The Alexandrian Platonist Philo, a Hellenized Jew, who wrote *On the Allegory of Laws* in the early years of the Christian era, inclined to the belief that Eden was only an allegory. He likens the trees in the Garden of Eden to the virtues planted by God in the soul:

> *Moses says that the tree was pleasant to the sight, which is a symbol of theoretical excellence; and likewise good for food, which is a token of useful and practical good. But the tree of life is that most general virtue which some people call*

goodness . . . And it is on this account that it is placed in the centre of the Paradise.[29]

The Eden story was interpreted in various ways, with a strong emphasis on the Fall. And it is in a garden that the disobedience of the Fall is reversed for the redemption of all mankind, with the spiritual struggle of Jesus in the garden of Gethsemane. Culminating in Jesus' death on the cross, it is followed by the Resurrection, which also takes place in a garden. Pagans who believed in an afterlife had a choice between cool intellectualism and the more emotive appeal of the mystery cults; Christians, through Jesus, had won immortality and could look forward to the resurrection of the body.

Early Christianity adopted both notions – of the earthly paradise in the Garden of Eden, and of paradise as the abode of the righteous after death. After the destruction of Jerusalem in 70 CE, Jews and Christians alike began to imagine the eternal, heavenly Jerusalem that would one day descend again to earth as the new earthly paradise. For the first Christians, essentially urban as they were, it must have been especially natural to imagine a heavenly city rather than an Edenic landscape; yet Eden's eternal cosmic symbols, the tree and the river of life, were transposed to the city. St John the Divine "saw the holy city, new Jerusalem, coming down from God out of heaven," and the "pure river of water of life, clear as crystal, proceeding out of the throne of God . . . In the midst of the street of it, and on either side of the river, was there the tree of life, which bare twelve manner of fruits, and yielded her fruit every month: and the leaves of the tree were for the healing of the nations."[30]

Almost from the start, Eastern (Greek) and Western (Latin) Christianity developed with differing, rival theologies. The Greek school provided allegorical interpretations of the earthly paradise. Clement of Alexandria (c.150-218CE) saw it as the symbol of the heavenly city. The Greek father Origen (c.185-284 CE) saw paradise as the church, the trees as the saints and the four rivers as the four gospels.

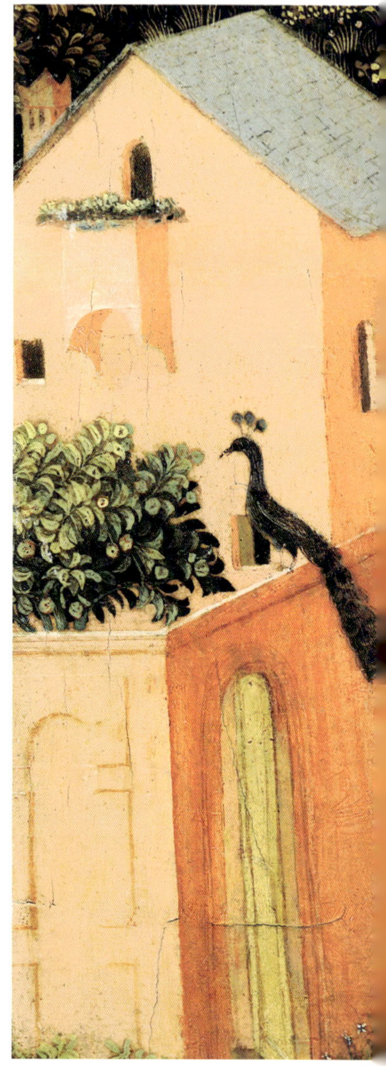

Illus. 11 *Fra Angelico , The Conversion of St Augustine. As a young man, Augustine had been attracted by Manichaeism, then by the Neoplatonist thought of Plotinus. These in turn led him to his momentous conversion to Christianity, which took place in a garden: Augustine, the successful young orator about to make a brilliant marriage, was in a garden near Milan with a friend when, deep in spiritual crisis, he heard a child's voice, outside the garden wall, saying "Tolle, lege – take and read" – and turned to the Bible, and away from worldly concerns. Musée d'Art, Thomas Henry, Cherbourg.*

In the Latin Church, many believed that the earthly paradise was a real place on earth. St. Augustine, one of the greatest of the African fathers of the Latin Church, whose conversion to Christianity took place in a garden on the eve of his marriage, shared this belief. He wrote:

Some allegorize all that concerns Paradise itself. . . And they understand all its trees and fruit-bearing

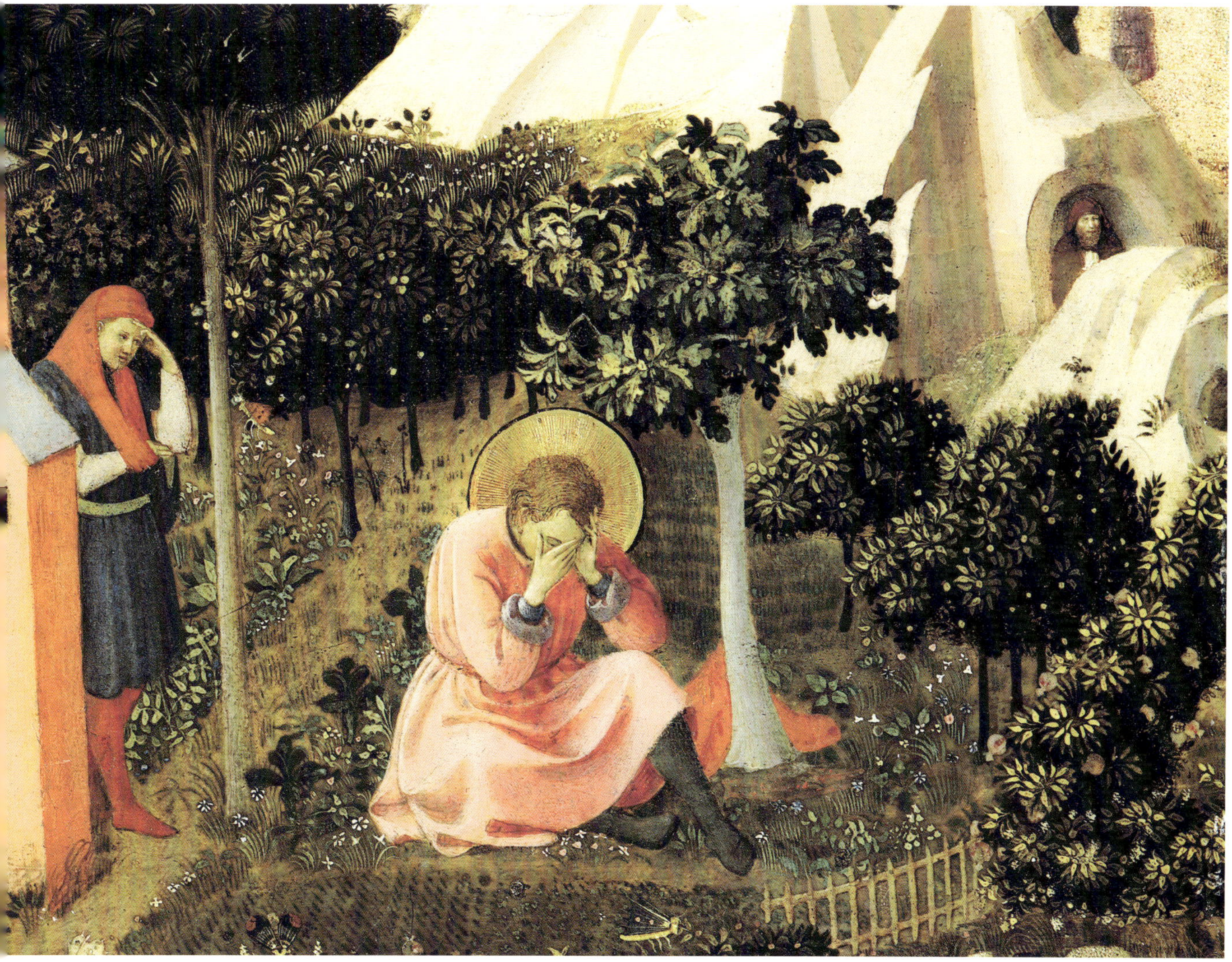

plants as virtues and habits of life, as if they had no existence in the external world but were only spoken of or related for the sake of spiritual meaning. As if there were no terrestrial Paradise! . .

A later and no less influential Christian thinker, St Thomas Aquinas (1225-74), sought to synthesize the theology of St Augustine with the Greek philosophy introduced to the west via the philosophers of Islam. He distinguished between the earthly paradise (a metaphor for the church militant) and the heavenly paradise (the church triumphant), without rejecting the idea that Eden actually existed somewhere on earth.

Paradise in Early Christian Architecture

From the earliest days, meanwhile, Christians had been making earthly imitations of paradise. In the early fourth century the Roman Emperor Constantine adopted Christianity, at least nominally, as his faith, ending the persecutions while allowing the old pagan public cults to continue. The great new churches built by Constantine and his successors in Constantinople, on the site of the ancient Greek city of Byzantium, were built in the image of the celestial city, of paradise. The altar, set in the east where Eden lay, was protected by a great door called the Door of Paradise. Their decoration of carvings and mosaics, too, displayed a love of nature. The court poet Paul the Silentiary, describing Santa Sophia on Christmas Eve, 563, evokes an idyllic pastoral scene:

> *Whosoever raises his eyes to the beauteous firmament of the roof, scarce dares to gaze on its rounded expanse, sprinkled with the stars of heaven, but turns to the fresh green marble below; seeming as it were, to see flower-bordered streams of Thessaly, and budding corn and woods thick with trees; leaping flocks, too, and twining olive-trees, and the vine with green tendrils and the deep blue peace of the summer sea.*[31]

Constantine also built a basilica (of nave and apse design) at Golgotha in Jerusalem, with a courtyard and garden, planted in memory of the garden where the risen Christ was seen by the women beside his empty tomb. Around 390 CE the Emperor Theodosius built a church on the site of the Garden of Gethsemane. The holy places became pilgrimage sites, and soon Golgotha became identified with the Garden of Eden itself, as the place where God had created Adam. Indeed, the porticoes adjoining the earliest Byzantine basilicas, planted as gardens, were referred to as paradises.

Monastic Gardens

The first earthly Christian gardens, pre-dating Constantine, had been those of the third century Egyptian cenobites, desert fathers who led solitary lives. The founder of the first Christian monastery, in 305, was St Antony (b. 251), another desert hermit, who had made a garden where he grew vines, and contrived to supply them with enough water. These early garden were no labour-free paradise, but were achieved with "the sweat of the face."[32] The fourth century saw the development of such monastic foundations, where men sought to live a holy life not in isolation but in community. The holy land began to attract monks from many parts of the Christian world who, like the Armenian Euthymius (d. 478), made gardens about their monasteries in the Judaean desert. There they could live like Adam in paradise, and fulfil the prophecy of Second Isaiah that "the desert shall rejoice, and blossom as the rose."[33] For despite its rigours, the desert also came to be seen in some sense as paradise.

Like the porticoes of the earliest Byzantine basilicas, later Byzantine monasteries, with their watered green gardens set in the dry Mediterranean landscape, were commonly referred to as a *paradeisos*, or garden, and their monks or nuns as plants and trees. The Eastern Church believed paradise to be within human reach, even if in fact closed to sinful humanity. The Roman notion of the garden as "embracing its surroundings," incorporating views of the landscape around it, was replaced by the ideas of enclosure and seclusion. Like the *hortus conclusus* of Western Christianity, the mediaeval Byzantine garden looked inward.

Despite its urban roots and desert tradition, Christianity clung to its imagery of a green, Edenic paradise. The third century African martyr Marian wrote in his memoirs that the road in his vision of Paradise led through meadows and green forests surrounding a hollow where flowed a crystal-clear fountain. The classical tradition also influenced early Christian concepts of paradise, especially in the Latin tradition. Tertullian (155-222) claimed that the pagan poets' descriptions of the Elysian Fields were taken from the earthly paradise. Later, Lactantius (260-325) is believed to be the author of what may be the earliest Christian poem describing the earthly paradise, *De Ave Phoenice*, where all the typical elements of paradise are present: eternal spring, flowing water, abundant fruit, and sweet fragrance.

Despite this literary tradition, Christians in the West, other than the Celtic monks, seem to have taken little interest in actual, earthly gardens until the development of the Benedictine monastic order. St Benedict (480-547) was an Italian nobleman who gave up his studies in Rome and retired to Subiaco to become a monk. Later, in 529, he founded a monastery on Monte Cassino in Italy and drew up the Rule of the Benedictine order, calling for six hours of manual toil in field and garden every day. The monastery garden was meant for practical use, not for pleasure, nor for mystical contemplation: it was a place to grow food for the refectory table and flowers for the altar. But St Benedict also saw manual work as a means to the soul's salvation. The mystic St Bernard (1090-1153 CE), Abbot of Clairvaux, a daughter foundation of the Cistercian order which aimed to observe the Benedictine rule to the full, also encouraged horticulture. In their heyday, the Cistercians would become Christianity's greatest monastic gardeners.

The layout of the Monte Cassino and other early monasteries derived from the Roman villa, adopted by the Goths and Franks – self-contained units with gardens for vegetables, fruit and flowers, around a central colonnaded atrium. A detailed plan of an ideal Benedictine monastery was made at St Gall in Switzerland, showing the central cloister (itself a symbol of paradise) with four squares around a central holy water stoup, and separate physic and vegetable gardens. So that the monks, after death, may lie in a place of both use and beauty, the cemetery is planted with fruit trees. The novices would also have studied in the monastery garden, as we learn from the 9th-century abbot of the Benedictine island monastery of Reichenau on Lake Constance, near St Gall, Walafrid Strabo, who wrote his book *Hortulus* just before the St Gall plan was made:

In the green darkness of the apple trees
Just where the peach tree casts its broken shade,
And they would gather you the shining fruit
With the soft down upon it; all your boys,
Your little laughing boys, your happy school,
And bring huge apples clasped in their two hands.

In Subiaco, St Benedict had had a small rose garden, with flowers to delight the senses – but also with thorns, to mortify the flesh. Radegunda (521-587), the widowed queen of Clotaire I (497-561), founded a nunnery outside Poitiers with a garden of apples and pears, where violets grew; and the gardens of queen Ultrogotha, widow of Childebert I (d. 558) were noted for their fragrant roses: "Paradisiacus spargit odore rosas." The early Church's constant concern was to subdue the senses, however, not to indulge them. Thus St Anselm (1033-1109), who knew something about the matter from his dissipated youth, saw a garden as a place of dangerous temptations to the senses, distracting men from their true vocation of contemplation and prayer. In these verses by St Peter Damian (1007-1072), the love of beauty, the appreciation of the joys of a garden, are sublimated into the imagining of paradise in the afterlife:

Winter's ire, summer's fire, that fair city never knows:
In its gardens, sweet with balsam, spring eternal breathes and blows,
White with lily, bright with crocus, red with ever-blooming rose.
Green its fields and clean its pastures; flow with honey stream and rill:
Fragrant scents and luscious juices aromatic herbs distill:
Fruits that fall not bend the laden boughs of orchards flowering still.

The Song of Songs

Both St Peter Damian and Abbot Walafrid bring to mind the Qur'anic descriptions of Paradise, where fruit clusters "hang meekly down" so the faithful may reach them simply by stretching out their hands.

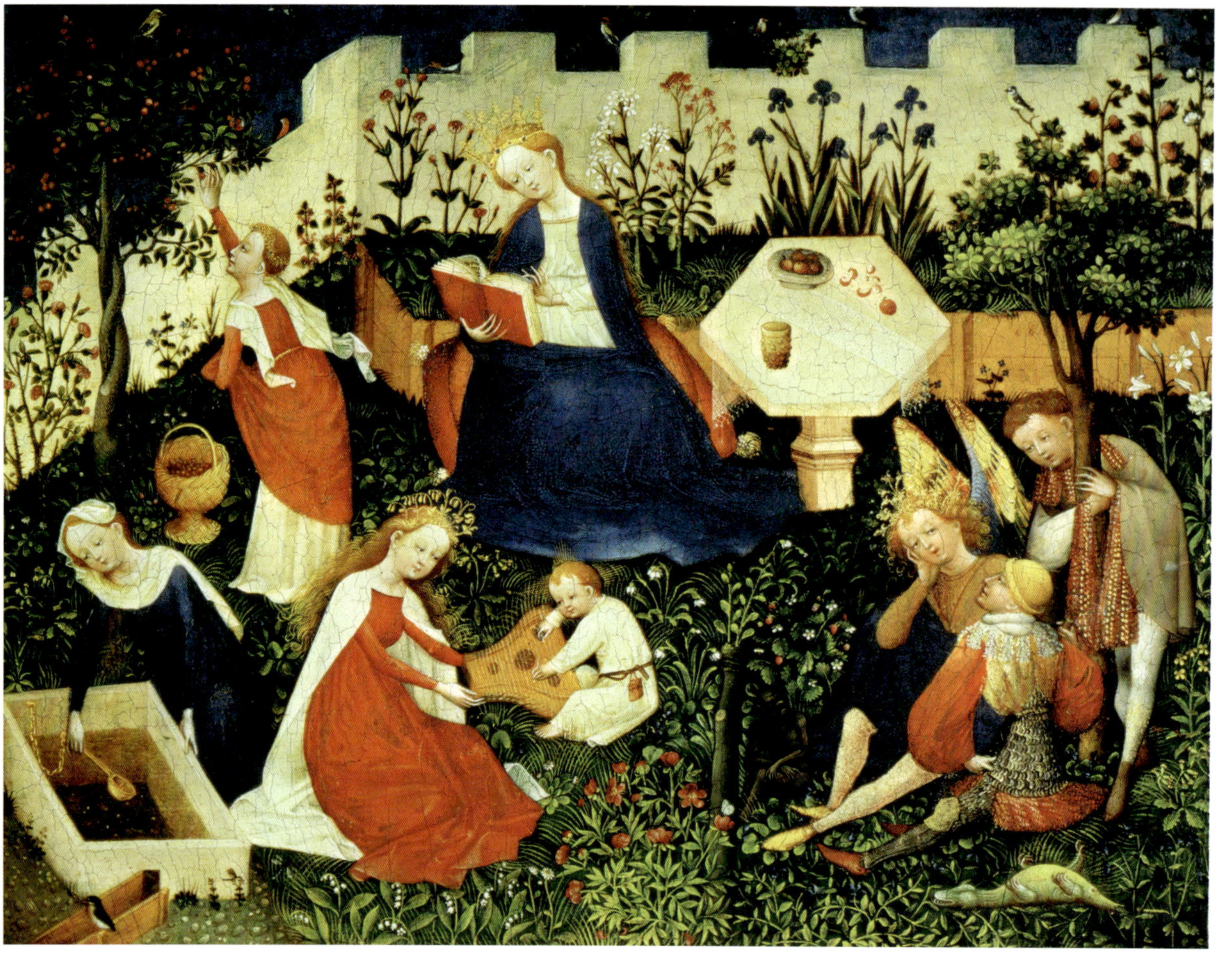

Illus. 12 *Oberrheinischer Meister (c. 1410) Paradise Garden. St Anselm would surely have disapproved, for not only are there here flowers to delight the eye and fill the air with fragrance, but fruit too for the sense of taste, while the ear is charmed by the sound of a zither as well as by the splashing of water. Just as in the Islamic paradise, however, these sensations, far from distracting the mind and soul from God, testify to His beneficence and mercy, and the picture is full of the Christian symbols that were familiar to all in the Middle Ages. Staedelsches Kunstinstitut, Frankfurt.*

This is a rare instance, in early Christianity, of an attitude approaching that of Islam, in which spiritual, aesthetic and sensual pleasures are united. From this perspective, the garden, in Islam, becomes a metaphor not only of paradise, but also of *tawhid*, the oneness of God and of all His gifts of creation. And almost certainly it was as a result of contacts with Islamic civilization during the Crusades and in Moorish Spain that, after Anselm, Christianity awoke to the symbolism of the paradise garden. From being a dangerous sensual distraction, the garden became a foretaste of paradise. The frank eroticism of the *Song of Songs* – "A garden inclosed is my sister, my spouse; a spring shut up, a fountain sealed" – is transmuted to an image of purity; the *Song* is seen as an allegory of the mystical union of the soul and its creator.

The *Song of Songs* also came to be seen as an allegory of Marian love, with the Blessed Virgin, the beloved of Christ, as the bride in the Canticle. St Ambrose, in the fourth century, was first to

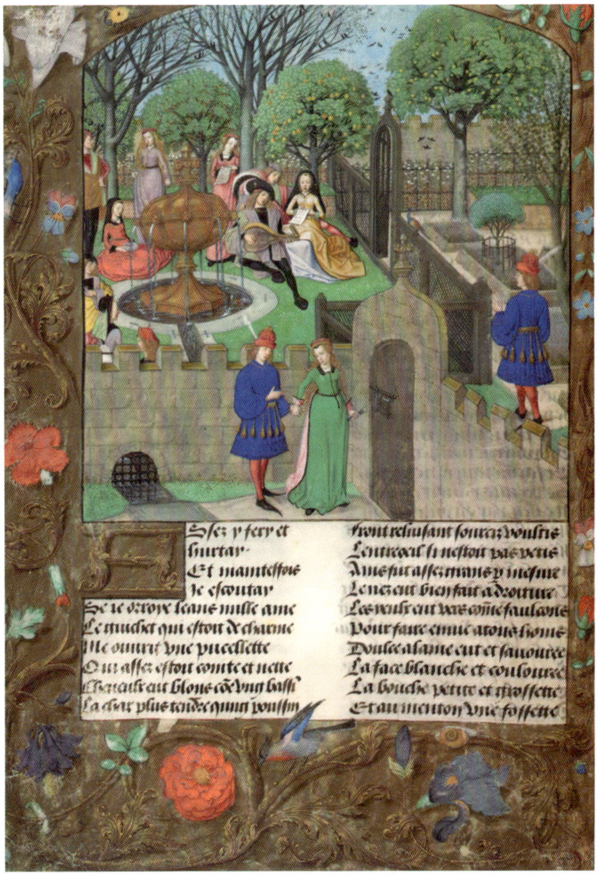

Illus. 13 *Le Roman de la rose, or the Garden of Pleasure, with lutanists and singers, late 15th century Flemish. British Library, London.*

equate the Virgin and the church with the bride of the *Song of Songs*. The cult of Mary as the Blessed Virgin, the Mystical Rose of Dante's *Paradiso*, first emerges in the seventh century, reaching its full expression in western Christianity in the twelfth century, inspired by St Bernard of Clairvaux.

With the Cistercians, for the first time, Mary is given the (feudal) title Our Lady, echoing the troubadour dedication to a Lady who, higher in rank and married to another, was unattainable. Artists of the fifteenth century, in particular, loved to depict Our Lady in a flower-spangled *hortus conclusus* (which must surely have derived from Persian miniatures).

The notion of the *hortus conclusus* or *giardino segreto*, enclosed against the harsh world, where love both human and divine could flourish, passed into the poetry of the troubadours. Their inspiration also came from Islam – as did the roses in the garden of the *Roman de la Rose*, which came from "the land of the Saracens."

The Islamic Paradise Garden

Islam spread rapidly from arid Arabia to fertile Byzantium and Persia. As the might and wealth of the Muslim rulers grew, they began to organize the paradisal elements of nature itself – water, trees, flowers and fruits – into splendid living gardens around their palaces: gardens in the image of the Qur'anic paradise.

The ancient city of Damascus, which gave its name to the fragrant Damask rose, was long thought by some to be the original Garden of Eden. The early seventeenth century Scottish traveller William Lithgow even related that the Turks had enclosed a garden there, in which the forbidden tree of Eden still grew. Among the very first pictorial representations from the Islamic world are those of the Great Mosque in Damascus (706-715 CE), dating from the first century of the Islamic era. These show Byzantine-style paradisal landscapes and trees.

It was Persia, however, that was to be the lasting inspiration for the Islamic paradise garden. The gardens that the new Muslim rulers found in Persia, built on the age-old and seemingly universal symbolic design of the cosmic cross, may have been inspired by the religion of Zoroaster. And long after the coming of Islam, the ancient myths were still vibrant in the Persian soul. The poet Abu-l Qasim, who took as his nom de plume the name Firdausi, "the garden of Paradise," completed his epic *Shah-nama* (Book of Kings) in about 1010. A copy dating from 1546 shows Jamshed, the semi-mythical monarch of Persia's golden age, in a garden. And when the survival of mankind, and of earth itself, was threatened by floods and burning summers, Jamshed was commanded by Ahura Mazda to save the animal kingdom from destruction in an underground fortress, his Var. But whereas God instructed Noah to fill the Ark with every kind of animal and bird, plants too were to be saved in these ancient Persian traditions. Jamshed was told:

> *Inside the Vara, make water flow in a canal... To that place carry the seeds of all trees which are most exalted and sweetest of odour on this earth, carry the seeds of all food most eatable in this world and sweetest of odour.*

The great enclosed palace gardens of the Achaemenids and the Sassanids, with their water-channels, symmetrically planted trees and the sweet air-borne fragrance of their flowers, seemed ready-made to express to perfection the often-repeated Qur'anic phrase "gardens beneath which rivers flow." They echo these lines from the beautiful Sura *al-Rahman*, with its musical refrain, *O which of your Lord's bounties will you and you deny?*, after each phrase:

> *But such as fear the Station of his Lord*
> *for them shall be two gardens*
> *abounding in branches*
> *therein two fountains of running water*
> *therein of every fruit two kinds*
> *reclining upon couches lined with brocade*
> *the fruits of the gardens nigh to gather*
> ...
> *And besides these shall be two gardens*
> *green, green pastures*
> *therein two fountains of gushing water*
> *therein fruits, and palm trees, and pomegranates*

This is just one of over 120 passages in the Qur'an describing paradise, as against none at all in the Hebrew Bible (as distinct from the Garden of Eden) and few in the New Testament. The garden of paradise is of boundless extent, "as the breadth of heaven and earth." Yet like the Persian *pairidaeza* it is also an enclosed garden, with gates that are opened to the deserving by gatekeepers. Ibn Abbas, who narrated many sayings by the Prophet Muhammad, described the gates as of gold inlaid with jewels, and in *Arousing the Heedless*, by Abu'l Layth al Samarqandi (d. 983), we read that the trees of Paradise have silver trunks and branches of pearl and emerald.

The Gardens of the Caliphs

The gardens of the Palace of Eternity, *Qasr al Khuld* (762 CE), outside the walls of the new Abbasid capital of Baghdad on the Tigris, were even said to rival the gardens of the Qur'an. And the palace of Jawsaq al Khaqani, in the temporary capital of Samarra, dating from the mid ninth century, had extensive courts and gardens with pavilions, canals and fountains. Ambassadors from Byzantine Emperor to the Abbasid Caliph al Muqtadir in Baghdad in 917 described the garden in the palace compound, with its pool and watercourses lined with metal "more lustrous than polished silver," and four hundred palm trees with dates ripe in all seasons. Another palace garden had an artificial tree with branches of silver and gold and leaves of various colours. Clearly, these gardens were of political as well as religious significance: caliphal ostentation and pious speculation on the nature of paradise complemented each other.

These Abbasid gardens have vanished entirely. Perhaps the caliphs should have taken greater note of the fate of the fabled *Gulistan-i Iram*, the garden said to have been made in Arabia Felix by the legendary King Shaddad. The paradigm of a garden as the expression of an impious aspiration to rival creation itself, it was destroyed by the Lord, the Qur'an tells us, in a "scourge of chastisement."

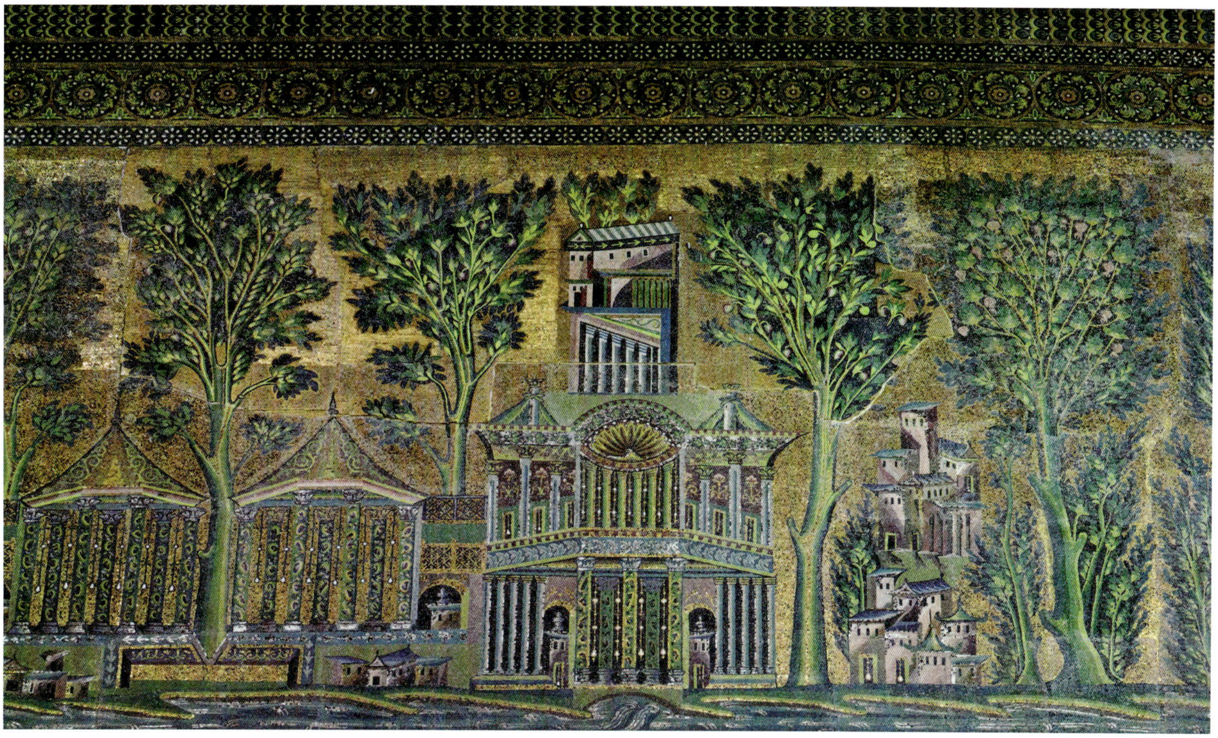

Illus. 14 *Great Mosque of Damascus, 87-96 AH (706-715 CE), Umayyad period: detail of mosaic in the Treasury Courtyard.*

Yet the lost glory of Shaddad's legendary garden came for many to symbolize the earthly paradise, and has inspired many poets – among them Omar Khayyam (1048–1131) and his interpreter to the English-speaking world, Edward Fitzgerald:

Iram indeed is gone with all its Rose,
And Jamshyd's Sev'n-ring'd Cup where no one knows;
But still the Vine her ancient Ruby yields,
And still a Garden by the Water blows.

And Hafiz, in the fourteenth century, also recalls the Garden of Iram:

In Iram's garden yesternight, when, in the grateful air,
The breeze of coming day stirred the tress of hyacinth fair,
I asked: "Throne of Jamshid, where is thy world-revealing cup?"

The Timurid and Mughal Tradition

In the early thirteenth century, Chengiz Khan had led the first Mongol invasion of present-day Afghanistan and eastern Persia. His son Kublai became the "Great Khan of Cathay" and made the gardens and pleasure dome of Xanadu, described in Samuel Taylor Coleridge's famous poem. Chengiz's descendants, the Ilkhans, adopted both Islam and the Persian garden tradition, and used the gardens as royal encampments. Such was the garden of the Golden Horde in Tabriz, made in 1302 as the setting to celebrate the completion of a copy of the Qur'an. After Timur (1336-1404), another Central Asian of nomadic stock, conquered Persia, he continued the Ilkhan habit of building magnificent *chahar-baghs* in his capital Samarqand in the shade

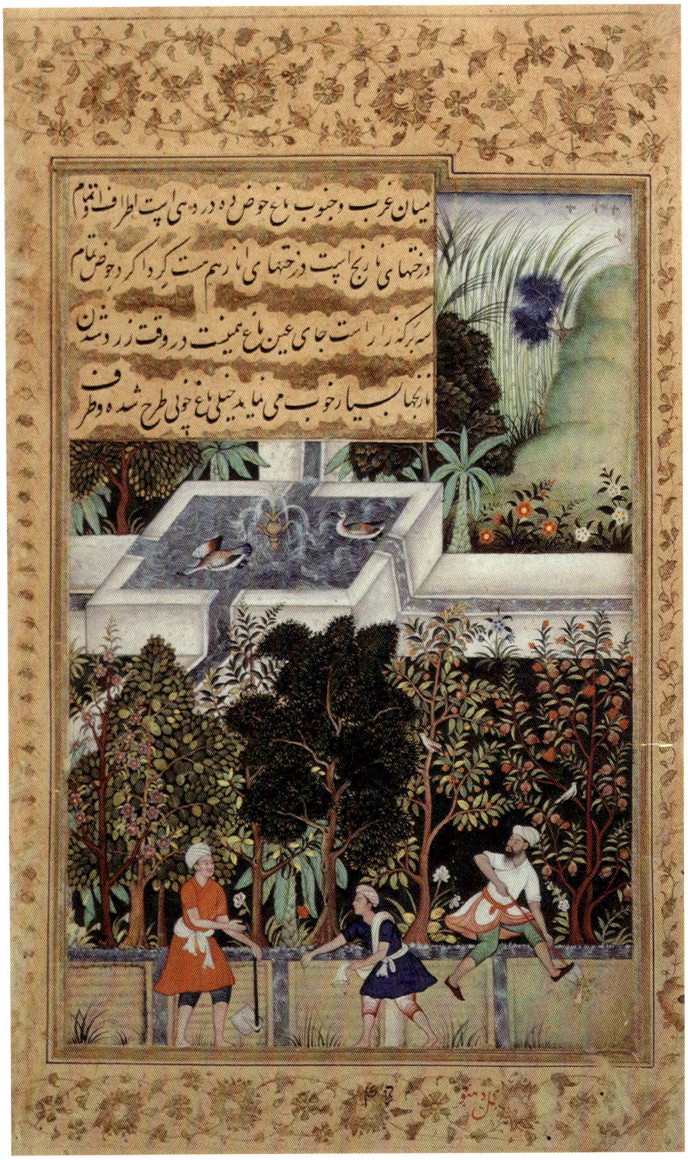

Illus. 15 *From the Babur Nama: the Bagh-i wafa showing not only the water-courses but also Babur's sugar cane and plantains, and pomegranate trees. British Museum, London. British Museum .*

of the chenars (plane trees, *Platanus orientalis*) for which the city had long been known. These gardens were given names such as *Bagh-i dilkusha* (garden of the heart's delight). They are described by Clavijo, who led an embassy from Henry III of Castile and Leon to Timur, as orchards with fruit trees, shady avenues, and pools surrounded by lawns.

Timur's son Shah Rukh followed his father's example in Herat; Shah Rukh's biographer describes a garden celebration in which "amber and musk perfumed the silken pavilions where musicians played the lute and lyre." Small wonder that the Timurid gardens, though imbued with political meaning and designed for pleasure, were often likened by their contemporaries to paradise, the reward of eternal bliss. Little now remains of the royal gardens of Herat, or of the expansive *Hasht Bihisht* (Eight Paradises) of Tabriz with its marble galleries, pavilions and fountains, its roses and jasmine. War and earthquake have wrought their destruction as they cannot in the true paradise.

A century after Timur, the memoirs of Babur, the first Mughal Emperor, are full of his descriptions of gardens he made or beautified in his native Kabul or in India. By origin a Timurid nomad from Central Asia, Babur marvelled at the garden cities of Samarqand and Herat, and created equally beautiful gardens in the cool climate and mountainous splendour of the Kabul valley. He describes how he improved the *Bagh-i kilan* or Great Garden outside the village of Istalif, where chenar, holm-oak and *arghwan* trees (*Bauhinia variegata*) grew around a spring called the *Khwaja Sih-yaran* (Three Friends), and a stream which formerly meandered irregularly was "made straight and orderly."

Among the most famous of his gardens is the *Bagh-i wafa* or Garden of Fidelity, depicted as a *chahar-bagh* where oranges, citrons and pomegranates grew, with plantains and sugarcane brought from Lahore. He loved to pause there in autumn, when the lawns were green with trefoil, the pomegranates ripened to their full cinnabar-red amid yellowing foliage, and the oranges just turning from green to the first hint of yellow. The loss is ours that almost without exception the original plantings of these and later Mughal gardens have not survived. Gone are the avenues of cypress trees and fruit trees, cherry or almond or citrus, the parterres of fragrant narcissi or of roses. Happily, we have many paintings of Mughal gardens, including the *Bagh-i wafa* itself, as well as literary records of the plantings in Mughal gardens.

In 1526, weeks before the decisive battle of Panipat that won Babur a new kingdom, he had already laid out his first *chahar-bagh* in India. His confidence was repaid: the Sultan's troops were routed, and Babur continued south to Agra. Though he found it at first "charmless and disorderly," he was fascinated by Hindustan, so different in every way from Kabul. He made *chahar-bagh* gardens of the basic paradise design, with terraces and watercourses, on the banks of the river Yamuna. All the Mughals, and Babur in particular, used their gardens in place of rather than as an adjunct to their palaces. In between the dust, heat and exhaustion of his campaigns, whether he was holding public audiences, entertaining courtiers and friends with music and poetry (often of his own composition), or writing his memoirs, Babur's life, both public and private, was led almost entirely in his *chahar-baghs* to the sound of cooling water.

Babur must have been aware that he was also fulfilling the Qur'anic dream; for *jannah* is unequivocally a garden, not a palace or a city, and it is in the gardens of delight that the deserving faithful will live,

upon close-wrought couches
reclining upon them, set face to face,
immortal youths going round about them
with goblets, and ewers, and a cup from a spring
(no brows throbbing, no intoxication)
and such fruits as they shall choose,
and such flesh of fowl as they desire,
and wide-eyed houris
as the likeness of hidden pearls. . .
mid thornless lote-trees and serried acacias,
and spreading shade and outpoured waters,
and fruits abounding
unfailing, unforbidden. . .[34]

Babur's successors followed his example, using new materials such as marble, but fundamentally changing none of his basic concepts. Symbolism appealed to the Mughals, who introduced their own modifications to the Persian, pre-Islamic model. The narrow rills of Persian design were expanded to the broad canals and brimming tanks of the Mughals. The original paradise gardens were flat, but the Mughals made use of differing levels, natural in Kashmir or artificial in the plains, to create fountains and waterfalls. Even on a flat site, they would contrive carved water chutes to form lacy "shawls" of falling water. Water dominated Babur's gardens and those of his successors. The central watercourse of the *chahar-bagh*, the bubbling fountains and water chutes and brimming tanks had a special magic in a dusty landscape, both sensuous – the moving water cooled the air, and falling, beguiled the ear and eye – and poetic.

The ultimate paradise garden was the *chahar-bagh* that enclosed a monumental tomb. The designs of tomb and garden were treated as one, in what became the Mughals' major contribution to garden architecture. Here the atmosphere was peaceful and harmonious, suggesting the repose that follows earthly life and the grief of death. This contrasted with the seductive, sensuous quality of the pleasure gardens and the emperors' residential *chahar-baghs*. The tomb of Humayun, the second Mughal emperor, though not the first of its kind, is one of the finest. After years in exile, he died falling from his library steps soon after reclaiming the Delhi throne. His tomb and its surrounding gardens, commissioned by his wife, were made according to the cosmic, paradise model (see Chapter V).

The architecture of Emperor Akbar (1556-1605)

was a synthesis of Persian Islamic and indigenous Indian elements, echoing the Emperor's syncretic beliefs. He built the great Lahore fort and palace, the Hari Parbat fort in Srinagar, the forts of Allahabad and Ajmer (where later Jahangir built a large *chahar-bagh*), the red sandstone Agra Fort, and his most ambitious project, the red city of Fatehpur Sikri. The architecture of these palaces and pavilions drew inspiration from the local, Hindu art. Akbar's own tomb at Sikandra, in its square walled garden, is also a hybrid, but the Qur'anic inscriptions on the entrance gateway – ending in the words "These are the gardens of Eden: enter them to dwell therein eternally" – make clear the association with the gardens of paradise.

The Great Mughal Gardens

Akbar's successors, Jahangir and Shah Jahan, shared their forefather Babur's passion for gardens. His eldest son, the Emperor Jahangir (1605-1627), especially loved Kashmir, which Jahangir described as "a garden of eternal spring . . . and a heart-expanding heritage for dervishes." No wonder he and his court made the difficult journey over the passes of the Pir Panjal no fewer than thirteen times. By the mid seventeenth century, the Vale of Kashmir was said to have 777 gardens, built by Jahangir and his Persian wife Nur Jahan, their son Shah Jahan, and their nobles. Their symbolic paradise design was enhanced by the natural beauty around them, and springs and streams from the mountains fed the gardens with abundant water. The narrow watercourses of earlier Mughal gardens expanded into wide, shallow canals and pools, with sparkling fountains, waterfalls and *chadar*s – inclined stone chutes, carved in chevron, fish-scale or scallop design, that made the water ripple and dance as it splashed musically down.

By contrast with the cool gardens of Kashmir in their spectacular mountain settings, the Mughal gardens of the plains were more self-contained, enclosed against the hot, dusty winds that had made Babur yearn for his cool Kabul and welcome the rains of the monsoon, and prompted the poets to sing of gardens in the rain. This is by Mir (c.1722-c.1808):

Chalte ho to chaman ko chaliye kehte heñ ke bahârâñ hay
Pât hare heñ phul khile heñ kam kam bâd o bârâñ hay.
Come, stroll in the garden, come; spring, they say, has come,
All is green, the flowers in bloom; a breeze, a shower of rain has come.

The Emperor Jahangir's last wish to be buried in Kashmir was disregarded. Instead, his tomb is in the Dilkusha bagh near Lahore (one-time capital of the Mughal Empire), set in a large walled enclosure divided into four *chahar-baghs*. It was already nearing dusk when I first visited the tomb of Jahangir, but the gatekeeper allowed us in, and the guardian of the tomb showed us round with grave courtesy. Above us, the pale green sky deepened to black, and kites wheeled and mewed, as though mourning the lost glory of the Mughals' paradise gardens. Also near Lahore, the great *Shalamar bagh*, made by the Emperor Shah Jahan (1627-1657), is a double *chahar-bagh* with a central water terrace. Alas, these are usually now silent and dry, the marble lotus buds from which they sprayed their mist-fine drops almost all gone.

Shah Jahan also built the *Lal Qila* or Red Fort in Shahjahanabad (now known as Old Delhi), the city he named for himself. The Fort was originally set in *chahar-bagh* gardens, now partly obliterated. However, part of a *chahar-bagh* survives, known as the *Hayat bakhsh bagh*, the "Life-bestowing Garden." This has a large central tank, canals with rows of fountains, and a marble pavilion at each end, named Bhadun Mahal and Sawan Mahal after the two monsoon months of the Hindu year. Here water and light were combined to great effect; water fell in an unbroken, vertical curtain in front of walls formed of white marble niches, in each of which by day stood gold and silver vases full of golden flowers, replaced at night by white wax candles. Water from the canal cascaded over carved chutes into a tank and out the other side. A water channel known as the *Nahr-i Bihisht*, the "Stream of Paradise," runs through the line of separate pavilions that form the private palace, on its way to the richly-planted Hayat Bakhsh. The marble piers of the *Diwan-i Khas* or Hall of private audience were decorated with delicate floral designs in *pietra dura* of inlaid semi-precious stones, and inscribed with these much-quoted lines in Persian, attributed to Amir Khusrau:

Agar firdaus bar rue zamin-ast, hamin asto hamin asto hamin ast
If there is Paradise on earth, it is here, it is here, it is here.

It needs a great exercise of the imagination today to call to mind the glory of Shahjahanabad, the white marble pavilions draped in scarlet silks, the gay *chattris* bright with gilded cupolas. It must have been especially magical after nightfall, when the air was drenched in the fragrance of *chambeli*, *motia* and *champa*, candlelight flickered in the niches of the pavilion walls, the sound of water and the strains of music floated on the moonlit air and the scent of sandalwood and rose water mingled with the perfumes of the *mahtab bagh*, the "Moonlit Garden."

Shah Jahan is best known for the Taj Mahal in Agra, his memorial to his beloved queen, Mumtaz Mahal. The marble building, glowing with rosy warmth at dawn, is dazzlingly white in the full light of the sun, almost incandescent at sunset, and luminescent by moonlight. Like its predecessors, it is set in expansive *chahar-bagh* gardens, here 300 metres wide. Shah Jahan's great innovation was to place the building, not in the centre, but at one end of the garden, next to the river Yamuna, on a platform of black and white marble of ripple pattern. In places the marble is inlaid, as is the *Diwan-i Khas* in the Red Fort of Delhi, with *pietra dura* floral decorations, while elsewhere flowers are carved in relief. Qur'anic inscriptions decorate the façades and entrance arch, none more poignantly evocative of Shah Jahan's grief than these:

O soul at peace, return unto thy Lord
well-pleased, well-pleasing.
Enter thou among My servants.
Enter thou My Paradise.

This is much more than a rhetorical expression of piety or a hope that the soul of the deceased will enter paradise. Research has convincingly demonstrated that the garden of the Taj Mahal was based on cosmological diagrams of paradise on the Day of Judgment, which also explains why the tomb stands at the end of the gardens rather than in the middle. It is more than simply a generic metaphor for paradise, as was, say, the garden of Humayun's tomb; it was designed as an exact replica. In it are not only the four water channels of the *chahar bagh*, as the four rivers of paradise, but also a single central tank, representing the celestial *hauz al-Kausar* where the Prophet Muhammad will stand before God on the Day of Judgment to intercede on behalf of the faithful.

Ottomans, Moors and Safavids

To the west of the Mughal Empire lay another great empire, that of the Ottomans, another people of Turkic origin whose empire lasted for over six centuries (1299-1922). In its heyday, the walls of the grander Ottoman mosques were often faced with floral Iznik tiles, transforming them into symbolic gardens of paradise. Royal tombs were set, not in an independent formal cross-axial garden as in Mughal India, but in garden-like funerary enclosures forming part of a mosque complex, guarded by cypresses, symbols of both death and immortality. The walls of the *türbe* (mausoleum) itself would be decorated with Iznik tiles, featuring blossoming trees, carnations, and tulips – the Ottomans' favourite flower, reminding them of their native steppes. Irises, the Muslim funerary flower, still bloom around the tomb of Sultan Süleyman the Magnificent (1520-1566) in the Süleymaniye complex in Istanbul, where the peristyle boasts two magnificent panels of Iznik tiles depicting stylized leaves and flowers. And in the türbe of his beloved son Şehzade Mehmet, the walls are tiled with floral panels in green, yellow and cobalt blue in an evocation of paradise.

By the time the Ottomans had extended their empire westwards to the Balkans in the mid fifteenth century, al Andalus in the Iberian peninsula (often called "Moorish Spain"), the former westernmost outpost of Islam, was in decline, soon to fall in 1492. The gardens of the first few centuries of al Andalus seem to have been more practical than paradisal: palace gardens symbolizing political power, or gardens laid out as productive country retreats. But the civil war of 1010 to 1013 led to the collapse of the Umayyad Caliphate, the destruction of the magnificent palaces and gardens of Madinat al-Zahra', the period of the rival Taifa rulers, and the gradual loss of al Andalus to the Christians. The Reconquista was a slow process; Toledo fell to the Christians in 1085, Cordoba in 1236, Seville in 1248, but Granada held out for another two and a half centuries. Perhaps it was the loss of more and more of al Andalus, evoking thoughts of a lost Paradise, that caused the shift in the symbolism underlying the gardens. In the eleventh century a public park in Cordoba was converted into a funerary garden. The notion of paradise was thus introduced to the garden, and with the passage of time, palace gardens too came to be viewed as paradise on earth.

A supreme example of these is the gardens of the Alhambra in Granada, last stronghold of the Muslim rulers of al Andalus, poised on its rocky eminence above the traffic and bustle of the modern town, imbued with the same pure air as flowed through these courts more than half a millennium ago. The tawny-pink "red castle" is adorned with plaster carved into lace-fine decoration or hanging in row upon row of delicate painted stalactites from intricate ceilings. Fountains fill the air with their water-lace in the courtyards, and arch in jets over the narrow central watercourse of the Generalife's Patio de la Acequia. Here one may imagine still the gardens of Murcia, of which the historian al Maqqari (c. 1578–1632) wrote that they were "filled with scented flowers, singing birds, and waterwheels with rumorous sound."

With the advance of Christendom the old *convivencia* of Muslim rule, with its rich, shared intellectual and spiritual life of Muslims, Jews and Christians, began to erode. After the fall of Granada and the expulsion of the Jews and later the Muslims, the rule of Their Most Catholic Majesties, Ferdinand and Isabella, brought a new, gloomier attitude towards life, especially after Cardinal Ximenes had persuaded Isabella to offer the Muslims a choice: conversion, or exile. Yet even a century after the fall of Seville to the Christians, the garden of the Alcazar was laid out by Muslim craftsmen – as evidenced by the inclusion of an inscription in Arabic of the short Sura *al Ikhlas* from the Qur'an, which refutes the very idea that God might have had a son.

Towards the east, in Persia, the Safavid Ismail captured Tabriz in 1501 and declared himself Shah of Persia – the first native ruler of the country for almost nine hundred years. Later, Shah Abbas (1587-1629) transformed the ancient city of Isfahan into a garden city, with fine buildings known for the limpid blue of their tiles, decorated with floral arabesques to evoke the gardens of Paradise, and

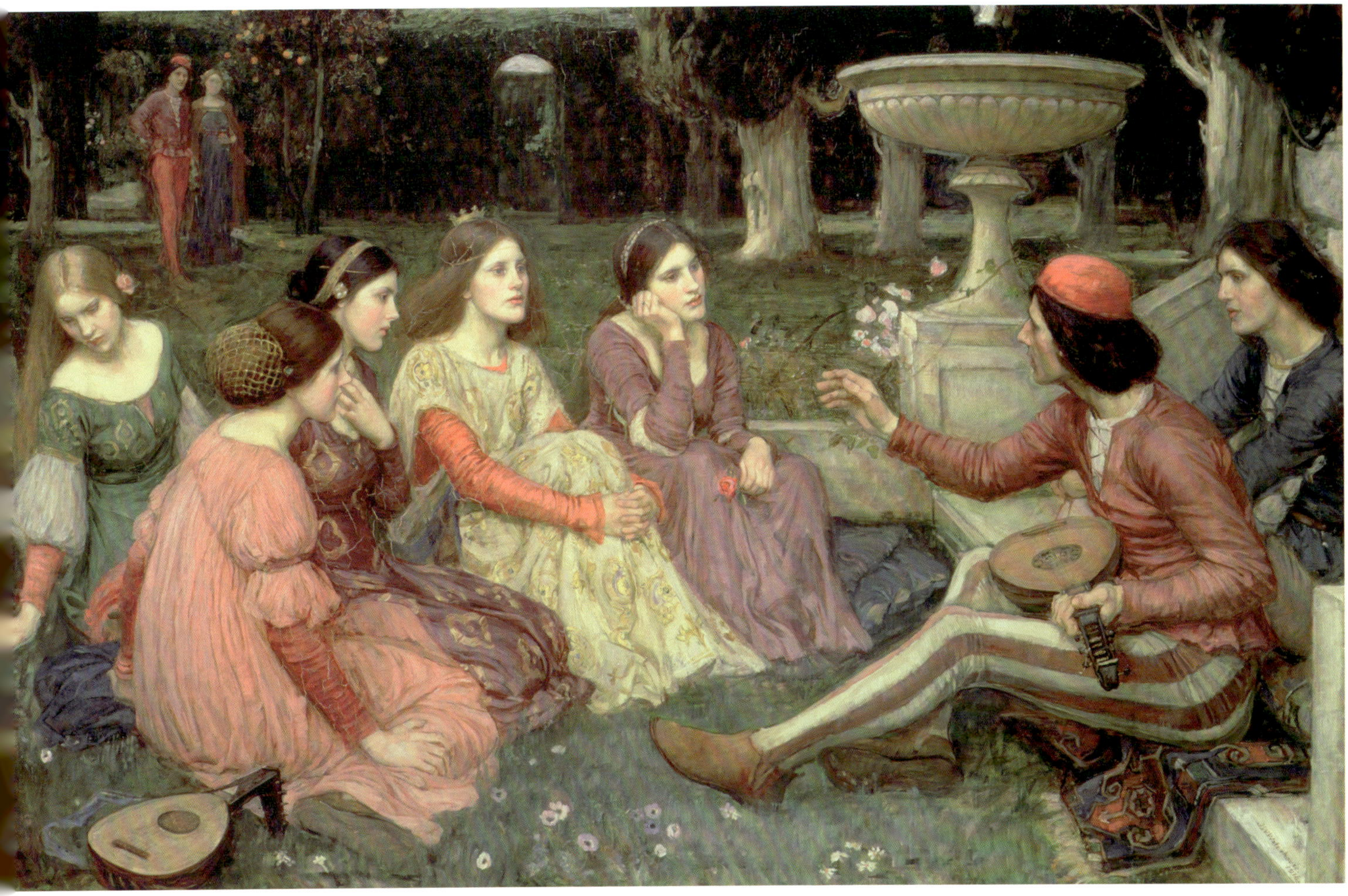

Illus. 16 *In 1350, inspired by Dante, Boccaccio began to compose his famous allegory known as the Decameron, in which ten young people who have sought refuge in a country garden from plague-ridden Florence tell a hundred stories. The book became hugely popular and many illustrated manuscripts of it were produced. This 19th-century painting was doubtless inspired by early illustrations of the Decameron garden. John William Waterhouse (1849-1917), The Decameron. Lady Lever Art Gallery, Liverpool.*

living gardens watered by stone-lined canals. The entire city, indeed, was designed on the *chahar bagh* principle, with the river Zayendehrud intersecting the Chahar Bagh avenue. This great avenue, shaded by stately chenars, was lined with palaces and gardens; one jewel-like palace, in the Garden of the Nightingale, bore the name *Hasht Bihisht* or Eight Paradises – a name often given to the finest gardens.

Paradise as a Garden in Christendom

Catholicism had triumphed over Islam in Spain, where monasticism, too, produced some fine gardens. The tranquillity of the monastic life was in sharp contrast to events in the outside world, for during the fifteenth and sixteenth centuries Europe also experienced the Italian Renaissance, the discovery of the New World, the first stirrings of the scientific revolution, the Reformation –

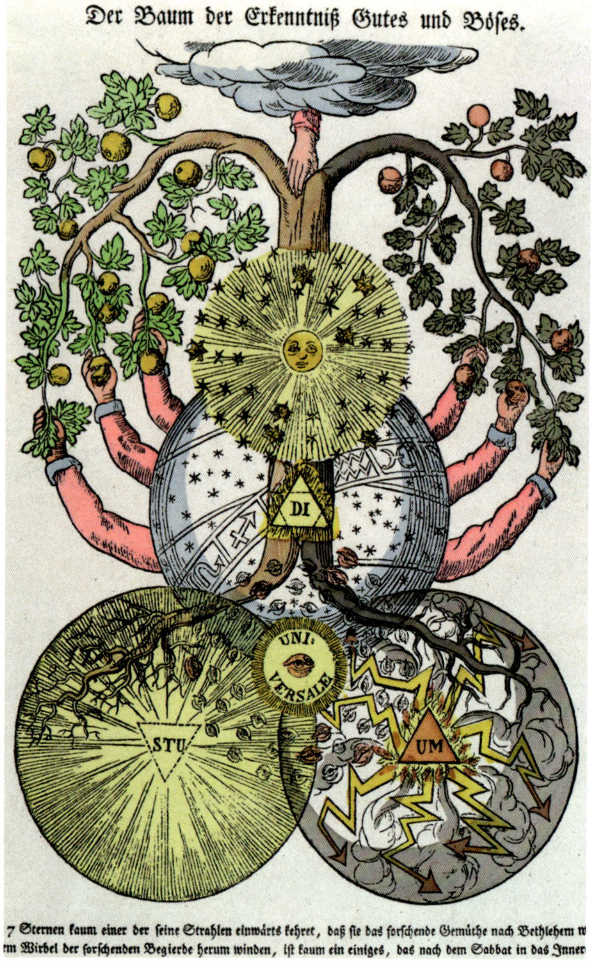

Illus. 17 *The Tree of Life, from a 1785 German manuscript, 'Secret Symbols of the Rosicrucians.' Bibliotheca Philosophica Hermetica, Amsterdam. Man as a tree, the masculine and feminine principles mirroring each other in the two halves of the tree.*

which divided western Europe into Catholic and Protestant – and the Catholic response in the Counter-reformation. To trace their impact on gardens, we need to step back in time to the cusp of the Middle Ages and the Renaissance.

The French-educated Florentine Petrarch (1304-1374) stimulated the revival of classical learning that became the foundation of one of the main strands of Renaissance humanism. Petrarch read and copied Virgil, Cicero, Seneca, and also St Augustine. He was not the first to turn to the past for inspiration; already in the time of Dante (1265-1321) the miserable conditions for most people in Italy were turning the thoughts of the educated classes not only to the Christian other world but also to the lost glories of imperial Rome. The classics were read once more, and Dante made Virgil his guide through Hell and his companion through Purgatory.

The rulers of the city-states of Renaissance Italy also looked to a pagan past, but a more glorious one, in worldly terms at least: to the grandeur of Imperial Rome. The villas and gardens of the Italian Renaissance were first conceived as the formal recreation of the classical Roman style. Cosimo de Medici (1389-1464) employed the Florentine Michelozzo (1396-1472) to remake the garden of his villa at Careggi on this model, with myrtle, bay and cypress trees. It was the setting for the literary and philosophical discussions of the Platonic Academy, of which Marsilio Ficino (1433-1499) was the first president and the Neo-Platonist and Kabbalist Pico della Mirandola (1463-1494) a prominent member. Cosimo and Ficino were convinced – wrongly – that in the manuscript known as the *Corpus hermeticum*, which they ascribed to Hermes Trismegistus, they had discovered the primordial revelation, the ancient Egyptian solar symbolism, preceding that of Moses, which had been the inspiration of the Persian Magi, Pythagoras, and Plato himself.

Throughout the fifteenth and sixteenth centuries, the men of the Renaissance expended immense energies on both biblical scholarship and efforts to identify the exact location of the historical paradise, as required by biblical exegesis, in their quest for the origins of humankind. They continued to be fascinated by the notion of the primordial revelation, one which both preceded and transcended the theological dogmas of mediaeval Christendom, and many shared Ficino's belief that they had found it in the Hermetic texts.

As the Thirty Years' War (1618-1648) ravaged a Europe divided between Catholics and Protestants, it remained to the Puritan poet John Milton (1608-1674) to bring home to western man just how completely paradise was lost to all of Christendom. In the Christian epic *Paradise Lost*, Milton describes Eden, "delicious Paradise," in images and symbols that amalgamate, in typically Renaissance fashion, both the Biblical and the classical traditions. But Milton's work may also be read as an esoteric work, replete with Hermetic symbolism: an allegory of mankind's spiritual history, interweaving the symbolism of the old religions and classical mythology into its exoteric account of the Fall. He compares man's spiritual growth to that of a tree:

. . . So from the root
Springs lighter the green stalk, from thence the leaves
More aerie, last the bright consummate floure
Spirits odorous breathes; flours and thir fruit
Mans nourishment, by gradual scale sublim'd
To vital Spirits aspire . . .
Your bodies may at last turn all to Spirit
Improv'd by tract of time, and wingd ascend
Ethereal, as wee, or may at choice
Here or in Heav'ly Paradises dwell.

Milton's earthly paradise is blessed with the perpetual spring of the classical Golden Age and the west wind that blows over Elysium, and with the four rivers and the Trees of Life and of the Knowledge of Good and Evil of Eden. It has the fragrance of the Christian Latin paradise, an abundance of ripe fruits yielding to the reclining Adam and Eve by the "compliant boughs" like the fruits of the Qur'anic *jannah* (but also fruit that recalls the golden apples of the Hesperides, "burnisht with Golden Rind"), and the songs of birds. It is a landscape of immense grandeur, dwarfing its human occupants.

The formality of the *hortus conclusus* is all that is missing from Milton's Eden, which is thus closer to Dante's Earthly Paradise, the Sacred Wood, and to the Virgilian Elysian Fields, than to the symmetry of the Islamic paradise garden.

As we have seen, the Qur'anic *jannah*, though etymologically derived from the *Gan Eden* of Genesis, is a very different garden from that of the earthly paradise. *Jannah* is unequivocally a metaphor for the hereafter, and its earthly equivalents, the paradise gardens, know themselves to be mere time-bound imitations. The Judaeo-Christian earthly paradise stands for the lost perfection when time was without meaning, and only later did the idea of paradise come to be assimilated to the eternal rewards of the after-life. In *jannah*, as in the paradise gardens of the Islamic world, beauty lies in order, in symmetry, in enclosure against hostile nature. In the earthly paradise, before the Fall, nature itself is perfection, plants and animals and man living in innocent, sexless harmony one with another, amid the timeless elements of beauty – trees, water, stone, the curve of a hill and the dip of a valley. As we shall see, the belief that it still existed somewhere on earth was to persist in Christendom well beyond the end of the Middle Ages, and to coexist with the new scientific frame of mind that marked the beginning of the modern era.

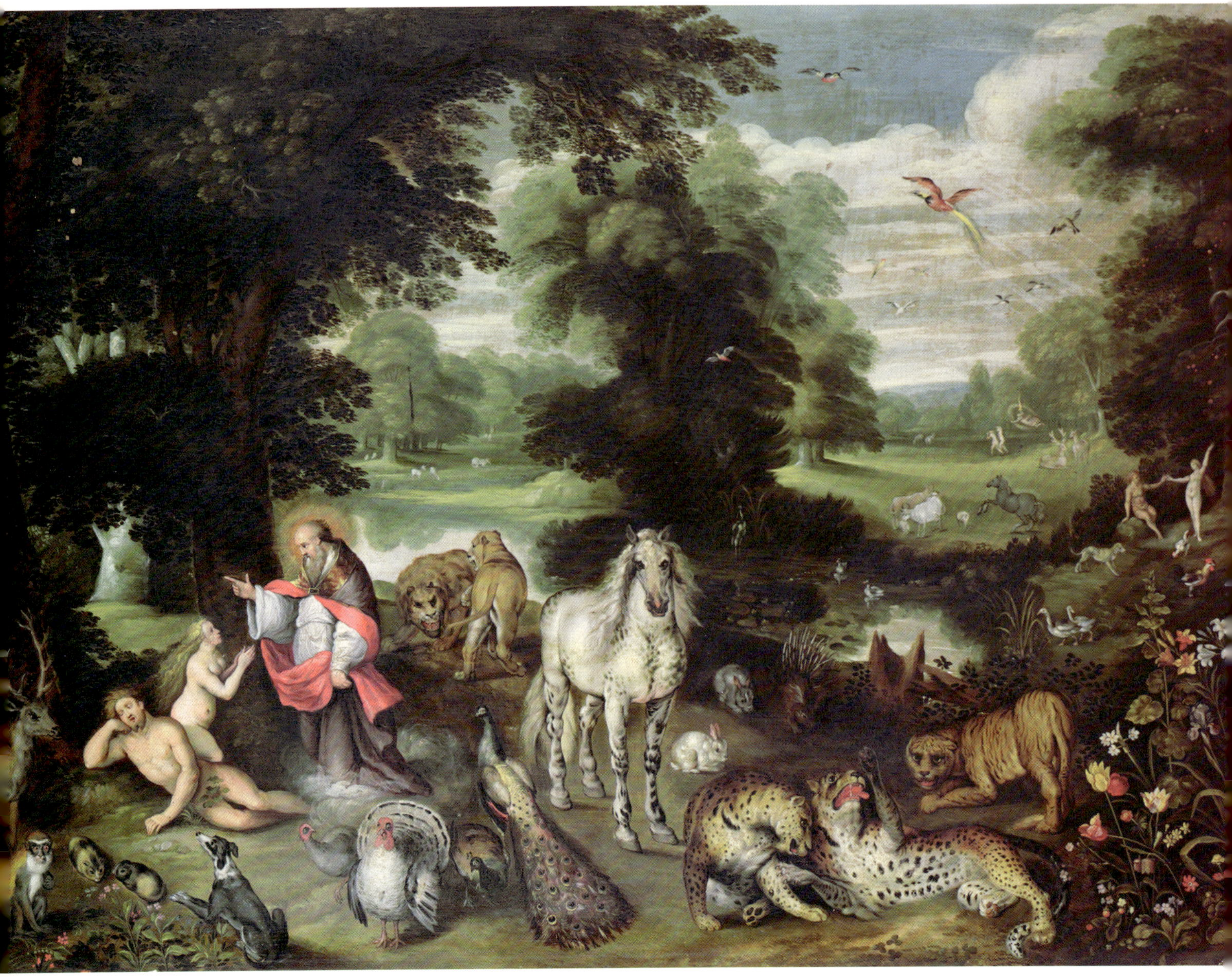

Illus. 18 *Jan Brueghel the Elder (1568-1625), The Garden of Eden. Flowers bloom and fruits ripen together, with sundry birds and beasts, including a couple of playful-looking leopards, living happily together in a landscape resembling a park informally planted with exotics. Though this is a typical representation of the Garden of Eden as an idealized "natural" landscape, there was also a widespread belief in Christendom, as in Islam, that the perfection of the first Garden lay in symmetry; that the irregularities of nature were not beautiful at all, but the result of the Fall, which disrupted the proper order of things. Alan Jacobs Gallery, London.*

Eden Recreated and Lost

Early Christians who believed in the physical reality of the earthly paradise thought that it must be located to the east of the inhabited earth, beyond the encircling ocean. Not only did it have a benign climate, in which trees bore fruit all year round, echoing the Tree of Life of the Book of Revelation; it was also known for its exquisite fragrances. And it was watered by four rivers, as described in Genesis, which early Christian writers saw as bringing the blessings of paradise to ordinary mortals, by flowing out into the four great rivers of the inhabited world.

In Christendom, men were to continue to search for the earthly paradise right up to and beyond the time of the great navigators. Columbus, Vasco da Gama, and others had more than purely commercial motives, seeking not only an alternative route to import costly spices but also the Garden of Eden. Columbus' innovation was that he thought he could find that "garden eastward in Eden" by sailing west. There were rival theories on the location of Eden. One held that since the precious, aromatic spices themselves originated in Eden, the fragrant airs of the southern seas suggested it might be found somewhere off Mozambique. As Milton would later say, paradise was a place of "groves whose rich trees wept odorous gums and balms."

Columbus never ceased to believe that the fresh water currents in the Gulf of Paria originated in the four rivers of Eden and that he had discovered, in Haiti, the Biblical Ophir. But despite the claims of other explorers, it slowly became clear that the original Garden of Eden had not been conclusively located in the new lands reached by the great navigators.

The conscious or unconscious yearning to regain the lost perfection of Eden continued to influence the making of gardens in the west as the mediaeval yielded to the modern era. This included the seemingly scientific endeavour of making gardens where plants from many parts of the world were the object of study. This was the era of the navigators, discovering new lands and new plants. The first modern botanical gardens looked both ways, back to the mediaeval conviction that Eden existed on earth, forward to the scientific spirit that took such a leap ahead in the years between 1500 and 1700. This was the period known as the Scientific Revolution, whose proponents also saw science and reason as a means of reimposing order on this disordered planet.

Precursors of the Modern Botanical Garden

The early botanical gardens of Europe were not the first such gardens to be made; merely the first in the Christian world. Those inquiring scientists, the Greeks, had got there first. Anticipating Linnaeus, Aristotle's pupil Theophrastus (327-287 BCE) wrote a treatise, *Enquiry Into Plants*, in which he attempted to develop a systematic botanical classification. He had plenty of material to work with, as he was in charge of the garden in the master's school at the Lyceum in Athens, which included plants brought back from Alexander's expeditions to the east. Pliny the Elder, who says that herbals of the first century BCE were often illustrated in colour, wrote his own *Natural History*, compiled from Greek sources, in the first century CE.

Another important botanical work, by Pliny's Greek contemporary Dioscorides, is known as *De Materia Medica*, the earliest known illustrated

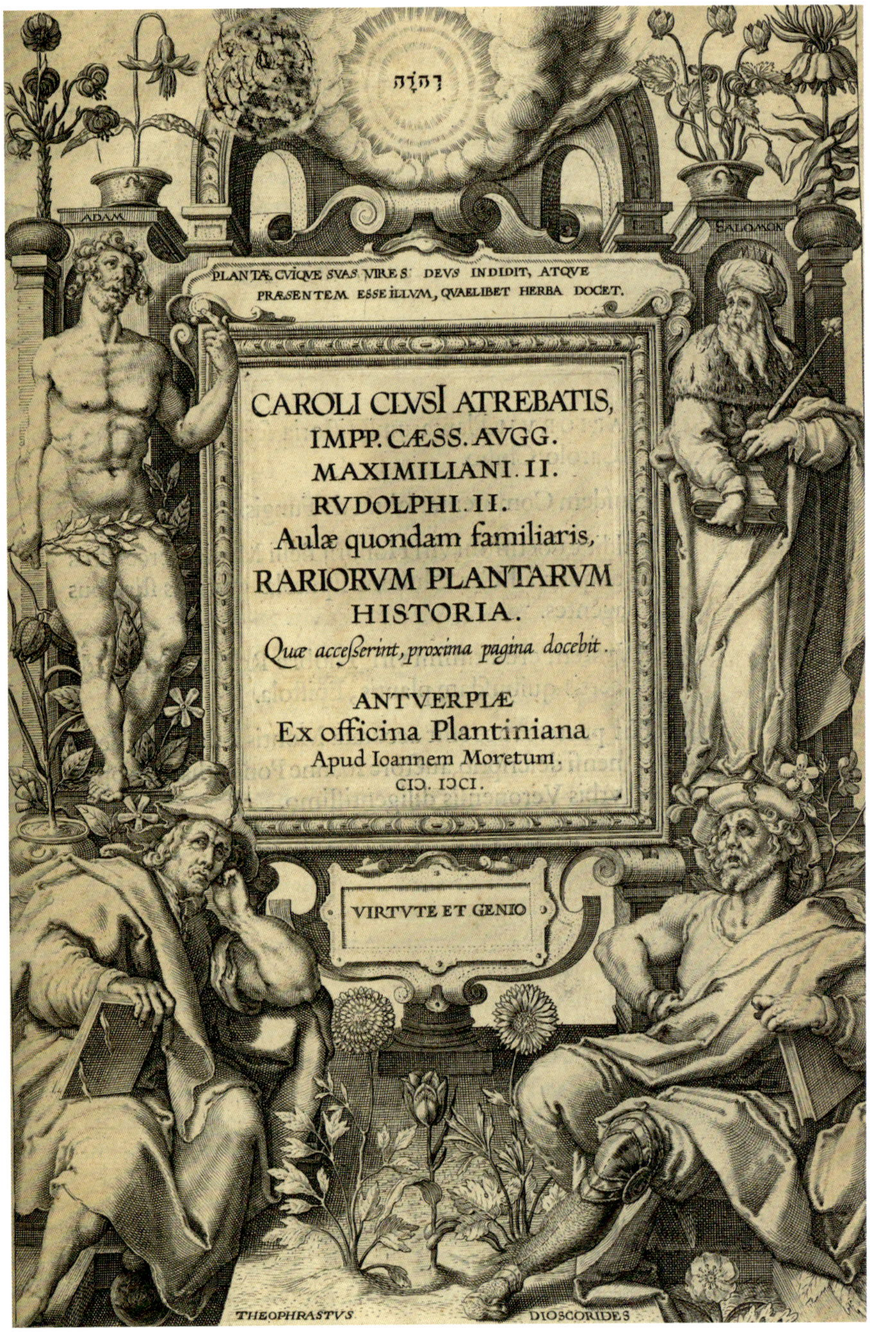

Illus. 19 *Title page of Clusius's Rariorum plantarum historia, Antwerp, 1601, featuring Adam, who named all the plants; Solomon, famed for his wisdom; Theophrastus, curator of the botanic garden of Aristotle's Lyceum; and Dioscorides, author of the classical work on pharmacology known as* De materia medica.

copy of which dates from about 512 CE. This encyclopaedia of herbal medicine continued in use in Christendom for centuries, and also reached the Islamic world, translated into Syriac and Arabic. The Islamic world in turn provided Christendom with its most important work of medicine and pharmacopoeia, *al qanun fil' tibb*, the *Canon of Medicine* of Ibn Sina (Avicenna: 980-1037), which drew upon both Hippocrates and Galen. Known in the west as early as the twelfth century, the *Canon* was still the standard work in the seventeenth, at the universities of Louvain and Montpellier.

The cultivation of plants for medicinal purposes continued, in monastery and manor and cottage garden alike. These mediaeval herb gardens, though essentially intended for practical use in the treatment of ailments rather than scientific study, are not unconnected in intent with the early botanical gardens. And indeed, there was good Biblical warrant for botanical gardens to be associated with pharmacology. The Genesis account merely says that the Lord God made "to grow every tree that is pleasant to the sight, and good for food," but Ezekiel's vision was of trees that bore not only fruit "for meat," but also "the leaf thereof for medicine."

The First Botanical Gardens

Wherever Eden may have been, the world after the Fall is disordered; plants no longer grow together, but are dispersed throughout the globe. The early botanical gardens of Europe were an attempt to bring together once more, as in Eden, "every herb bearing seed, which is upon the face of all the earth, and every tree, in the which is the fruit of a tree yielding seed."[35] And with the discovery of the Americas such a project seemed, for the first time, a practical possibility. Once a specimen of every kind of plant had been discovered, perhaps the true identity of the Tree of Life and of the Tree of Knowledge of Good and Evil could be established. At the same time, assembled in one place, every other plant could be named, and their value to mankind, for medicinal or other purposes, properly determined.

The earliest modern botanical gardens, such as those of Padua, Leiden and Montpellier, were established in the sixteenth century, followed by Oxford, Paris (the Jardin du Roi, renamed after the Revolution as the Jardin des Plantes) and Uppsala, in the seventeenth century. They were laid out in a formal, symmetrical design, derived from the *hortus conclusus*, often in four quarters representing the age-old cosmic symbolism of the four quarters of the world. They were thus by no means empty of religious significance. The botanical garden at Padua was designed as a microcosm of the world, and that at Leiden combined the Celestial City with the Garden of Eden. The rectangular or radiating beds, the geometric layout, certainly facilitated scientific study and research. But more than scientific curiosity alone motivated the makers of these botanical gardens, who sought not only to study but also to reassemble the elements of the lost paradise that had been dispersed by the Fall.

For both practical and symbolic reasons, animals were not kept in the botanical gardens, but in separate enclosures. The botanical garden was to be a place of happy sexlessness, like the first Eden. Though the sexual reproduction of plants was barely recognized, with the exception of the date palm – which, as Theophrastus already knew, had separate male and female forms – no one could be blind to the fact that animals not only reproduced sexually, like mankind, but were remarkably shameless about it. Birds, however, were allowed, or encouraged, into the sexless paradise of the orchard or botanical garden as Eden. Their sex lives were not too obtrusive as a rule, and could be overlooked for the sake of the greater symbolism – winged, their natural element the air, they were regarded as midway between man and the angels.

The spiritual dimension of the garden as Eden is quite explicit in Ralph Austen's seventeenth century

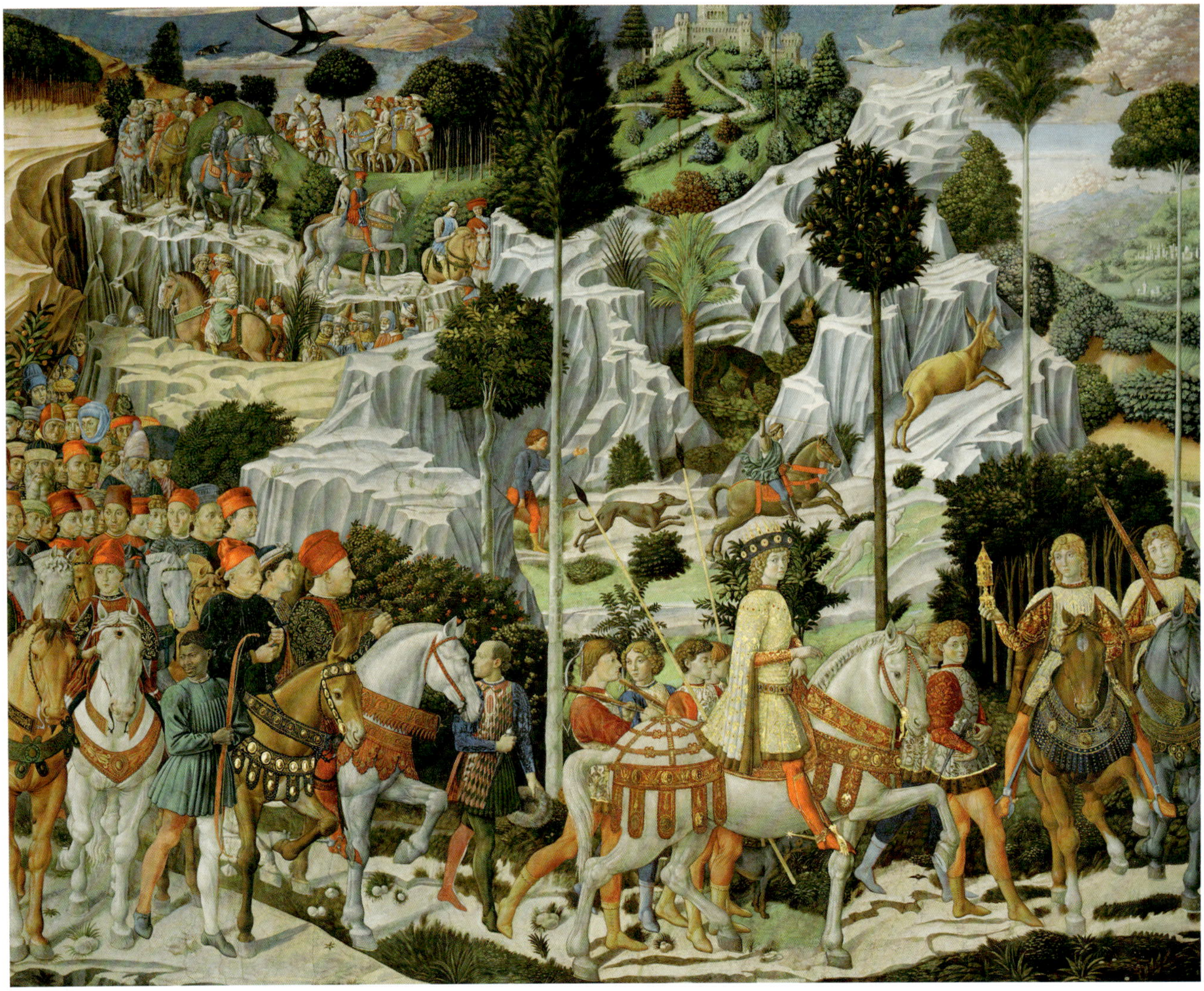

Illus. 20 *Benozzo Gozzoli (15th century), Journey of the Magi, in the Palazzo Medici Riccardi in Florence (1459–61)*

allegorical work "The Spirituall use of an Orchard: Held forth in divers Similitudes betweene Naturall & Spirituall Fruit trees: according to Scripture and Experience." The trees in the orchards of Austen's day were often set out in a pattern of quincunxes, which Austen's contemporary, the philosopher Sir Thomas Browne, considered as a revelation of "the mystical mathematics of the city of Heaven." The same pattern was to be found in Eden, according to Browne: "Since even in Paradise itself, the tree of knowledge was placed in the middle of the Garden, whatever was the ambient figure, there wanted not a centre."

Gardens of the Italian Renaissance and Baroque

The development of the pleasure garden in the West was taking place in an increasingly secularized world, which was shifting towards a more sensate attitude towards life. In Europe, at least, the formal gardens of the period from the early Renaissance to the early eighteenth century were an expression of this new outlook. The villas and gardens of the Italian Renaissance were principally conceived as a formal re-creation of the classical Roman style, though traces of the *hortus conclusus* were to linger on. Garden-making in Rome became a fine art, entrusted to architects and painters; and again, Greece and, above all, Imperial Rome were the source of their inspiration. It began with Pope Julius II (1503-1513), who engaged Bramante (1444-1514) to make the Belvedere Court and Statue Court in the Vatican. At much the same time, Cardinal Giuliano de Medici commissioned Raphael (1483-1520) to assist in making the Villa Madama, a series of garden rooms rather than a house, between 1516 and 1520. With Bramante and Raphael there began the classicizing of Roman gardens. At the entrance to the Statue Court – which housed Pope Julius' collection of statues and was planted with orange trees – stood a statue of Hercules, as if guarding a sacred precinct, where the fruit of the oranges brought to mind the golden apples of the Hesperides. The theme of Hercules and the Hesperides appeared in other Roman Renaissance gardens, too, including those of the Villa d'Este.

The gardens of the Villa d'Este at Tivoli, made for the Cardinal Ippolito d'Este by Pirro Ligorio (1493-1580) are without doubt the most famous of Italian Renaissance gardens, with their astonishing cascades and fountains on a series of terraces below the house. As in the paradise gardens of Persia and Mughal India, water is the central element; but rather than being musical and peaceful, at the Villa d'Este its dominant impression is of noise and constant, restless movement. Even here, the other world was not wholly set aside by the motives of self-aggrandisement. The hydraulics and mechanics that created these spectacular effects also illustrated the laws of nature, the creation of God. Classical and Christian mythology blend here: the statue of Hercules holding the three golden apples of the Hesperides merges with the symbolism of the Garden of Eden.

The Church preserved the Christian concept of the earthly paradise that was so strongly influenced by the pagan poets of classical Rome. Christian symbols were still strongly present in Renaissance Italy, alongside the passionate rediscovery of an antique past. One of those symbols was the mediaeval *hortus conclusus*. Thus in Benozzo Gozzoli's fresco of 1459, the *Journey of the Magi* in the chapel of the Palazzo Medici-Riccardi in Florence, the procession, winding its way through a formalized landscape of the Val d'Arno, arrives at the *hortus conclusus* of the sanctuary of the chapel.

The garden of the Jesuit novitiate on Quirinal hill in Rome was created with explicitly Christian themes. The garden was destroyed in the nineteenth century, but a description of it by the French Jesuit Louis Richeome dating from 1611 survives. A statue of the Virgin stood at the entrance to the upper garden, while within was Christ surrounded by fragrant plants – hyssop, lilies, roses, balsam – and a quotation from the Song of Songs: "I am come into my garden, my sister, my spouse; I have gathered my myrrh with my spices."

The gardens of Bernini (1598-1680), in the flamboyant style known as baroque, are said to have been influenced by the Jesuits. Indeed, the baroque, like the Jesuits themselves, emerged during the Counter-Reformation, in reaction against puritan austerity. Forsaking the static classical stability, the baroque appeals to the senses, seeking to surprise, to dazzle, to excite the imagination; it is an art of movement, of light, of contrast.

The extravagances of the baroque provoked, in turn, a counter-reaction, in the shape of the Accademia dell'Arcadia, a literary and artistic academy founded in Rome in 1690. Its members – scientists, aristocrats and princes of the Church – sought to break away from the Petrarchian tradition and to rediscover the classical models: Virgil, Theocritus, Pindar, Anacreon. They affected simple ways, meeting in the open at the

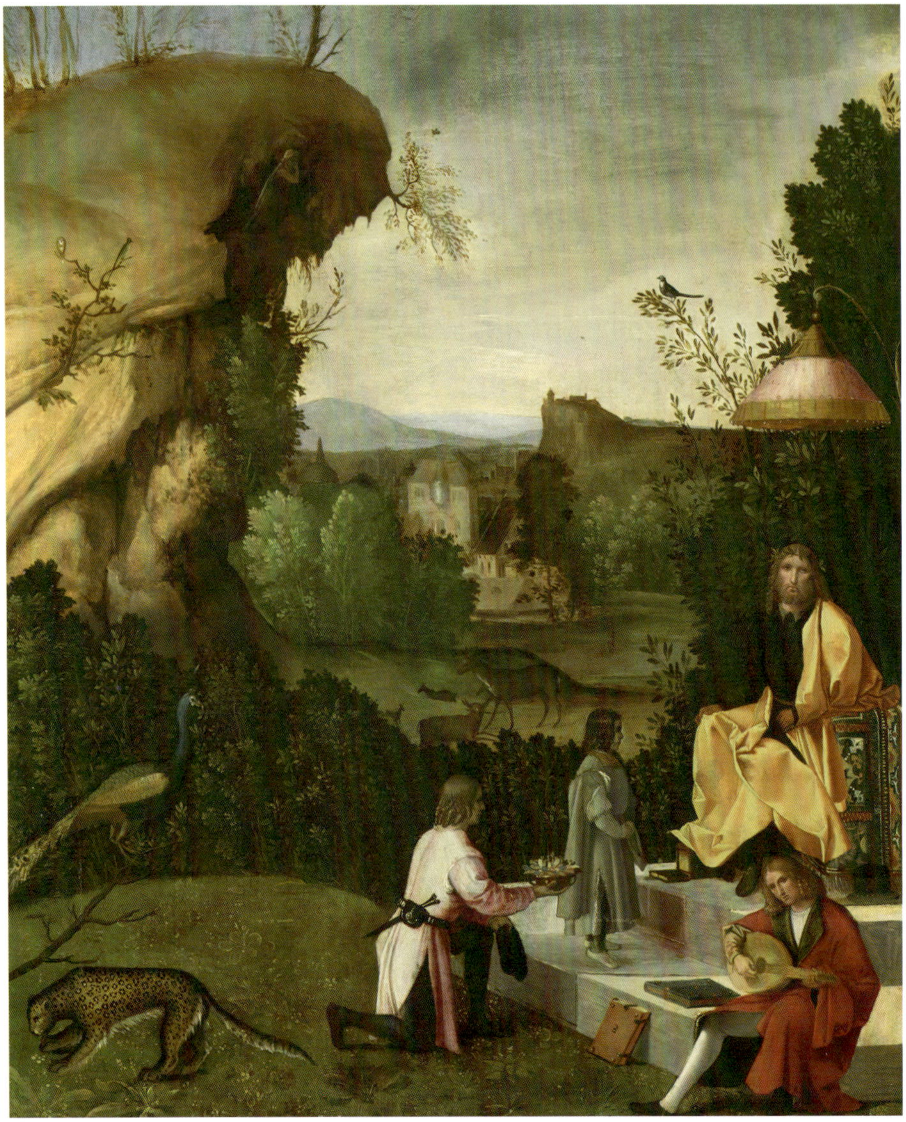

Illus. 21 *The Baroque was in part inspired by the pastoral novel of Sannazaro, Arcadia, published in 1504, full of descriptions which were also to influence landscape painting in Venice, and ultimately the landscapes of Claude. The Arcadian spirit is beautifully expressed in a painting by a follower of Giorgione (early 16th century) entitled Homage to a Poet – tellingly, it was previously known as The Golden Age – in which an Arcadian poet is accompanied by a pard and a peacock painted in heraldic style on a carpet of flowers.*

Illus. 23 *"An agreeable mixture of garden and forest" – the grounds of the Palace of Versailles, with the Orangery*

Bosco Parrasio in Rome, and adopted the names of rustic Arcadian shepherds. The classical Greek, Roman and Renaissance tradition of the garden as the setting for poets and philosophers to meet had re-emerged.

The Gardens of France

Fine gardens were not unknown in France when the great Italian gardens were first being made. The fifteenth century dukes of Burgundy made a magnificent park and garden at Hesdin, and René d'Anjou (1409-1480) made gardens in both Anjou and Aix en Provence, with roses and fruit trees of the newest and best varieties. But tradition has it that it was the visit of Charles VIII (1483-1498) to Italy in the 1490s that gave rise to the Renaissance garden in France. Of his visit to Naples, he wrote: "You would not believe the beautiful gardens I have [seen] in this city, for, upon my word, it seems that only Adam and Eve are lacking to make it a

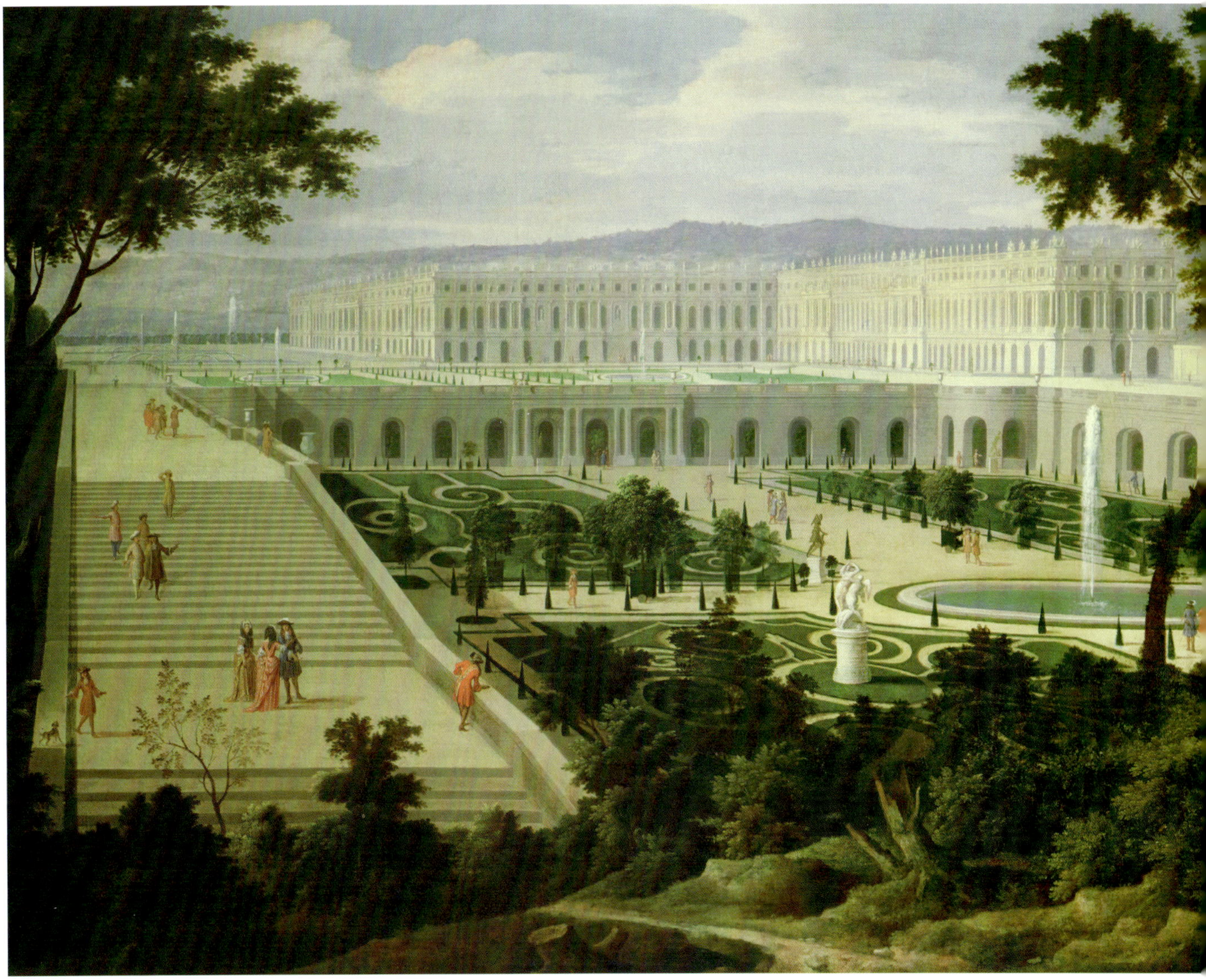

terrestrial paradise, it is so lovely." Charles engaged an Italian to beautify royal Blois and Amboise in the Italian style. The garden of François I (1515-1547) at Fontainebleau was also embellished in the Italian style.

The old ways were not entirely discarded, however. In the sixteenth century garden of the château of Villandry, the intricate geometry owes much to the mediaeval monastic garden, and the parterre closest to the house is a *Jardin d'amour*, an allegory of the four kinds of love (tragic, passionate, adulterous, tender) laid out in clipped box.

Love may have reigned at Villandry, but the sixteenth century was a century of war – first with Spain, and then the Wars of Religion that effectively destroyed the Renaissance civilization of France, brought to an end only by the Edict of Nantes of 1598. The peace and growing prosperity that followed allowed the French aristocracy to develop their vast gardens. Marie de Medicis, wife of Henri of Navarre, who became king in 1594, commissioned Jacques Boyceau to beautify the Jardin du Luxembourg between 1611 and 1620 after Henri was assassinated. It has been an inspiration to many writers and artists, from John Evelyn to Watteau, Rousseau, Rilke and others. The seventeenth century, when the Sun King Louis XIV reigned, was also the century of two great families of royal gardeners, the Mollets and the Le Nôtres. It was the genius of André Le Nôtre that created the grandiose formal French parterres, canals and avenues of Fouquet's Vaux-le-Vicomte and of Louis XIV's Versailles.

The Myth Endures

Whether in the shape of the Eden of Genesis or the classical Golden Age, the paradise myth was too deeply rooted in the human psyche to fade easily before the advance of science and temporal power. Religious belief in the existence of paradise was waning, but the myth was preserved in the literary genre of the utopia, a creation of the Renaissance and the Reformation. Like most of his Christian contemporaries, Sir Thomas More, author of *Utopia*, an allegory of a fictional, seemingly perfect island society, continued to believe that the original paradise still existed somewhere on this earth. Thus John Evelyn (1620-1706) urged, in one of his lesser known works, the *Kalendarium hortense* of 1664, that gardens should be made to resemble as nearly as possible the Garden of Eden. He was well aware, though, that "nor will our Gardens (as near as we can contrive them to the resemblance of that blessed abode), remain long in their perfection, unless they are also continually cultivated."

For Evelyn, gardens "signifie . . . *rem sacram et divinam*," a sacred and divine reality. He spoke of the Garden of Eden as the paradise of God and of the garden as "the church Catholic on Earth" and "Triumphant in Heaven."[36] Kings and philosophers, he claimed, "when they would frame a type of Heaven . . . describe a garden." This is strikingly close to the concept of the Islamic paradise garden of the Mughal or Safavid dynasties. But unlike the Islamic garden, Evelyn's perfect garden for kings and princes included a botanical garden of the Leiden, Padua, Oxford or Paris type, where plants from all over the world would be gathered.

Abraham Cowley (1618-1667), apostrophizing John Evelyn in his ode *The Garden*, was in no doubt that the purpose of the garden-maker's art was to recreate the lost Eden:

. . . we count it to excel,
If it a docile scholar can appear
To Nature, and but imitate her well,
It over-rules, and is her master here.
It imitates her Maker's power divine,
And changes her sometimes, and sometimes does refine;
It does, like Grace, the fallen tree restore
To its blest state of Paradise before.

What the garden maker could not do, of course, was to restore the perpetual yet fruitful spring of Eden. Impossible this universal dream may be, but that did not prevent gardeners from planting new and improved varieties of fruit, and trying to cheat the seasons. Francis Bacon, in his 1625 Essay *On Gardens*, which begins with the words "God Almighty first planted a garden," gives a list of the flowers and fruits that can be enjoyed month by month. He begins with "December and January and the latter part of November," when "you must take such things as are green all winter: . . . orange-trees, lemon-trees, and myrtles, if they be stoved," and concluding "that you may have *ver perpetuum*, as the place affords."

Another reason for the decline of the botanical garden as Eden ideal was the growing awareness that there were far too many plants in the world to be brought together in one place. The day of the enclosed garden was, for a time at least, at an end. There were political and ideological reasons for this, too. The great formal gardens of Europe, whether or not they were consciously made in the image of paradise, were the direct expression of the Hobbesian quest for domination. The powerful and the wealthy had both the desire and the ability to impose upon their lands an image of the social hierarchy which they dominated. This they did by extending outwards into the surrounding country in vast avenues, or by adding formal garden upon formal garden for as long as the owner's resources or interest lasted.

The English Landscape Garden

Like the early botanical gardens, Tudor gardens in sixteenth century England were an evolution of the *hortus conclusus*, with elaborate knot gardens of clipped evergreens, topiary, and pleached trees. Francis Bacon regarded knot gardens as "toys," but there were those who perceived in them a clear religious meaning. Though there were grand formal gardens in the French style in seventeenth century Britain, the ostentatious splendour of the great French gardens suited the British taste less well than the more intimate, domesticated formal gardens of Holland, introduced with William of Orange to England in 1688. But in England a revolution in garden art would soon take place in which the formal style, as an expression of wealth and power, was swept aside.

By the early eighteenth century, the Dutch-style formal gardens were beginning to look old-fashioned, under the impact of the ideas of Anthony Ashley Cooper, 3rd Earl of Shaftesbury (1671-1713), Joseph Addison (1672-1719) and Alexander Pope (1688-1744), who published essays in which they recognized the awe-inspiring beauty of untamed nature. They were influenced by the gardens of Italy so much admired by Englishmen on the Grand Tour, as well as by the accounts of Chinese gardens brought back by Christian missionaries. The great formal gardens of France, which led the eye to distant vistas and merged into the surrounding forest plantations, also appealed to them. Addison, a proponent of the new appreciation of nature, considered that

> *our English gardens are not so entertaining to the fancy as those of France and Italy, where we see a large extent of ground covered over with an agreeable mixture of garden and forest, which represent everywhere an artificial rudeness, much more charming than that neatness and elegancy we meet with in those of our own country.*[37]

The time was ripe for the English landscape gardeners to evolve their idealized landscapes. Pope recommended the description of the gardens of Alcinous in Homer's *Odyssey*, for offering "all the justest rules and provisions which can go toward composing the best gardens." These gardens were "fenced with a green enclosure all around," just as the great Capability Brown landscapes were surrounded by belts of trees for privacy.

Addison and Pope were not alone in their views. Stephen Switzer affirmed in his *Ichnographia Rustica* of 1718 that "those who were most capable of art were always most fond of nature." And Batty Langley, whose *New Principles of Gardening* appeared in 1728, though he still proposed parterres, avenues and labyrinths, was moving away from the stiff formality of the great set-piece gardens of France. He called for the "truly grand and noble after nature's own manner." In Europe, and especially in Britain, the idea that nature herself was beautiful, in all her diversity – as the Chinese had long known – was displacing the old conviction that nothing had been as it should be since the Fall. But even nature was still in need of improvement; and the "improvers" were there to respond to the demands of the wealthy, who were willing to lay out huge sums for the purpose.

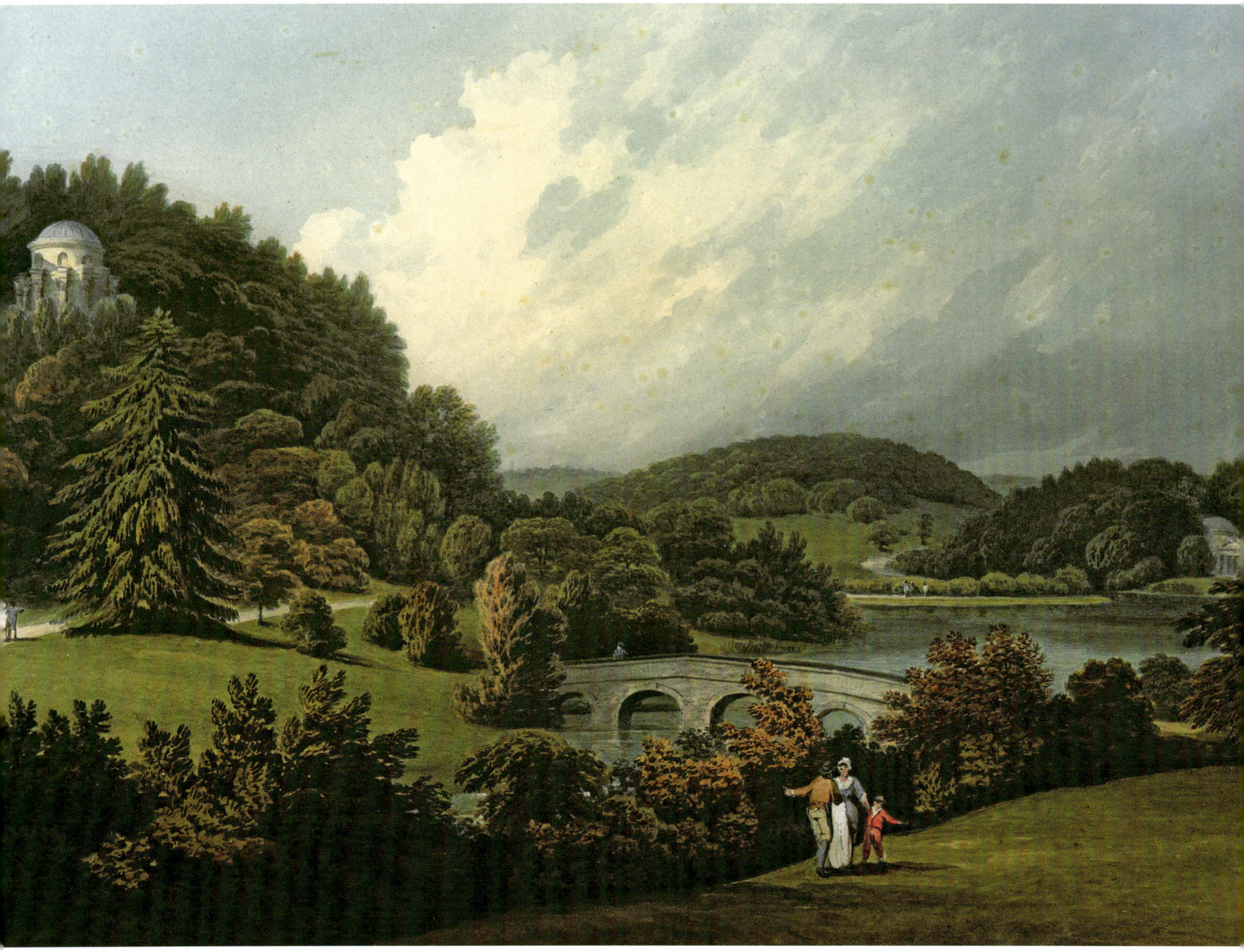

Illus. 24 *Francis Nicholson (1753-1844), Stourhead, watercolour on paper.*

In the hands of the professional landscape gardeners William Kent (1684-1748) and Lancelot "Capability" Brown (1715-1783), the ideas of Addison and Pope, Switzer and Langley were transformed into an entirely different expression of the garden as metaphor for paradise – or more exactly, the garden as nature perfected. No longer was the garden enclosed against hostile nature. Instead, with the new confidence in human capacity to dominate nature that developed with the rise of rationalism, it was conceived as an idealized landscape, looking outward. The art historian and man of letters Horace Walpole (1717-1797) said of Kent that "He leaped the fence and saw that all Nature was a garden." [38] Walpole wrote of Brown that:

With one lost Paradise the name
Of our first ancestor is stained;
Brown shall enjoy unsullied fame
For many a Paradise regained.[39]

Now the poets no longer evoke the imagined earthly paradise or its parody, the enchanted garden. It is the real landscape garden itself that they extol, and to which they attribute Edenic epithets. In his essay *On Modern Gardening*,[40] Horace Walpole said of John Milton:

He seems with the prophetic eye of taste . . . to have foreseen modern gardening. . . The description of Eden is a warmer and more just picture of the present style than Claude Lorraine could have painted from Hagley or Stourhead.

Kent and Brown swept away enclosures, brought close-cropped grass right to the walls of the stately houses of their clients, and devised the ha-ha (a sunken fence or wall and ditch) to prevent the cattle, sheep and deer in the parks from straying too close to the house without visual interruption to the apparently unbroken sweep of grass. And they improved on nature by planting trees in carefully-sited clumps and belts, excavating lakes and damming and diverting rivers. The idealized landscapes they thus created were adorned with Palladian temples and graceful bridges, and set with statuary. One of the most perfect of these great landscape gardens is Stowe, completed by William Kent after others (Vanbrugh, Gibbs, and in particular Charles Bridgeman) had worked on it. As James Thomson wrote in *The Seasons*:

The fair majestic paradise of Stowe!
Not Persian Cyrus on Ionia's shore
E'er saw such sylvan scenes, such various art
By genius fired, such ardent genius tamed
By cool judicious art, that in the strife
All-beauteous Nature fears to be outdone.[41]

More irreverently, Nathaniel Cotton (1705-1788) wrote these lines On Lord Cobham's Garden:

It puzzles much the sages' brains,
Where Eden stood of yore;
Some place it in Arabia's plains
Some say it is no more.
But Cobham can these tales confute,
As all the curious know;
For he hath proved, beyond dispute,
That Paradise is Stowe.

The men who made these idealized landscapes drew their inspiration from Poussin and Claude Lorrain. Though these artists painted Biblical as well as classical themes, they looked for their inspiration primarily to the Virgilian Golden Age, or to Arcadia. The men of the Renaissance and their heirs looked back to ancient Greece and Rome as well as to their own Judaeo-Christian heritage. The classical education essential to the making of a gentleman until well into the early years of the twentieth century ensured that to the owners of Stowe and the other great landscape gardens, such as Henry Hoare's Stourhead, every element had symbolic meaning, evoking the Graeco-Roman past, at least at the intellectual and aesthetic level. It is less clear whether their makers were also conscious that they were echoing in aesthetic terms the ancient sacred landscape of stone, tree, water.

Horace Walpole liked to think that the English landscape garden was entirely an English creation and was distinctly sniffy about both what he called the "fantastic" *sharawadgi* (a word first used by William Temple in his *Gardens of Epicurus*) or "whimsical irregularity" of Chinese gardens and the geometric formality of French gardens. Continental European writers, however, found no difficulty in suggesting that the inspiration for these great landscapes was not the English spirit, but rather English borrowings from Chinese gardening art – indeed,

English landscape gardens were known as "le jardin anglo-chinois." The Chinese had always regarded a longing for mountains and water as an expression of the spiritual life, and appreciated the beauty of stone and water as well as plants in their gardens. A "Confucian" view of life, rationalist and somewhat resistant to transcendental religion, was shared by the Chinese and the English gentry. Perhaps this combined with the sophisticated Chinese spiritual appreciation of nature and the European "Back to Nature" movement of the eighteenth century to generate the same kind of "poetic" garden art. But even allowing for the eighteenth century English fashion for grottoes, there was a clear difference between the broad expanses of grass, water and trees of the English landscape garden, and the lawnless Chinese garden, which had numerous buildings grouped in courtyards set with fantastically shaped rocks piled one against or upon the other in a manner that would seem cramped and frenetic to the European eye.

The landscape movement was comparatively short-lived, though several of these great landscapes still survive, showing in maturity the reach of their makers' vision. In their early years, the saplings yet to grow into noble trees, they must have seemed, to many, simply bare and monotonous. It is perhaps no wonder that people regretted the loss of the old flower gardens. The reaction came soon after Brown's death, stimulated in part by the introduction of more and more exotic plants from Central Asia, the Americas, China, and Japan. The reaction was also prompted in part by the aesthetic beliefs of men such as William Gilpin (1724-1804) who in 1791 published *Three Essays on Picturesque Beauty, on Picturesque Travel and on Sketching Landscape*, Sir Uvedale Price, whose *Essay on the Picturesque* of 1794 also inspired the Picturesque movement, and the professional landscape gardener Humphrey Repton (1752-1818). Repton at first resisted, and then accepted Gilpin's and Price's arguments against Brown – which were partly founded on the accusation that Brown's landscapes were flat and insipid, too smooth, too unlike nature.

Yet what emerged in England under the influence of the Picturesque movement was not so much "natural" gardens as a more restrained, self-conscious formality. The proponents of the Picturesque, gentry all, in a faint echo of the old myth of the Golden Age looked nostalgically back to an earlier age, an idyllic, imaginary past when all was well with the world. But their past was no more distant than Tudor times, and their style of cottage and garden was merely a dilute Gothic. Like Marie Antoinette, playing at *la vie champêtre* with her ladies of the court, they were pretending to pursue the rustic life, but suffered none of its inconveniences.

The nineteenth century saw a great growth in the wealth of the middle class in the West. In Britain, many of the newly-prosperous built villas with gardens near the cities and manufacturing towns that were the source of their wealth. People such as these became the clients of Repton, who had to devise ways of concealing the views of neighbouring houses, or worse still factories and smokestacks, by planting trees and shrubs so as to create an impression of seclusion. Flowers, banished by Brown from the environs of the house, were brought back by Repton. The Scottish botanist and garden designer John Claudius Loudon (1783-1843), responding to the growing demand for private gardens, brought out his great *Encyclopedia of Gardening* in 1822, and from 1826 until his death his *Gardeners' Magazine* appeared monthly. He and his wife Jane produced many designs for their readers, the owners of villa and suburban gardens, in which formal and informal combined in what he called the "gardenesque" style. The desire for an illusory perfection was still there; only its expression had altered yet again.

The new attitudes to garden art occurred at a time of wider-ranging change in aesthetic views. In England the poetry of the Lake poets, Coleridge

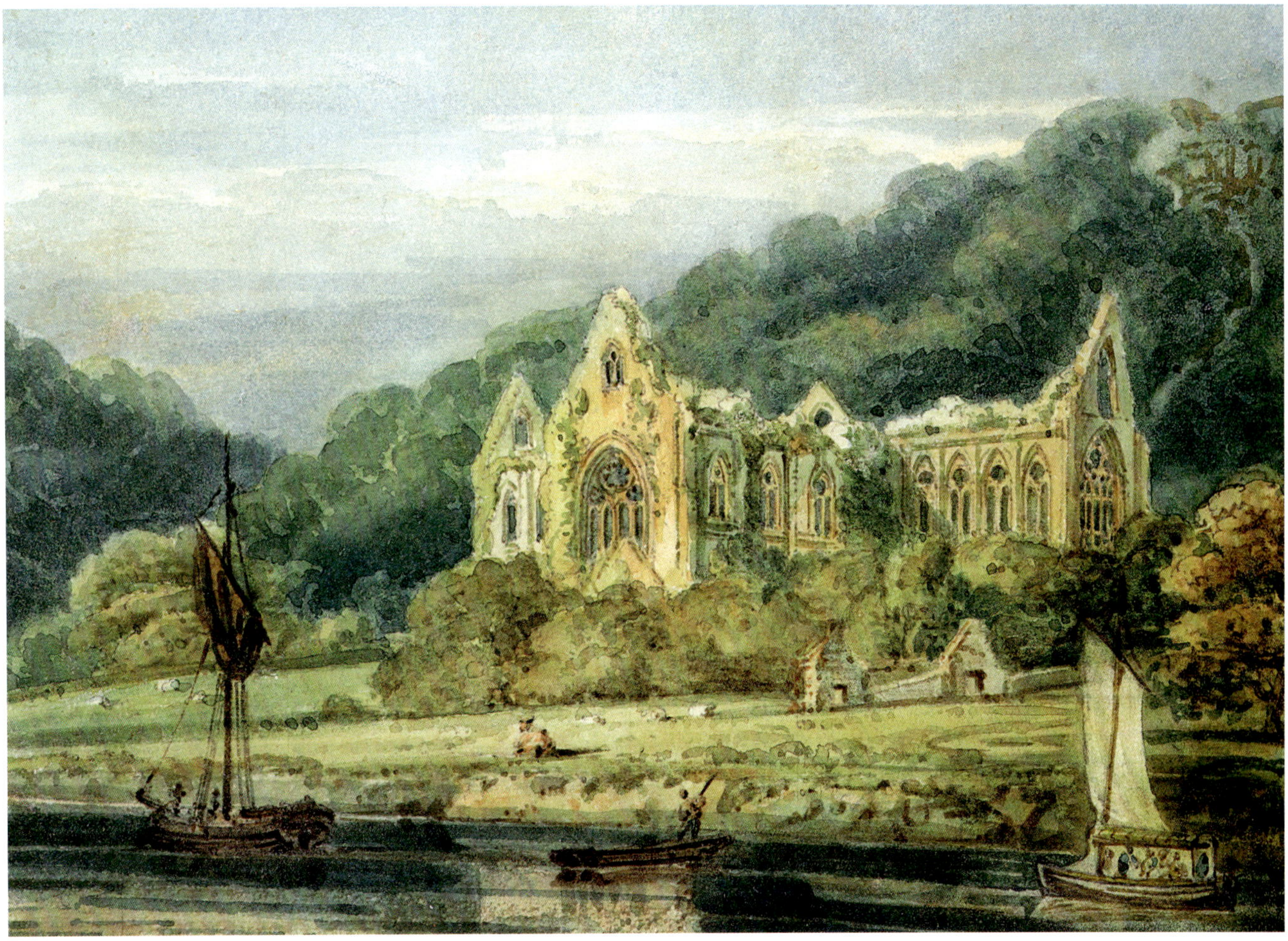

Illus. 25 *Thomas Girtin (1775-1802), Tintern Abbey, watercolour on paper.*

and his close contemporary William Wordsworth (1770-1850), like the paintings of J M W Turner (1775-1851) and John Constable (1776-1837), was setting new trends. The poets turned to an exploration of the inner self in reaction against the aggressive external reality of the Industrial Revolution. French and German Romantics, too, were beginning to explore the subliminal mind. At the same time, the philosophy of nature – the *Naturphilosophie* of Friedrich von Schelling (1775-1854) – which inspired the poets and painters, led them to hold one great idea in common with the industrialists. Both believed that nature is the source of power, and that all forms of power – the water, wind, sun, coal and steam which powered the new factories – are expressions of a single, central force, the force of energy.

The late eighteenth century also saw reversal of the assumption that every kind of plant was already present in Eden. One of the precursors of the German Romantics was the protean Goethe (1749-1832), whose scientific works include *Versuch die metamorphose der Pflanzen zu erklären* (Essay on the metamorphosis of plants) of 1790. In it he develops a notion that came to him while visiting the botanical garden of Padua: the utopian idea

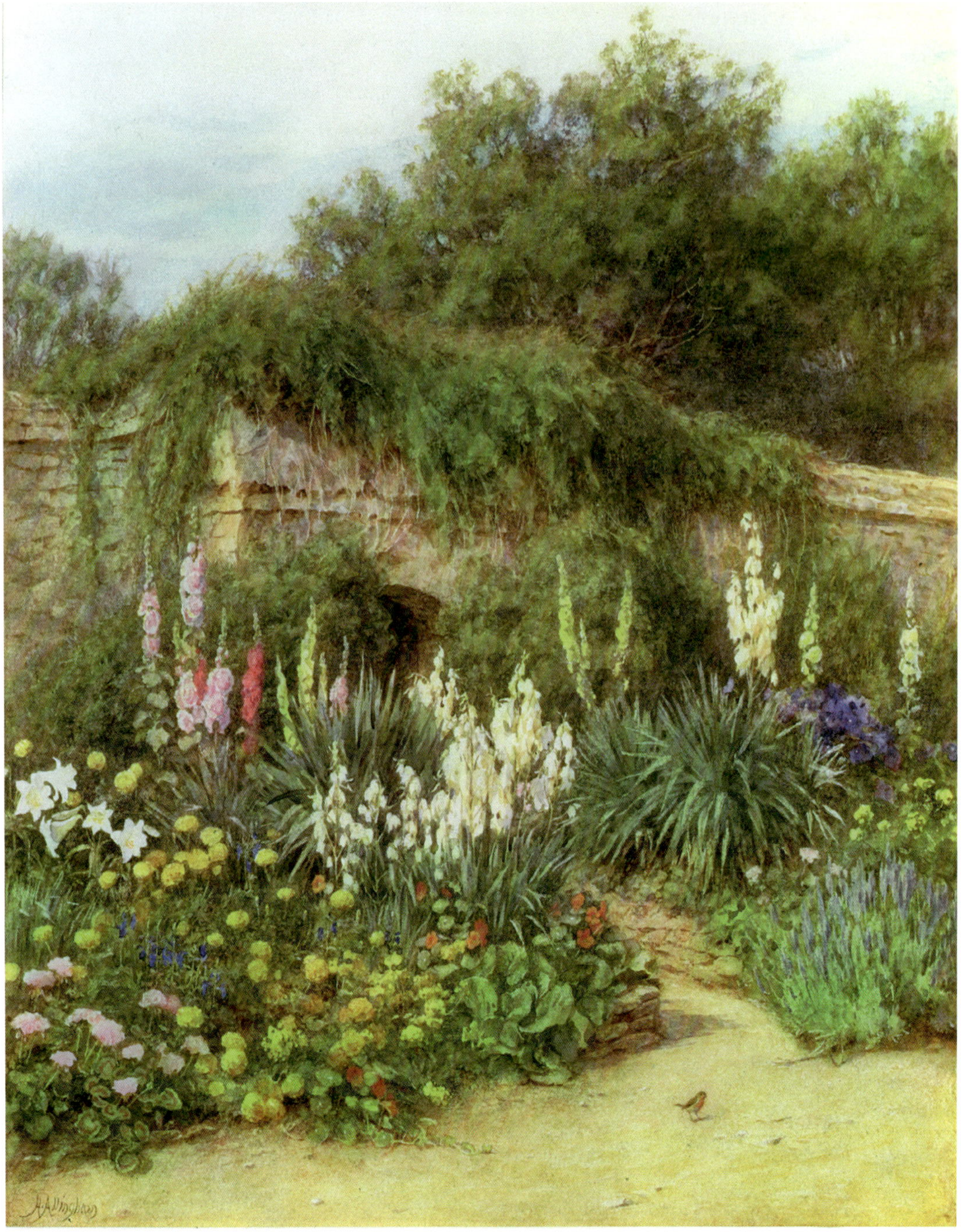

Illus. 26 *Helen Allingham (1848-1926), In Munstead Wood Garden (1903). Gertrude Jekyll's garden, in Godalming, Surrey.*

of an *Urpflanze*, a sole original type-plant from which all others had evolved. Goethe makes this his starting point for an examination of the evolution of the organic life of plants.

This is a diametrically different view of the natural world from that of the makers of the botanical gardens. In *Lines Composed a Few Miles Above Tintern Abbey, 13 July 1798*, Wordsworth (1770-1850) declares that:

. . . I have felt
A presence that disturbs me with the joy
Of elevated thoughts; a sense sublime
Of something far more deeply interfused,

Whose dwelling is the light of setting suns,
And the round ocean, and the living air,
And the blue sky, and in the mind of man:
A motion and a spirit, that impels
All thinking things, all objects of all thought,
And rolls through all things. Therefore am I still
A lover of the meadows and the woods,
And mountains. . .

This feeling for nature was unquestionably a spiritual one, but what of the garden? It can still move the emotions; but its appeal to the spirit as the symbol of paradise had by now perhaps been displaced by the new response to nature. In words that complement his far more famous phrase "emotion recollected in tranquillity," Wordsworth also wrote about the art of gardening that:

Laying out grounds may be considered a liberal art in some sort like poetry and painting and its object is or ought to be, to move the affections under the control of reason.

The hope that the botanical garden would recreate Eden had long been dashed. But with the introductions to western gardens in the nineteenth century of rhododendrons and other flowering shrubs from the Himalayas, a style of gardening evolved, in Britain in particular, which has been called the paradise garden. It was achieved by assembling plants from many regions, not in the formal layout of the botanical garden, but in great, naturalistic woodland gardens. Each of these was a leafy and eclectic Eden, composed of plants combined as never they were by nature in flawed, post-lapsarian Eden, for nature had carelessly allowed them to evolve in different continents.

The great woodland gardens were not for everyone; with some exceptions, they were successful only in the milder climates of the western seaboard, on acid soils. Climate and soil were less critical to the gardens of Edwardian England typified by the "wild garden" of William Robinson (1838-1935), embellished with exotics, and to the more formally structured, lavishly and artistically planted gardens of Sir Edwin Lutyens (1869-1944) and his partner in garden-making Miss Jekyll (1843-1932). Robinson and Jekyll were to inspire countless idealized cottage gardens. Lutyens consciously designed houses in the vernacular style, following the Pre-Raphaelite philosophy of John Ruskin (1819-1900) and William Morris (1834-1896). Like Ruskin, Morris, the father of the Arts and Crafts movement, turned away from mass-produced goods to the old arts and crafts, to the mediaeval and the Gothic for his inspiration. Writing of gardens, indeed, Morris clearly had the *hortus conclusus* in mind when he urged that they be "well-fenced from the outside world" and should avoid any imitation of "either the wilfulness or the wildness of nature."

However beautiful the Abrahamic gardens of Paradise made on earth may be, for those who share Alexander the Great's astonishment that anyone should wish for immortality they are freighted with associations quite different from those intended by their makers. For such people, the oriental notion of ultimate extinction holds a stronger appeal. In nirvana, surely – rather than in the inconceivable timelessness of eternal existence, however idyllic the surroundings – lies bliss: the irrevocable bliss of ceasing to be, deliverance from the seemingly endless cycle of temporal drudgery to a non-existence. As those who seek the *religio perennis* assure us, in nirvana, as in paradise, neither time nor eternity has meaning. It is time to turn to the faiths of the East, and to the gardens of China, Japan and non-Mughal India, to consider whether the quest for paradise, and in particular for paradise as a garden, has any meaning in these very different spiritual traditions.

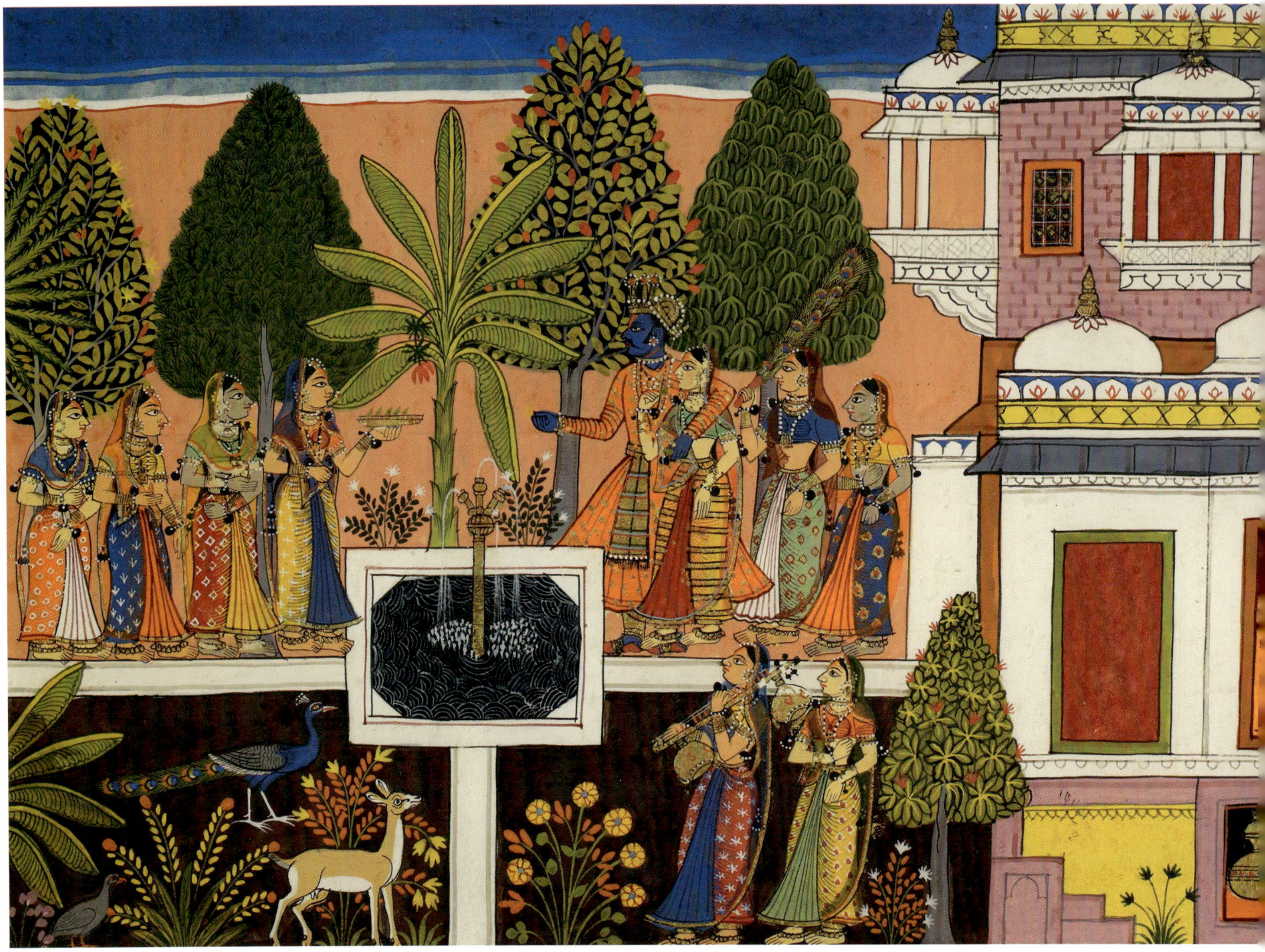

Illus. 27 *A Mughal chahar-bagh in a Hindu setting. Detail from a copy of the last Book of the* Ramayana, *made for a Hindu patron at Udaipur, 1653, British Library, London.*

Gardens and the Eastern Faiths

The concept of circular time, from which the timeless extinction of self in nirvana is a blissful escape, is not absent from the intellectual traditions of the West any more than it is from the mystical. Plato defined time as that which is measured by the revolution of the celestial spheres, and which accordingly progresses in a circle, in an unending succession of cycles. Notwithstanding the influence of Hellenic thought on the Abrahamic faiths, however, the emphasis of the scriptures on situating the sacred within history definitively imposed a linear concept of time on the western mind. Paradise lost and the life to come became the twin poles of past and future, birth and death, origin and return.

In the Indian and Far Eastern traditions, in contrast, everything returns, and escape from the inexorability of cyclical time is to be found in the ultimate extinction of the self in the unity of all things. This sense of cyclical time, recognized by mystics everywhere, permeates the great faiths that arose in India and spread eastwards to China and Japan, as it does the indigenous Chinese and Japanese beliefs. In the Vedic tradition, the Brahmanic sacrifice symbolizes the recovery of the primordial wholeness that preceded the created world. The Buddha's Awakening is also the spiritual recognition of that all-encompassing unity. Buddhism soon spread eastwards throughout the Asian land-mass, and in the Daoism of China, in particular, it encountered the same aspiration to unity. The Daoist belief is that the same essential *qi* or breath forms everything in existence, whether pure and heavenly or impure and earth-bound. China has an ancient tradition of gardening, in which the concept of *qi* plays a central part, as it did in the closely allied art of landscape painting.

Pre-Islamic Garden Traditions in India

But I begin with India, and from there shall follow the path of the sacred Lotus, the spread of Buddhism. India, a land where the great religious and spiritual traditions of the East have their origins, is also a land where Islam, above all, gained many converts. This was chiefly through encounters with Sufis, the mystics of Islam, who themselves were influenced by Vedantic and Buddhist thought. Gardens in the subcontinent have over past centuries been dominated by the Mughal "paradise" gardens which, though deriving from the Persian and Timurid model, were influenced by the indigenous traditions. The Mughals borrowed such motifs as the lotus, flower of Vishnu, of Brahma, of the Buddha, which gives its outline – in bud or fully expanded – to pools and column bases, and the serpent pattern representing Nāga, the holy water snake. The protean nature of the Indian traditions allowed for the adaptation of the Persian chahar-bagh design to Hindu cosmology. At the same time, Indian originality, in particular the creativity of the Rajputs in the eighteenth century, gave rise to a new indigenous style. Examples of this can be seen at Deeg, made by the Maharajah of Bharatpur, or in the palace complex at Amber, by the Maharajah of Jaipur, both dating from the eighteenth century.

Gardens of the kind introduced by the Muslims were a novelty in India, where the very concept of a formal garden was foreign. For, as Sima Sharma writes, "there is a radical[ly different] approach between the ancient Vedic tradition and the others. The contexts and the landscapes are different – the lush and all-sustaining forests of the Indo Gangetic plains as distinct from the hot desert or the cold and bleak climes. In the North civilization sprang from the

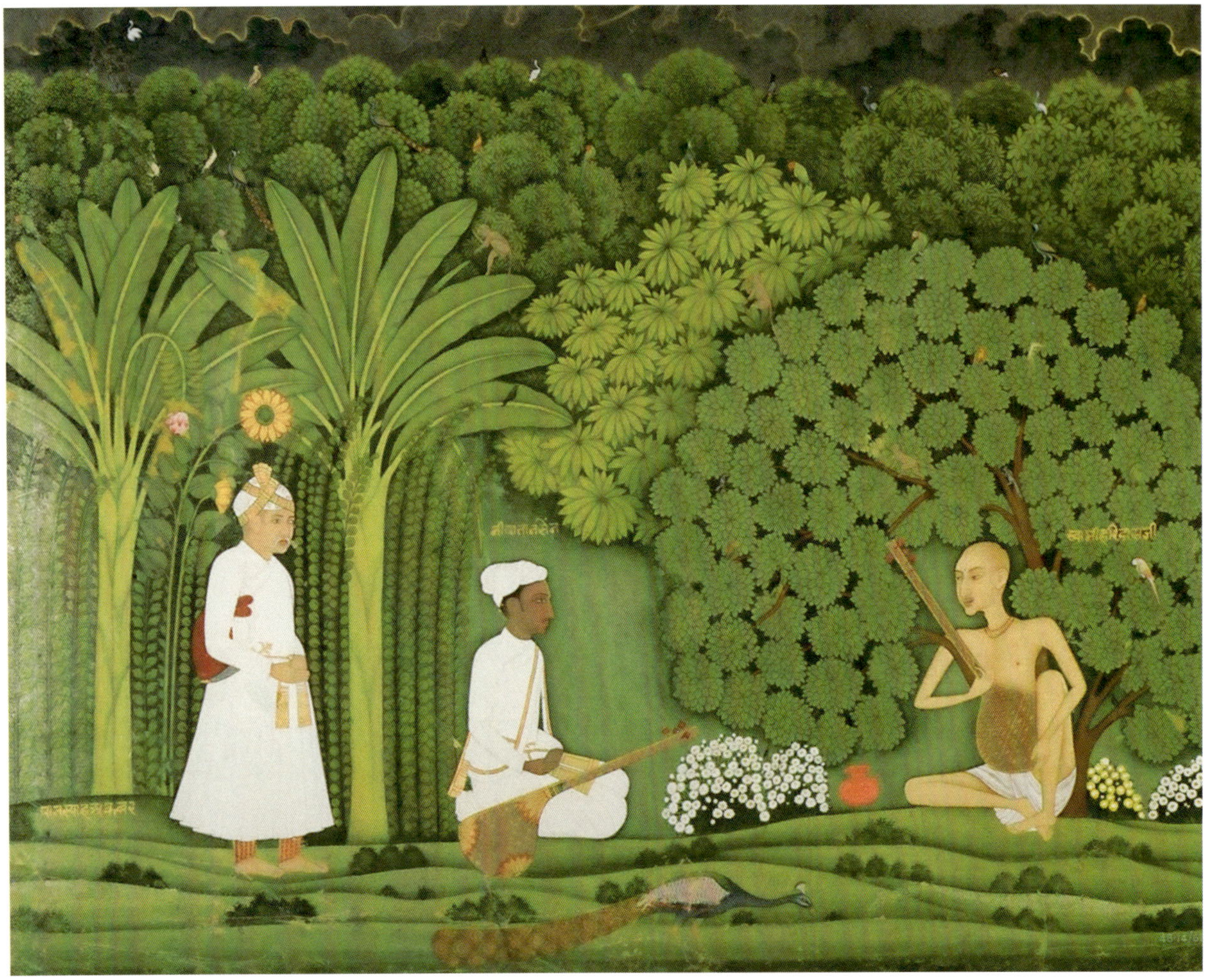

Illus. 28 *The Emperor Akbar with Swami Haridas, listening to the court musician Tansen playing the sitar and singing. Kishangarh, Rajasthan, c. 1670. National Museum, New Delhi.*

observation of the rather hostile, wild and disorderly Nature and the desire to bring about an ideal order and then to possess and subjugate. The Indian . . . sprang from the observation of a marvellously precise and ordered Nature to which the heart yearns only to belong – to participate in her rhythms and patterns which are perfection. Hence the retreat to the forests – Aranyas – to contemplate and let the wisdom descend from the broad-leaved trees so often repeated in metaphors in poetry and scriptures."[42]

These ancient sylvan colonies, where people lived a simple but spiritually rich life, are described in a number of poems. Forests are painted in exquisite detail, every leaf distinct, in many miniatures, depicting such scenes as an ashram in a forest or visions of the gods in lush garden or forest landscapes. A popular subject is Krishna and the *gopis* in a landscape of sacred groves. In the physical landscape, these groves formed the earthly equivalent of a mandala, embodying sacred geometry and myth. The Buddha himself was a forest-dwelling ascetic before he attained enlightenment under the Bodhi-tree – which then became a sacred object of reverence to his followers.

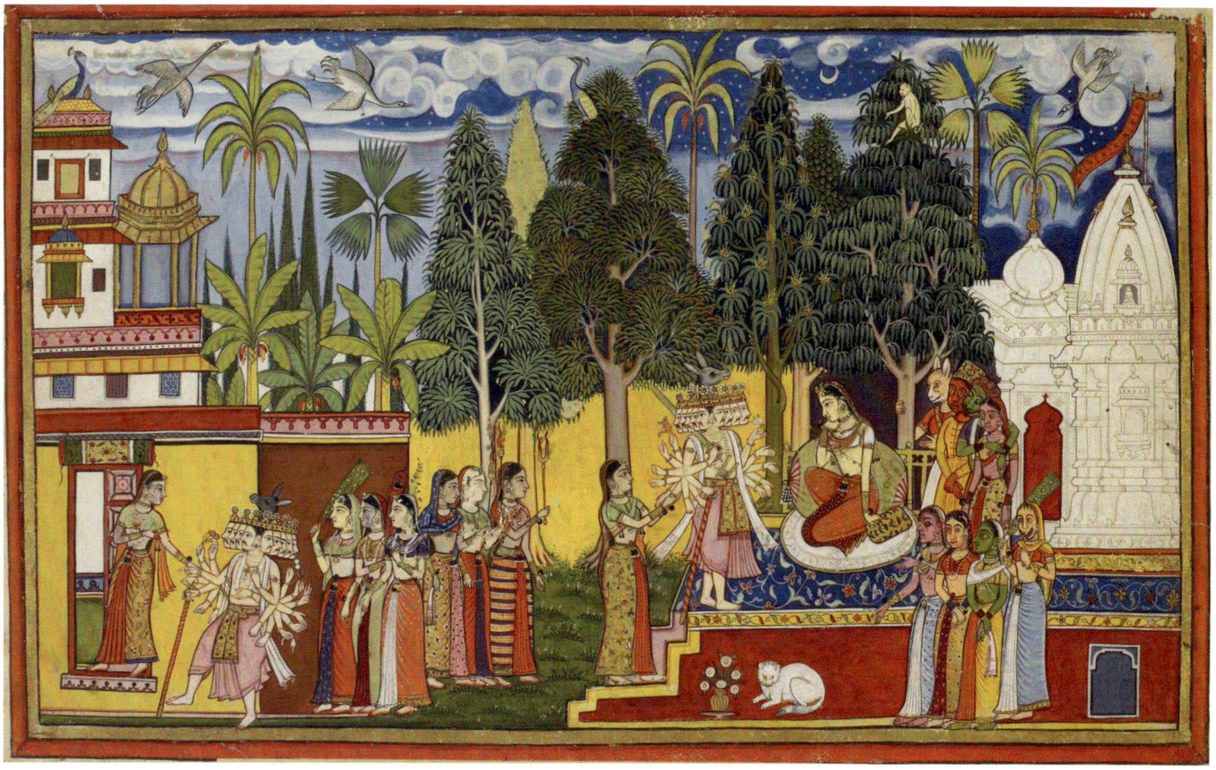

Illus. 29A *scene from the Ramayana showing Sita in a temple grove at Ashokavana. Mewar, commissioned by Maharana Jagat Singh (1628-1652).*

What, then, were Indian gardens and sacred landscapes like before the Mughals introduced the formality of the *chahar-bagh* into the Indian landscape? The *Brihatsamhita*, an early Hindu text on astronomy, tells us that gardens are the abode of the gods: "The gods always play where groves are, near rivers, mountains and springs, and in towns with pleasure gardens." The ancient sacred texts speak of the great parks in which the gods and goddesses lived, on the hills around the cosmic Mount Meru. On these hills grew mango, rose-berry and banyan trees, and lakes of milk, honey, sugar-cane juice and sugar. One of these groves, the Chaitra-ratha, is said to be comparable to a paradise, where rare and beautiful flowers grow. The *Mahabharata* also describes the pleasure gardens of the worldly kingdom of the Pandavas. The Pandavas' capital, Kandavaprastha, was surrounded by pleasure gardens, in which there were artificial hills, lakes of pure water where lotuses grew and ponds with fish and waterfowl. Everywhere were flowers and fruits – the same that grow in India today, mangoes, the asoka with its brilliant vermilion flowers sacred to Shiva, the fragrant champa and screw pine, sal trees, bignonia, and oleander. The gardens must surely also have been filled with fragrance, in emulation of the tree of paradise, Parijata, the fragrance of whose flowers perfumed all the world below. Birds flew among the branches, peacocks uttered their plangent screams and the koel or Indian cuckoo its song.

Descriptions of the features to be found in gardens have also come down to us from Hindu *shastras* or ancient treatises on the construction of sacred buildings, courtyards and temple gardens. The lotus motif recurs again and again, with lotus-shaped pools and the lotus motif as decoration. There are pavilions, for the enjoyment of the monsoon rains, and swings, favoured during the hottest season when their leisurely movement through the air brought some relief. We also have early Western accounts of Indian gardens. The garden of Chandragupta Maurya is described by Megasthenes, the Seleucid envoy to the Mauryan court in the fourth century BCE, who speaks of shady bowers woven from the branches of trees, cultivated plants, fish ponds, and tame peacocks and "birds of fine colours."[43] Writing during the reign of the Roman Emperor Hadrian (117-38 CE), the historian Aelian describes Indian royal gardens with their shady groves of trees both native and imported "with circumspect care from other parts, [that] with their beauty enhance the charms of the landscape."[44]

A few centuries later came the accounts of two Chinese Buddhist monks, visiting the country where the founder of their faith was born. Faxian (Fa Hsien), in the early fifth century, and Xuanzang (Hsuan Tsang), in the first half of the seventh century, described the custom of making garlands and scattering flowers during religious ceremonies, and the gardens of flowering trees around the temples and shrines, planted with the same trees as those mentioned in the Mahabharata. Faxian describes a shrine by the Sarasvati River, with "ponds of water clear and pure, thickets of trees always luxuriant, and numerous flowers of various hues." Xuanzang refers to a shrine at the place where the Buddha died, planted with trees at the corners of the shrine. He also speaks of the formal tanks that were a feature of Buddhist shrine gardens, as at Bodh Gaya, where the Buddha received enlightenment, and at a monastery in Nalanda, where there were "deep, translucent pools bearing on their surface the blue lotus intermingled with the Kie-ni of deep red colour."[45]

Gardens in China

China's great indigenous traditions, Confucianism and Daoism, influenced garden design when, after centuries of turmoil, peace returned to China under the short-lived Qin dynasty (221-206 BCE) and its successor, the Han dynasty (206 BCE-220 CE). Calmer conditions gave the gracious arts of living the chance to expand, and different types of classical Chinese gardens to develop. There were the private pleasure gardens of officials and merchants; the scholar gardens of writers and painters who, disillusioned with their political careers and Confucian values, turned to Daoism and the values of nature even as they continued to live in the city; and the imperial parks, with which we shall begin. Qin Shi Huang Di collected plants and animals for the Shang-lin Park, an old hunting enclosure, which had eight rivers winding through cinnamon forests and meadows, great expanses of fragrant flowers, sweet fountains and an abundance of fruit. And the Han emperors were drawing upon an earlier tradition when they enclosed large expanses of land to build pavilions and turn nature into a garden-park for the refreshment of the spirit.

Indeed, these parks are thought to have derived from the royal sacred parks of ancient times. In the *Songs of Chu*, from one of the fourth century BCE southern kingdoms of the Yangtze valley, a shaman singer describes the palace with its lattice-work doors and its galleries, musical with the sound of water. It had vermilion balustrades leaning out over the serpentine pools where scented lotus grow, and terraces and pavilions with views to the distant hills. The song is a "Summons to the Soul," in which the shaman seeks to entice the soul of the dying king back to his old abode, represented as a perfect place: the garden as paradise.

It seems, too, that there was already a tradition, in ancient Chinese oral myths and legends, of a place called Xuanpu, a kind of paradise in the K'un-lun Mountains (the Himalayas), also imagined as the gateway to heaven. The Kunlun tradition was one of the two principal mythological traditions in ancient China, belonging to the western plateaux.

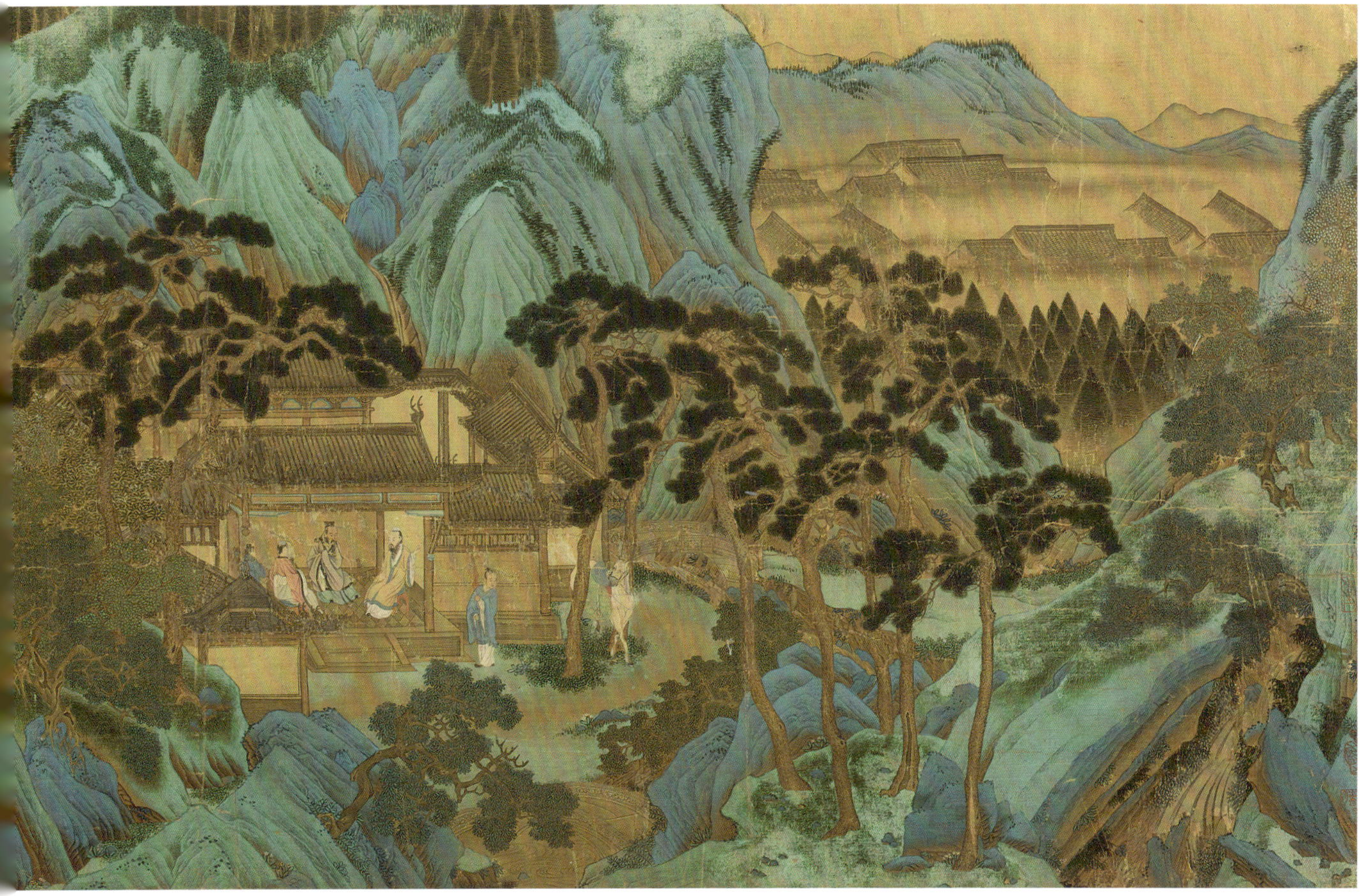

Illus. 30 *Qiu Ying (Chinese, c. 1494-1552),* The Shanglin Park: Imperial Hunt, *mid to late16th century, Ming dynasty, ink and colour on silk. Freer Gallery, Washington D.C.*

The other was the Penglai tradition of the eastern coastal regions, where there is also a paradise for immortals, consisting of three island mountains in the ocean. The first Qin emperor had wanted to find the mystical islands of the *Hsien*, the Immortals, who could vanish with the wind and fly on the backs of cranes. To this end, he sent an expedition to the Eastern Seas, but as his expedition neared the rocky islands, it disappeared into the mist. The Han emperor Wudi (140-87 BCE) tried another tactic; he tried to bring the Immortals to him. He created a vast lake in his hunting park, with three islands set with artificial crags in emulation of the soaring peaks of Mount K'un-lun in the far west, where the Immortals lived in their remote palaces. It was planted with the most beautiful trees and flowers to lure the Immortals down to earth. The Immortals were not tempted, but henceforth, as we shall see, almost every small garden of the professional classes in China would echo Wudi's dream in miniature.

The establishment of the Tang dynasty in 618 CE marked the start of a century of extraordinary artistic achievement. Landscape paintings, and landscape itself, are called *shan shui* or 'mountains and water'. In fact, it was often the greatest painters, such as Wang Wei (701-761 CE), who also created the most beautiful gardens in China. Not everyone was skilled with the brush; not everyone could

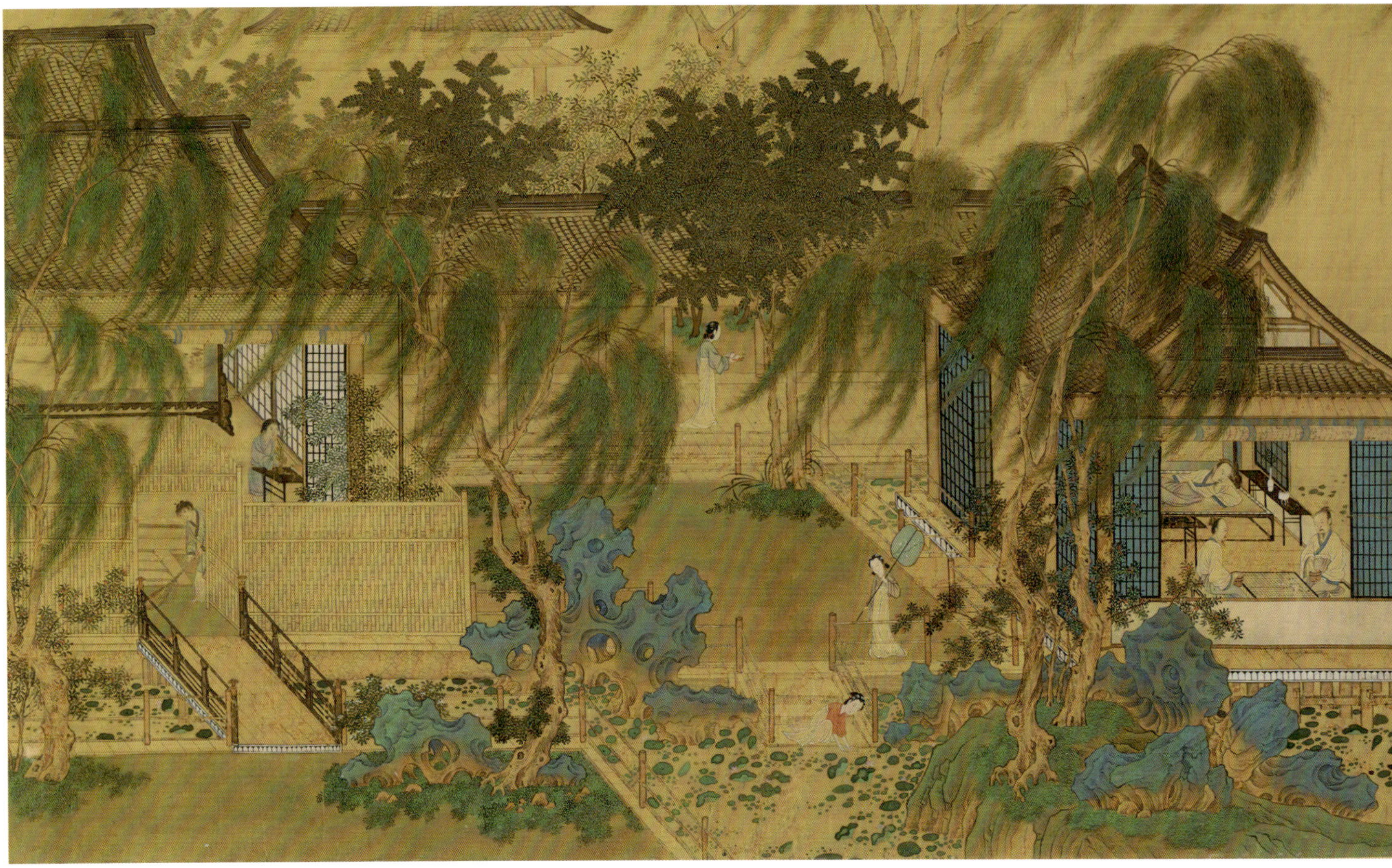

Illus. 31 *Leng Qian (Chinese, 14th century). The scroll (Qing dynasty, an 18th century copy of a lost work) describes this as "Immortals Playing Weiqi on Penglai," but the pavilion and garden resemble a wealthy scholar's private retreat, Freer Gallery, Washington D.C.*

retire to a mountain retreat and build a pavilion, however modest, from which to contemplate nature, magnificent and unspoiled. This was particularly true of the professional classes, bound by their official duties in town and the Confucian values that informed those duties. But they could replicate nature in a small town garden, or a miniature rocky landscape in a bowl, and concentrate in this tiny compass the symbols of Daoist mysticism, to contain a "world in a grain of sand." Thus scholar-gardeners sought to recreate in a smaller scale what the emperors aspired to on the grand scale – the totality of nature. These tiny gardens, composed of the primal elements of earth, stone, trees in miniature, and water, were as sacred places, analogous to a temple, and their creation was a ritual action. In the microcosmic scale of the garden, the *yang*, the active masculine principle of rock, is balanced with the *yin*, the passive, moist, feminine principle of water. Rock and water thus mirror the harmony of the macrocosm of mountains and rivers. For the Chinese, nature wild and untamed, which to early Christian Europe seemed threatening or even terrifying, had long since come to represent the spiritual, the fundamental unity of all things.

Vibrantly fresh and naturalistic paintings of

flowers, as well as of landscape, survive from the Tang and, especially, from the Song period (960-1127). This was a time when scholar officials were actively making gardens both in towns, as refreshment for the spirit, and in rural retreats, perhaps as consolation for being banished to a remote area or even dismissed from service. The Song Emperor Hui-tsung himself (1100-1126) was a talented painter and a passionate garden-maker. His imperial gardens contained an immense artificial mountain landscape, set among thousands of plum trees and adorned with grotesquely contorted pine trees and eroded stones of fantastical shape. It was a paradise for the Immortals which he named Ken-yu, or the "Impregnable Mountain." He must have believed he was close to luring the Immortals into his paradise when the mushrooms of Immortality were found growing on one of the peaks. But Hui-tsung's confidence was misplaced. His extravagance broke the dynasty, which was driven south by the Mongol invasions, to survive as the Southern Song dynasty in Hangzhou between 1127 and 1279. The southern Chinese garden was typically composed of water – either assembled in pools or dispersed among rocks; mountains – with a single fine rock, or many piled up to form an artificial mountain; and buildings – the house, pavilions and verandas. Plants were relatively unimportant in this style of garden, though fine old trees were much prized and preserved whenever possible. And each season had its typical flowers -- magnolia and peony for spring, roses and lotus for summer, chrysanthemum and maple for autumn, and camellias, bamboo and winter plum for the coldest months.

Chinese 'Paradise' Myths

With the exception – an important one, it is true, in terms of its influence – of Wu's lake and islands, it appears that garden design was influenced principally by the spirituality of Chinese philosophical traditions rather than by specific myths. Certainly, other Chinese "paradise" myths do not seem to have had an impact on garden design in the same way as the scriptural gardens of the Abrahamic faiths, although they speak of gardens and beautiful landscapes. One tells of the August Personage of Jade, who lives in the topmost level of heaven on K'un-lun Mountain. His wife, Mother Empress Wang (represented as a young and beautiful woman, apparently another face of Hsi Wang-mu, the Mother Empress of the West, an elderly lady), presides over the banquets of immortality at which the peaches of immortality are offered. These peaches ripen once every 3,000 years on the peach trees of the imperial orchard, and thus the peach is symbolic of longevity. The only humans allowed in this palace (built entirely of jade, with nine storeys) are those permitted by the gods to eat the peaches of immortality as a reward for their virtue.

The Romance of the Emperor Mu (1001-947 BCE) tells of the banquet the Mother Empress gave Mu at Jasper Lake in her country far to the west. With the introduction of Buddhism to China, she became the Guardian of the Western Realm of Heaven, the Lands of Immortality. Later still she became synonymous with Kuan-yin, the Bodhisattva of compassion, who also dwells in the Lands of Immortality in the West.

Chinese myths were often formed in this way out of a fusion of Daoist and Buddhist beliefs and folklore. Righteous persons admitted to the bliss of eternal life go to the Land of Extreme Felicity in the west, an enclosed place of delights, with seven terraces and seven rows of trees whose branches are precious stones which chime musically in the wind. There are lakes flowering with lotuses, many-coloured birds with divine voices, showers of blossom falling on the ground. Every morning the righteous go at dawn to offer flowers to the Buddhas of other worlds. At the hour of their death the souls of those who call upon Amitabha in their lifetime are received by Buddha, who places them in the lotuses of the lakes. There

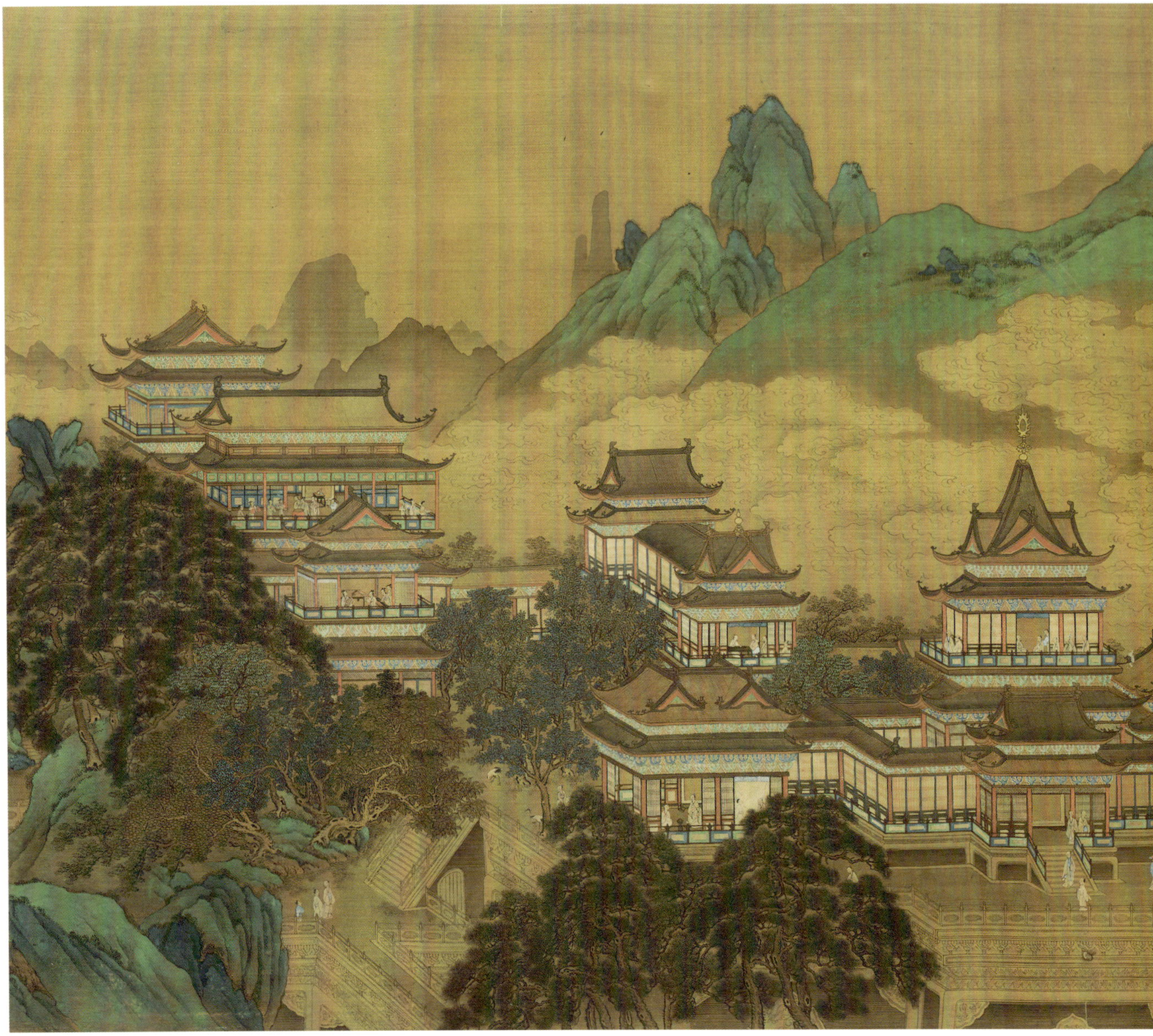

Illus. 32 *Fang Chuniang (c. 1225-1264), The Peach Festival of the Queen Mother of the West, 17th-18th century, Ming or Qing dynasty, ink and colour on silk. Freer Gallery, Washington D.C.*

they remain until cleansed from all impurities, when the flowers open and they go to mingle with the just in the Land of Extreme Felicity.

Many Buddhist missionaries from India and Nepal came to China during the latter years of the Han dynasty and later. They won many converts, their message finding an echo in both Confucian practical morality and Daoist other-worldliness. The Buddhist concept of the universe, with its central cosmic mountain (the Great Meru or Mount Sumeru), was readily adaptable to existing Chinese mountain worship. It seems, too, that

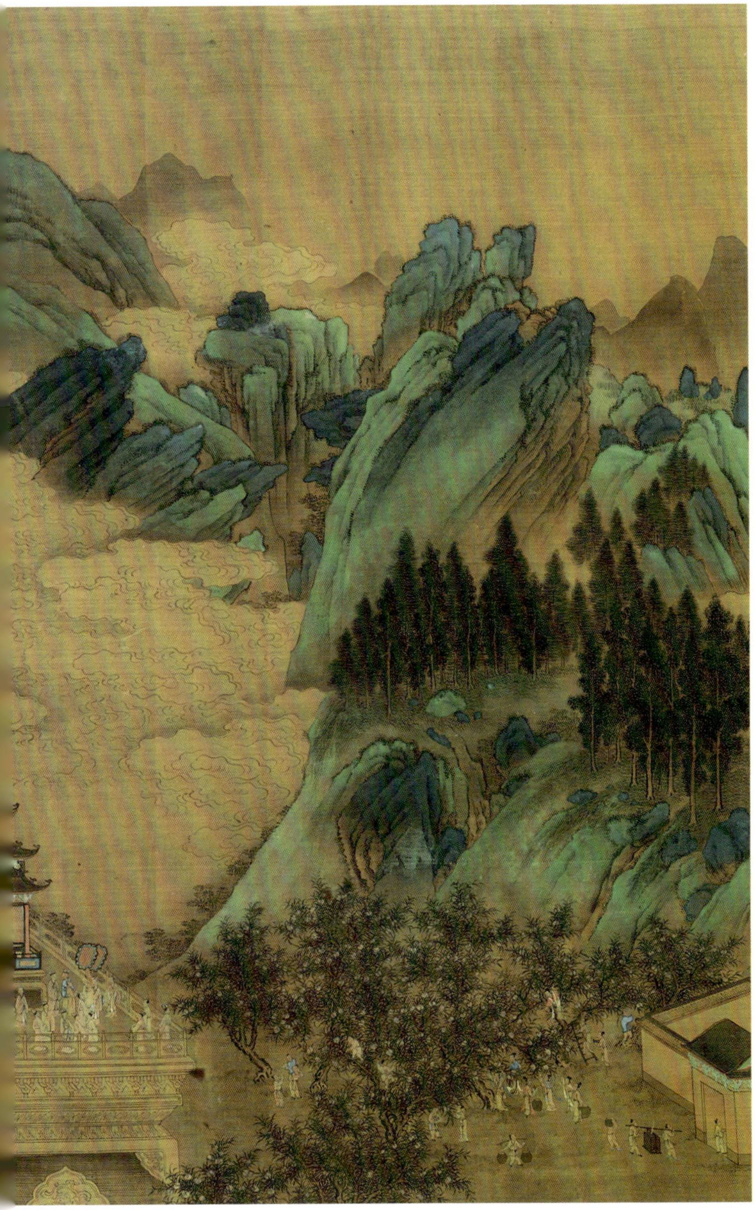

books of Buddhist wisdom, brought to China in late Han times along the Silk Road, told of another paradise – the paradise of Amida, a garden with soaring mountains, misty abysses, seas and islands, resembling the Daoist abode of the immortals.

Although Daoism regards heaven as a place where those who live good lives gain their reward (and evil its retribution), in Chinese Buddhism paradise is not to be compared with the Abrahamic concept, a reward for virtue in this life. However beautiful it may be, it can only be a stage on the way to nirvana, to the final dissolving of duality, the loss of self in unity.

Buddhism encouraged a monastic way of life, and – as with Christian monasticism – we may surmise that the gardens of Buddhist temples, which were built in places of great natural beauty, would be a place to grow flowers as ritual offerings at the shrines as well as vegetables and herbal remedies for the monks. Here, too, the monks preserved trees that elsewhere would have been cut down for fuel before they could grow to any size: junipers, cypresses, pines and ginkgo, set among blossoming plum and apricot. The monks in their remote temple are the Buddhist equivalent of the solitary Daoist in the mountains; the first seeking spiritual enlightenment in community, the second experiencing, alone, the unity of all things.

With the passage of time the "barbarian" Mongols, too, acquired the Chinese love of gardens. Kublai Khan (1215-1294), in particular, who established the Yuan dynasty in 1271, was strongly attracted to Chinese culture, and studied Buddhist philosophy. We know from Marco Polo, who met Kublai Khan in 1275, that the emperor made a royal park in Shangdu (Xanadu) and another in Beijing (Kaan-baligh, city of the Khan). Kublai Khan's Xanadu was a combination of hunting park and mountains of the Immortals, modelled perhaps on the royal park of Hangzhou. This Marco Polo also described, along with the city's many temples and gardens, its lake set among hills, its noble trees and blossom. "In heaven there is Paradise – on earth, Soochow and Hangchow," the old saying goes. But Kublai's "mountains" were made of lapis lazuli, and later he added two palaces rising out of the waters of the lakes, decorated with crystals to look like ice palaces. He planted mature trees in the grassy parks that were an echo of the steppes whence came his forebears.

The oldest surviving treatise on Chinese gardens, Ji Cheng's *Yuan Yeh,* dates from between 1631 and 1634, at the end of the Ming period, another turbulent time for China. Ji Cheng signed his author's preface by his pen-name, "The Negative Daoist," and the Daoist ideal of unity permeates his treatise. Ji Cheng designed gardens to lift the soul beyond the mundane concerns of this world. There are comparatively few plants – most important are the "three auspicious things," plum, pine and bamboo, symbolizing eternity. The essentials are water and rocks. Water features not in the artificiality of fountains, but as streams, lakes and waterfalls. Rocks, weathered by wind and water into fantastical shapes, are assembled into steeply graded representations of mountains. Together, water and stone are the garden equivalent of the *shan shui* – mountains and water – of Chinese landscape paintings, the symbol of the life of the spirit.

The Chinese garden as a whole symbolizes its owner's life and character, and even the universe as a whole. The garden may be considered as a religious space; and like all such spaces, it constitutes a break in mundane time, an entry into timelessness. What appears to European sensibility as its crowded, frenetic nature is in fact to be experienced as a seemingly endless experience, in which time and space lose their day-to-day meanings. The classical Chinese garden is not merely the framework for this experience, but the embodiment of poetry in stone and water, space and form. Specific poems, indeed, were frequently the inspiration for a particular garden, and poetry is an integral part of many gardens (and essential to a scholar's garden): verses in fine calligraphy adorn gateways and doors, or are carved on stone tables and rocks.

Japan, a Land of Two Faiths

The indigenous tradition of Japan is Shintoism, an animistic worship of trees, mountains, and the sun goddess Amaterasu from whom the imperial family had sprung. In the Shinto tradition, heaven is not a distant and inaccessible place, but a landscape much like that of Japan itself, traversed by the heavenly river, Ama no Gawa. Japan is rich in trees of great beauty, and in Shinto tradition fine trees are venerated – especially the *sakaki* (*Cleyera japonica*), because it was the tree chosen by the gods on which to hang the mirror during the ceremony to tempt the sun goddess from her cave. All Shinto shrines are surrounded by groves of *sakaki* and other trees, and *sakaki* branches are laid before the altars.

In 552, the first Buddhist missionaries reached Japan from Korea, gaining Japanese converts to Buddhism from Shintoism. To this day, however, the two faiths, indigenous and introduced, live amicably side by side, even within the same family or person. Far more significant for Japanese society than the endeavours of these missionaries was the decision of the Japanese emperor, in the early seventh century, to send a succession of envoys to the Chinese emperor Yang Ti, with instructions to learn all they could about China – its society, its culture, its political systems.

Almost everything Chinese was then adopted in Japan – not just the centralized political structures and Buddhism, but also the conception of the universe, tea-drinking, and garden design. Indeed, an early Japanese name for garden was *shima*, meaning island. It happened that in 607, the year of the first Japanese mission to China, the emperor of China had embarked upon the construction of a magnificent imperial park, with lakes, hills and islands. The largest lake, like Wu's before it, was graced with islands representing the three mystic isles of the Immortals. The Japanese envoy returned with tales of this wonder, and in 611, work began on a similar garden of lakes, islands and hills alongside the Japanese emperor's palace in Nara, near Kyoto. The new imperial garden had a bridge and a "mountain," perhaps a representation of Sumeru, the mountain at the centre of the Buddhist concept of the universe. If so, it anticipates a later style based on temple gardens made as an earthly form of the Buddhist paradise described in the Lotus Sutra.

The Sino-Japanese garden style known as Shinden-Zukuir developed in the Heian period (794-1185), a time when Japanese high society cultivated aesthetic sensibilities and exquisite courtesy. In Japan, as in China, gardens were composed of trees, stones, rocks and water. A courtyard to the south of the *Shinden*, the Principal Chamber, was an expanse of white sand landscaped with a stream called the *yarimizu*, an irregularly-shaped pond with one or more islands, carefully placed rocks, and plantings known as *senzai*.

In these gardens, both the artistic and the spiritual were given due weight, symbolizing nature and the cosmic forces. The ever-changing aspects of the garden matched the Japanese understanding of eternity as a pattern of changes. Each element of the garden, including sound and space, was believed to have its own essence. The garden-maker's task was to sense and respect that essence, *kowan ni shigatsu* – "following the request of the stone." However, the more metaphorical Japanese mind turned away from the Chinese love of naturalistic lakes and waterfalls, the piled rock "mountains," the individual rocks weathered to resemble animal or mythical forms; instead, the Japanese began to make dry waterfalls of rocks without water, of which the earliest survival is probably that of Saga-no-in, where the Emperor Saga retired in 823.

By the end of the twelfth century, the principles of gardening had been formalized. A compilation of these tenets, the *Sakuteiki*, includes severe proscriptions against practices originating in the geomantic taboos based on Chinese *feng-shui* or wind-and-water. In the tenth century, or perhaps even earlier, the belief had arisen in China that the forces running through the earth affected the fortunes of men. *Feng-shui* was the art of placing oneself, and harmonizing the landscape in which one lived, so as to maximize the flows of positive energy and minimize the negative or evil forces. Though the taboos were strict, the Japanese sought inventive ways to circumvent them by "curing" unfavourable sites and orientations, rather than allowing them to curb their creativity.

Japanese gardens of the late Heian and Kamakura (1185-1333) periods were influenced both by the gardens of the Chinese Southern Song dynasty, and by Chinese landscape painting, especially the monochromatic landscapes of the Song school, depicting sacred Buddhist mountains, waterfalls, lakes and seas. Toba Rikyu, the Bird's Feather Summer Palace, made in 1086, was very much like the Chinese gardens inspired by the islands of the immortals. The Chinese influence lasted into the Momoyama and Edo period (1574-1867). Thus the Three Treasures Garden at Daigo-ji temple, built in the Momoyama period in 1589, was based on the principle of "one pond and three hills," and by the Edo period the "divine islands and holy mountains" theme was the inspiration for many palace, monastery and private gardens.

The Japanese Concept of Paradise

The Japanese veneration for nature as itself an ideal, the concept of paradise as a perfect other world, has less meaning than in the Abrahamic traditions. However, especially during the later Heian period, the civil wars and destruction that rent Japan led to a heightened sense of the transitory, illusory nature of life in this world and the hope for compensatory bliss in the next. As a result, concepts such as *gongu jodo*, the search for paradise, began to emerge. The Buddhism that dominated this period was largely esoteric. Everything in nature was considered as a mandala, as a "picture of the Buddha," the earthly embodiment of the spiritual world. The gardens of temples and residences, too, although they were not geometrically regular, were made according to mandalistic concepts.

In popular understanding the mandala represented paradise, composed of seven parts – *bugaku-e*, a place for music and dance; *raibutsu-e*, a place for saints; *hochi-e* or treasure pond; *juge-e* or holy place beneath the trees; *sanzon-e* or place for the Amitabha in triple form; *horo-kyuden-e* or treasure hall; and *koku-e* or gathering place for the angels and holy animals, where the angels play musical instruments and the sky is filled with falling petals. These would often be arranged in a circle, the whole forming a complex with no beginning or end.

Paradise gardens, like the mandala itself, were designed to be seen from above, as though those who visited them could soar above them rather than experiencing them as a series of events representing the different parts of paradise. Several paradise gardens of the eleventh, twelfth and thirteenth centuries show a similar pattern. The treasure hall of the mandala is the central hall of the garden, the lotus pool represents the *hochi-e*, and a bridge over the pool symbolizes the *guzei*, the bridge across which the blessed are led to paradise. An island in the pool is the place for Amitabha in triple form.

One of the strands of Buddhism that especially led to the creation of paradise gardens was the Jodo-shu or Pure Land sect, founded by the priest Honen (1133-1212). This introduced the notion of a paradise that to some extent replaces nirvana. It is governed by Amida, most famous of the Dhyani Buddhas of Japan, the protector and comforter, who lives in his western celestial realm helping sentient beings to attain salvation. He has vowed not to enter nirvana until he has saved all mankind; his paradise in the west is open to all. As belief in the Pure Land developed in the late Heian period, gaining widespread acceptance in the Kamakura period, it was thought that Amida descended from the Pure Land or Western Paradise to welcome believers at the hour of their death.

As in other paradise traditions, the realm of Amida was a place of peace and beauty, in contrast to the drudgery of life on this earth. Mandalas depict the Amida Buddha before a heavenly pond adorned with Buddhist symbols. Gardens of the Pure Land sect, such as Saiho-ji in Kyoto, were intended to evoke Amida's paradise, for which the familiar lake-island theme was ideally suited. Composed of a lower Chinese-style garden and a "stroll garden" in the upper forest, Saiho-ji is still mysterious and alluring in its deep, mossy forest shade, dry cascades of rocks falling from the woodland "spring" of moss, and still waters forming the heart of the garden. Though it has been somewhat modified by later Zen influences, it remains one of the finest surviving examples of the Japanese paradise garden.

The Zen Gardens of Japan

During the Kamakura period (1185-1392), Zen Buddhism brought to Japan a new, ascetic spirituality and practice which influenced monastery gardens. Once again, painting and gardening were to be closely associated, this time in the hands of Zen priests. The temple garden at Saiho-ji was made by the Buddhist abbot Musö Soseki (1275-1351; also known as Musö Kokushi) on the site of the earlier Pure Land paradise garden. Musö Soseki was known for his ability to create beautiful and inspiring gardens using the natural features of hills and valleys, sometimes making literal representations of actual paintings. He regarded the appreciation of these scenic gardens, in which distant views were an important factor, as a spiritual experience. In Saiho-ji, he made one of the most dramatic examples of a dry cascade, which was later to evolve into the meditation garden. Indeed, he is said to have introduced the notion of the garden as a medium for meditation. Tenryu-ji (Temple of the Heavenly Dragon), another paradise garden in Kyoto that, like Saiho-ji, centres on a pool, was also the work of Musö Soseki. To an earlier Shinden style garden from the Heian period, Musö added dry landscape (*kare san sui*) elements. Tenryu-ji

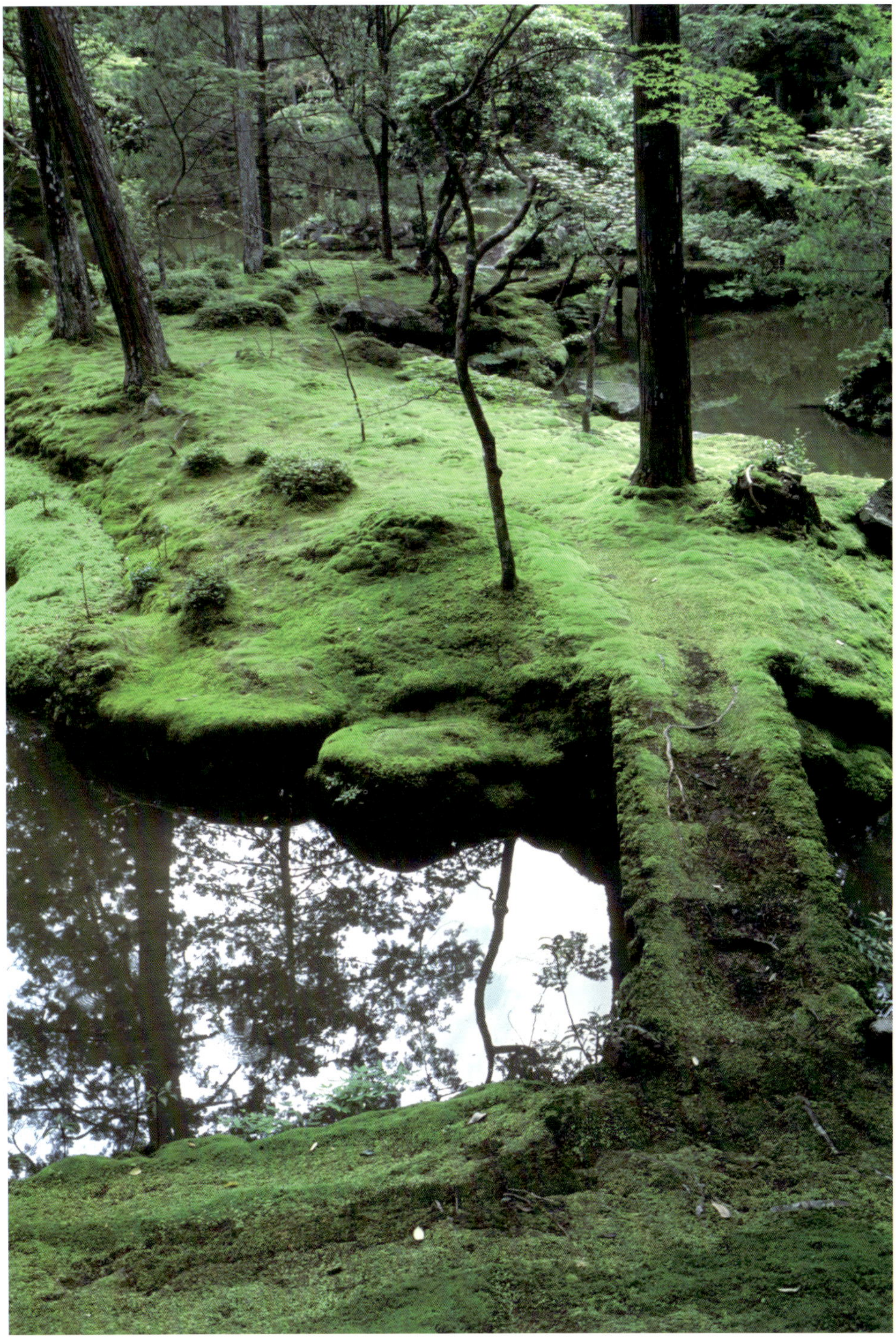

Illus.33 *The moss garden of Saiho-ji, Kyoto, a Pure Land garden.*

marks a shift from the earlier naturalistic landscape to a more symbolic style, a microcosm of the entire universe. Individual groups of stones also become symbolic. A gardening manual of the fifteenth century, *Senzui harabi in yagyo no zu* (Illustrated designs for mountain, water and hill landscapes), written by the Buddhist priest Zoen, shows the Buddhist triad – three stones, with the largest at the centre, assembled to reflect the trinity of Buddhist images in Buddhist temples.

The Zen emphasis on simplicity and humility corresponded more closely to the Japanese spirit than the Chinese-influenced Buddhism of the mandala. The Zen gardens of Kyoto made from the end of the fifteenth century onwards were gardens of contemplation and meditation. In complete contrast to the lush greenery of the Jodo paradise gardens of Saiho-ji and its like, they were gardens of raked gravel and rocks, composed with the simplicity of extreme spiritual sophistication, with the Zen feeling for abbreviation and symbolism. (It is surely not coincidental that since ancient times, sacred places in the Shinto tradition had been indicated by gravel and sand.) Economic factors, as well as spiritual, may well have influenced this new style, however. After the Onin war of the mid fifteenth century, when the great Zen temples of Kyoto were burned down and their gardens destroyed, the painter-priests had to rebuild them with minimal resources. Water was scarce too, so they developed a style that did not need water. Instead, there was an expanse of raked gravel or white sand in which, in this hushed setting, the spiritually adept might come to hear the mystic sound of water. These were gardens not only to be seen, but above all to be experienced, in which the rocks and sand are not just representations of mountains and water. They are there to bring out the inner forms of nature, to discover the eternal in the finite. Buddhism sees life as in a constant state of flux, and this notion of mutability is reflected in the asymmetry of Japanese gardens, in marked contrast to the geometrical regularity of the Islamic chahar bagh or the formal gardens of Western Europe.

The natural rocks which complete the landscape must thus be placed asymmetrically; not arbitrarily, but in meaningful relation to each other, with most of their mass buried. These rocks would be brought to the garden site by night, being considered as sacred objects, perhaps deriving from the ancient belief that spirits dwell in stones. Once delivered they would be set in place by *ishitate-so*, stone-setting priests, for their positioning was as much a spiritual as an aesthetic discipline, requiring a knowledge of esoteric Buddhism. Only when set in their positions, emerging like mountain-peaks from the cloudy mass of the white gravel, or like islands from the sea, could they be seen by ordinary mortals. To the western mind, it may seem strange that priests were so closely associated with the making of gardens; yet even the training undergone by gardeners was seen as an esoteric skill.

Among surviving gardens of the Zen type in Kyoto are the Daisen-in garden of the Daitokuji Temple, inspired by the painter Soami, who was also regarded as a great garden artist; and Ryoan-ji, founded in 1499 and one of the sparest of temple gardens, with just five groups of rocks in a raked sea of sand. Ryoan-ji may have been made by the Zen priest Tessen Soki, who wrote in his gardening manual *Ka Senzui no Fu* that the garden should condense thirty thousand miles into a few feet or inches. Whether intentionally or not, the garden at Ryoan-ji can be seen as an echo of the Chinese myths of the islands of the Immortals, emerging from the eastern sea. Another interpretation is that the rocks are for the Arhat, the five hundred disciples of Buddha, to cross the sea of sand. But it need have no "meaning" at all; it is above all a focus for meditation. Zen belief is that spiritual awakening comes intuitively, through contemplation of the simplest forms of nature.

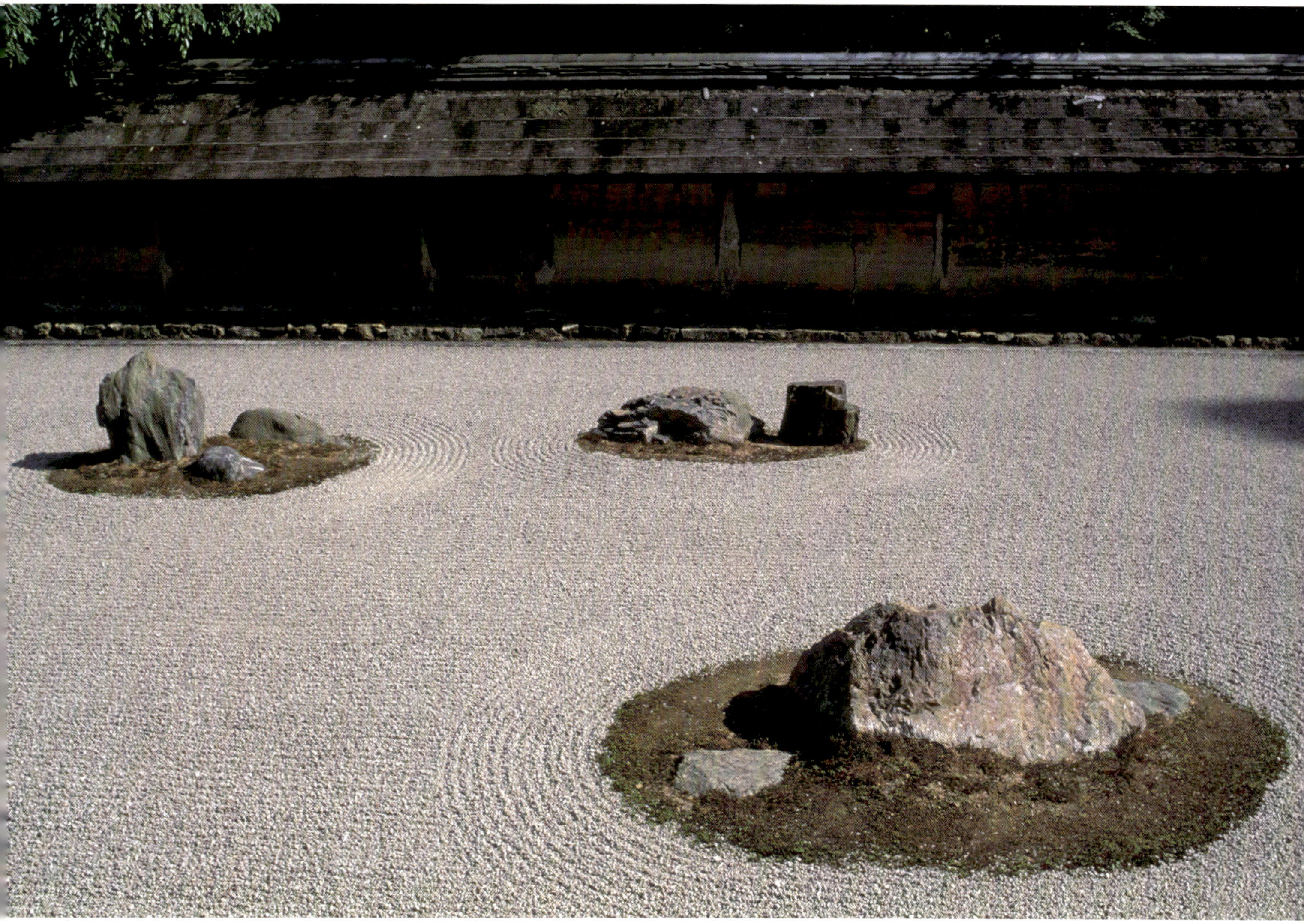

Illus. 34 *The karesansui garden at Ryoan-ji Zen Buddhist temple, Kyoto.*

The Tea Ceremony

The tea plant, a member of the same family as the camellia, is indigenous to China and had long been used as a stimulant. Chinese monks would drink a foamy brew made from its leaves to help them keep awake during long hours of meditation. In time, the drinking itself developed into a ceremony honouring Bodhidharma, who was thought to have discovered the tea plant. In Japan, too, tea-drinking became a quasi-religious ceremony among monks. Specifically, it was a monk by the name of Shuko Murata (1423-1502) who first transformed what had become a social habit into a ritual. Among his followers, men who valued the spiritual graces, were some who became "tea masters." The greatest of them was Sen no Rikyu (1521-1591), who elevated the tea ceremony to an art with moral and spiritual meaning, in which the ritual of drinking is performed in a hut set in a tea garden or *cha niwa*. The approach through the garden is itself an essential part of the ritual. Varying shades of green predominate, with the natural colours of

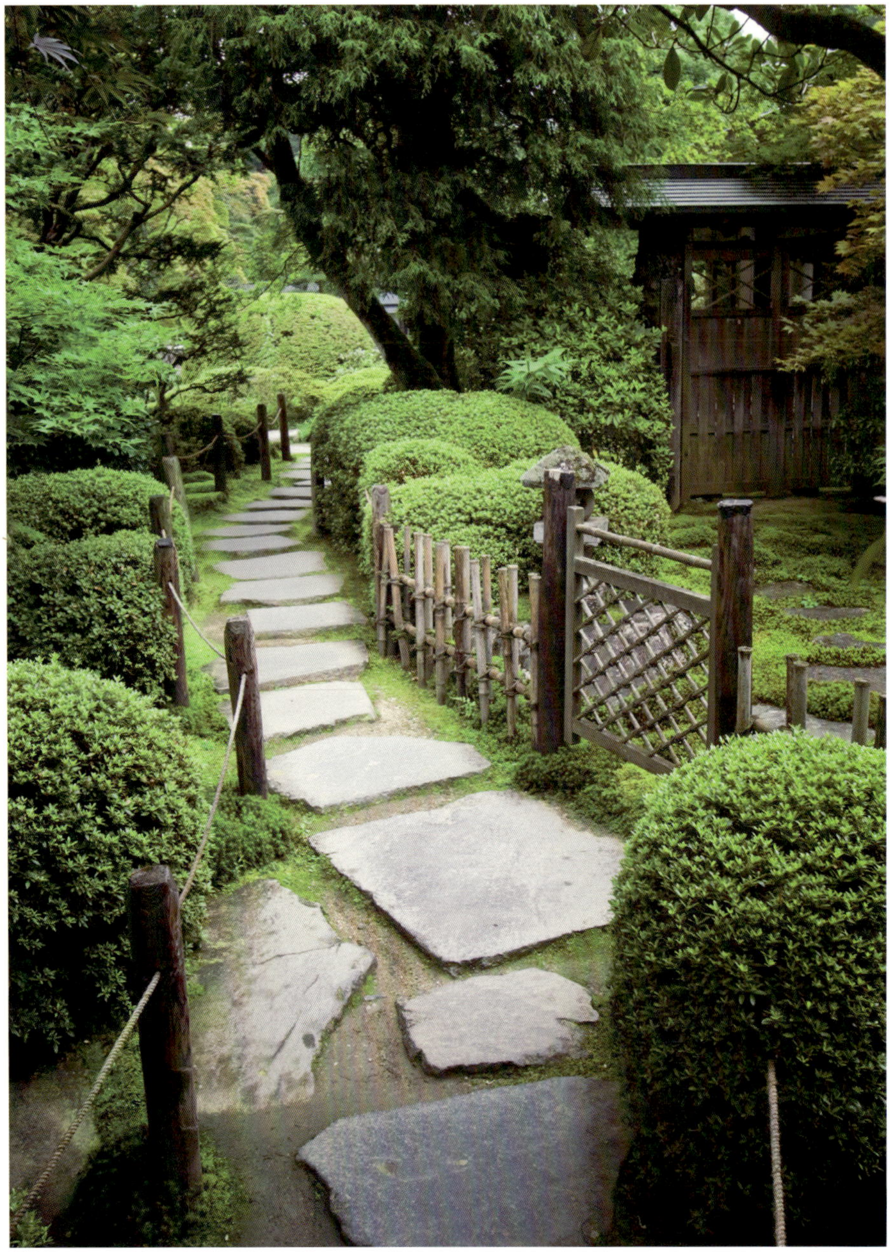

Illus. 35 *Shoyoen tea garden, Nikko, Japan.*

bark and stone, and the subtle tints of bamboo stems in green, ochre or black. There must be no bright, distracting flowers, but the vivid autumn colours of maple leaves are admissible. Stepping stones guide the visitor through the garden, and through the ceremony; they also serve to keep the moss that carpets the ground fresh and unbruised. The other essential elements are stone lanterns (for the ceremony is often held at night) and a stone water-basin and dipper for the ritual ablution. The entire ceremony is a series of movements designed to enhance and concentrate the feelings of harmony (*wa*), tranquillity (*jakui*), reverence (*kei*) and purity (*sei*) induced by the calm beauty of the garden.

The Emperor Hideyoshi (1584-1598) is said to have held many a discussion on life with Sen no Rikyu in the garden the Emperor made in his chosen place of retreat, Sambo-in, part of the monastery of Daigo near Kyoto. Begun at the very end of Hideyoshi's reign, and supposedly inspired by the Emperor's admiration for an ancient cherry tree at Daigo, Sambo-in is said to have been completed by the tea master Kobosi Enshu (1579-1647). In complete contrast to the rigorous asceticism of "flat gardens" such as Daisen-in and Ryoan-ji, Sambo-in is in the *tsuki-yama* style, with mountains, the Emperor's collection of fine stones, water, and a seasonal succession of flowers.

Under the Tokugawa shogunate (1636-1858) Japan was entirely sealed off from the outside world. The *daimyo*, the feudal lords, nostalgic for the classical Heian period, made gardens that drew entirely on earlier traditions, blending the Heian Shinden design with both Jodo and Zen concepts. Obliged by the shogunate to spend at least part of the time in Edo (modern Tokyo), as a means of limiting their power and wealth, the *daimyo* made grand gardens there, hiring professional garden-makers from the gardeners' trade guilds. Gardening ceased to be primarily an art of spiritual or philosophical inspiration and degenerated into a stereotyped craft. The stroll garden, the invention of which is attributed to the *daimyo* Kobori Enshu (1579-1647), was larger and more ostentatious than the tea garden, more concerned with vistas than detail. One of the largest of the Edo period *daimyo* stroll gardens is Kenroku-en in Kanazawa. Begun in 1676 and completed only in 1837, it incorporates elements of every garden style from the eleventh century onwards.

In China, by contrast, the scholar's garden was still regarded as a place for contemplation and spiritual refreshment, as it had been since the end of the Han dynasty, and was considered artistically superior to parks and even to temple gardens. Linqing (1791-1846), a senior Manchu official, heard of a garden near the Forbidden City in Beijing, known as Banmu Yuan (the Half-acre Garden), long renowned for its natural beauty and its excellent tea water. Years later, he acquired it and began restoring it in 1840, keeping a record of the work, illustrated with woodcuts. One of the features of Linqing's garden was the pavilion for the contemplation of the moon, built on stilts over a lotus pool, with a zigzag bridge leading to the shore. The pavilion overlooks the entire garden, as is typical of classical Chinese gardens, designed to be viewed from a single point.

Revival of the Imperial Park

At about the time Japan closed itself off from the rest of the world, a revival of an earlier style also took place in China. The emperors of the Ming dynasty did not make any grand imperial parks; the revival of this tradition came only with the advent of another non-Chinese imperial family, the Manchus, who founded the Qing dynasty in 1644. Three summer palaces are associated with the Qing emperors. One is in the mountains some 150 kilometres north-east of Beijing at Chengde, where in 1703 the Kangxi Emperor (1662-1722) began the construction of a summer retreat, called Bishushanzhuang ("Mountain Hamlet Far from the Heat"), with a large natural lake, filled with lotuses. The famous Yuan Ming Yuan or Garden of Perfect Brightness, built by the Qian-long emperor (1736-96), is another. The neighbouring summer palace of Yi he yuan, was remade by the Qia-long emperor in 1750 with imitations of southern gardens and a mock Suzhou, his mother's favourite city, in honour of her sixtieth birthday. This summer palace was also sacked in 1860 and further damaged by foreign troops after the Boxer uprising of 1900, but twice restored by the Dowager Empress Cixi.

A return to older ways is often seen as retrograde by the Western mindset, for which time is linear and its forward march implies the idea of progress, of improvement. Measured in terms of increased material comforts for the fortunate minority, this may be true; in terms of man's spiritual growth, the thesis is harder to defend. For a mindset that sees everything as turning and returning, drawing sustenance from old ways, old symbols, is not retrograde but revivifying. And to the symbolism of gardens and their elements I now turn.

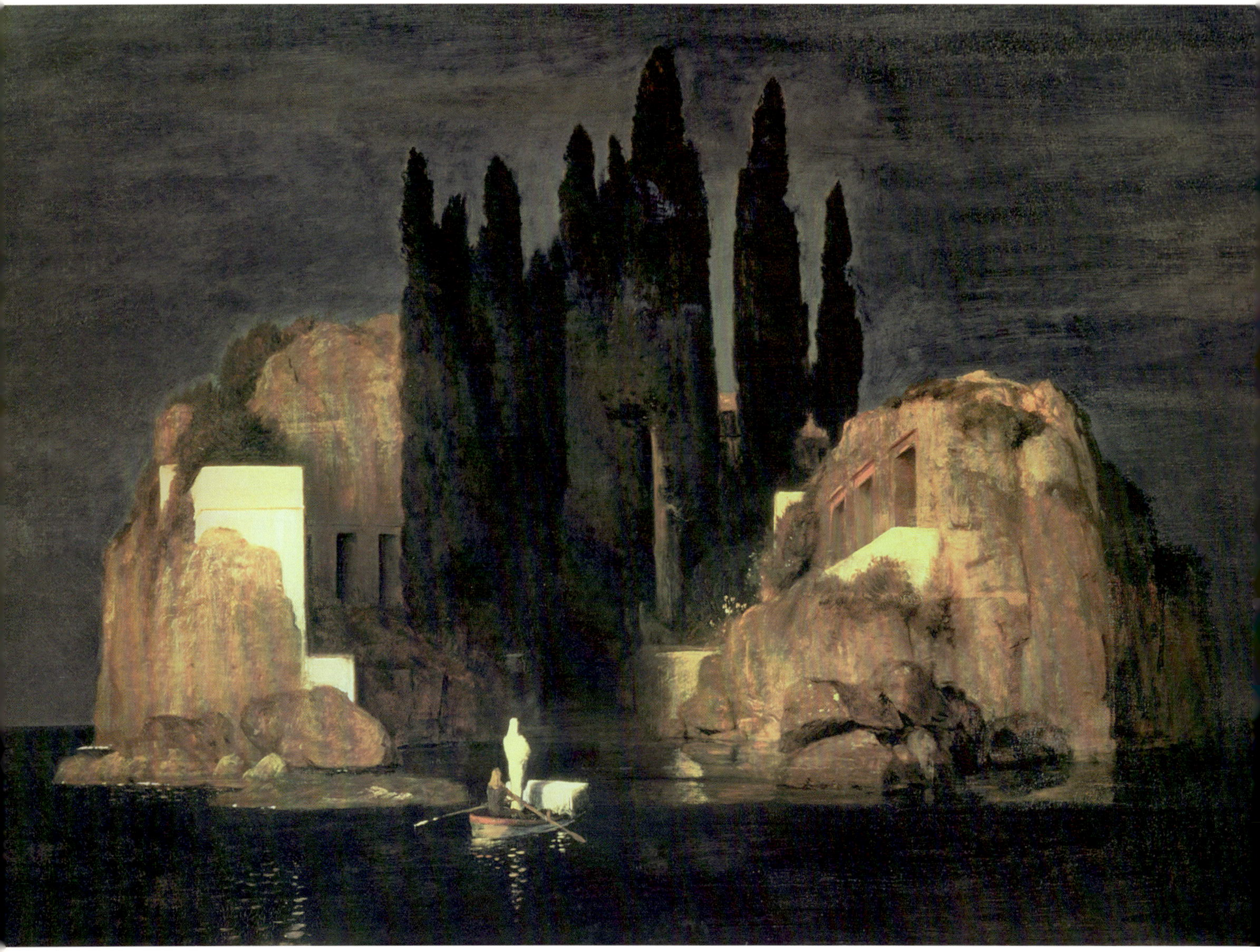

Illus.36 *Arnold Böcklin (1827-1901), L'ile des morts, 1885-1886, oil on canvas. Kunstmuseum, Basle.*

Symbolism and Evocations

The basic elements that form a garden – trees, water, stone – are also the elements that from time immemorial have composed a sacred space. Each is imbued with symbolic meaning. The stone represents indestructibility, permanence; the tree, the power of regeneration; water, purity, the source of life itself. And the sacred space itself, which represents a centre, is intimately linked to the nostalgia for paradise. Above, there is only the sky, the dwelling-place of the Supreme Being of primitive faiths: an omnipotent creator, utterly remote, as infinite, awe-inspiring and transcendent as the sky itself.

The Holy Mountain

Mountains are the meeting point of earth and sky, often considered as the *axis mundi*, the "centre." It is for this reason that so many sacred sites are in high places, real or symbolic. The Mesopotamian ziggurat, the Buddhist stupa, and the Chinese pagoda are all variants of the cosmic mountain. In Chinese mythology, the cosmic mountain K'un-lun, the abode of the immortals and of the Queen Mother of the West, rises nine levels high from the Western sea. In the Buddhist tradition, the cosmic Mount Sumeru (surrounded by eight seas) is the central mountain of the world, clad in fragrant trees. At its summit is the palace of Indra, and on its slopes the four Celestial Kings guarding the cardinal points of the compass.

The prophet Ezekiel located Eden, the garden of God, on the holy mountain of God. In the apocryphal Book of Jubilees (4:26), however, "the Lord hath four places on the earth: the Garden of Eden and the Mount of the East, and this mountain on which thou art this day, Mount Sinai, and Mount Zion." The great Biblical prophet Isaiah prophesied that "it shall come to pass in the last days that the mountain of the Lord's house shall be established in the top of the mountains. . . For the day of the Lord of hosts shall be . . . upon all the high mountains."[46]

Sacred Groves and Trees

Yet in Isaiah's view, the kings of Israel committed sacrilege by setting up images and groves in every high hill, and under every tree, where they burned incense and worshipped Baal.[47]

The altar in a grove, often with its sacred spring, is the universal trinity of stone, tree, water. It took time to eradicate the old ways; but finally the symbolism of the grove came to be equated not with the sacred, but with empty idolatry. Only during the Hellenizing period, under Antiochus, was the Temple Mount in Jerusalem (a symbolic "high place") again transformed, for a while, into a sacred grove with trees around the altar. Its desecration, as devout Jews saw it, fed the apocalyptic piety and mystical visions of Enoch and others like him.

To those who worshipped many gods rather than the stern God of the Jews, the grove around an altar was, like the Temple itself, a form of sacred space. The groves were cared for under the direction of the priests, and protected by decrees regulating replanting and preservation. Each species of tree had its own special associations. The oak belonged to Zeus/Jupiter, and one of the most sacred places in Greece was the sanctuary at Dodona with its oracular oak, taken over by Zeus from Dione. The oak was also the tree of the Druids, on which the sacred mistletoe grew. And the oaks which so troubled Isaiah were the prickly oak of the Mediterranean and Near East, for this is the tree of El, the great god of the western Semites.

Certain trees were particularly associated with the afterlife. Black poplars were sacred to Hecate, the death goddess, and to Persephone, the goddess of death-in-life, who had a black poplar grove in the far West. The wild pear was the tree of both Hera and Athene. In pre-Hellenic times, an apple-spray was the promise of immortality to the sacred king, whose fate it was to be killed; a hero was a sacred king who had been sacrificed to Hera, and whose soul was enjoying her paradise in the far West. The sunset was a symbol of the sacred king's death; and in both Greek and Celtic myth the golden apples (see Chapter I) were originally the passports to this paradise.

In Celtic mythology, two trees shared the winter solstice – the fir, the birth tree, and yew, the death tree (which was also sacred to Hecate). These associations are long since lost; but to this day yew trees, some of great age, survive in many English churchyards, among the gravestones. For the Romans, the cypress was the tree of death, of Dis, lord of the underworld; and in many cemeteries in Europe the cypress takes the place of the yews of English churchyard.

Yet the cypress that we consider so typical of the Mediterranean landscape may not be native to the region at all, but was perhaps introduced by the Phoenicians from western Asia or the Himalayas, reaching Cyprus by about 1000 BCE. It seems even then to have symbolized immortality, as it still does in Persia and south Asia. In Persian and Mughal paintings depicting gardens, again and again the slender, dark cypress is paired with the frail beauty of fruit blossom, representing eternity against the ephemerality of life. Further east, in China, fleeting blossom and evergreen constancy recur in the "three friends in winter" – the pine (standing for the meditative qualities of silence and solitude), winter-blooming plum and straight-stemmed bamboo. These often feature in both gardens and poetry, exemplifying the human characteristics valued by Confucianism of loftiness, purity and tenacity.

The great chenars or plane trees which are so characteristic a feature of the more northerly Mughal gardens are valued not only for their presence and their welcome shade, but also because their five-pointed leaves are like hands held out in prayer in the graceful Muslim gesture. The ivy and the vine were the symbols of Dionysus, the Orphic god, and his Roman counterpart Bacchus. The laurel was Apollo's, and the prize for victory at the Olympic games, a religious as much as a sporting festival, was a laurel wreath. The winner of an event might also be given an olive branch. It is said that when Apollo was born of a myrrh tree on Delos, the island blossomed and the leaves of the olive turned gold.

The olive tree was sacred to Athene. The sacred olive tree in the Academy was a scion from the original tree of the Acropolis, planted by Athene herself. All the olive trees in Attica with this pedigree were treated as protected state property and regularly inspected. Pindar's third Olympian Ode tells how Heracles brought the olive-trees of Olympia from the Hyperboreans, from the land at the back of the north wind. This was not an ice-bound polar waste, but a mythical land blessed with the warm-temperate climate in which alone the olive flourishes. The fallen fruit of the olive seems to have been especially valued as an offering to the gods, in memory perhaps of the Golden Age when fruit dropped unasked into the hands of the first men. Athenaeus (2nd-3rd century) tells us that the ritual meal offered by the Athenians to the Dioscuri consisted of cheese, barley cake, and fallen olives and pears.

The olive is invested with mystical qualities in the Islamic tradition, as the famous Light Verse of the Qur'an reveals:

God is the Light of the heavens and the earth;
the likeness of His Light is as a niche
wherein is a lamp

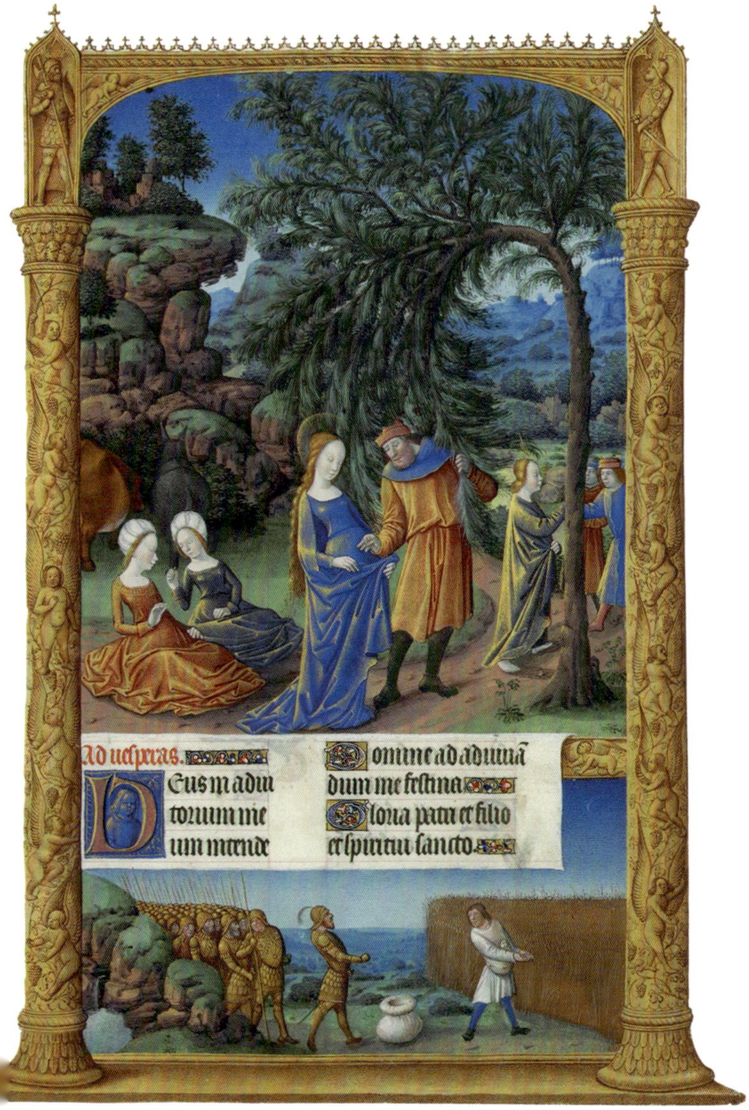

Illus. 37 *The date palm bends its fruit to the Virgin Mary on the flight to Egypt: miniature from Les Très riches heures du Duc de Berry, fol. 57r. Musée Condé, Chantilly.*

(the lamp in a glass,
the glass as it were a glittering star)
kindled from a Blessed Tree,
an olive that is neither of the East nor of the West
whose oil wellnigh would shine, even if no fire touched it;
Light upon Light

The date palm is as important to the southern Mediterranean and the Arabian peninsula as the olive is to the northern Mediterranean. It was sacred to Isis and Lat, and to the Egyptian gods Re and Min. The olive and the palm both came to have a central symbolic meaning in the Abrahamic traditions. The palm and olive frame the life of Jesus: the apocryphal Book of James recounts how a palm tree bent its fruit to the Holy Family on the flight to Egypt, and when Jesus rode into Jerusalem before Passover, the people "took branches of palm trees, and went forth to meet him, and cried, Hosanna." And after the feast of Passover, which came to be known as the Last Supper, Jesus went "as he was wont, to the mount of Olives."[48]

In the Islamic tradition, Mary gave birth to the infant Jesus under a palm tree, the birth tree of antiquity. The fruit of the date palm is important to Muslims for more than just its economic importance, which has become sacralized. To this day. In imitation of the Prophet Muhammad, Muslims traditionally break their fast each evening at sundown during the month of Ramadan with a handful of dates. Other paradigmatic fruits in the Qur'anic garden are the grape and the fig – one Qur'anic Sura even begins with the words *wa'l tîni wa'l zaytûn*: "By the fig and the olive."[49]

However fiercely prophets and the guardians of scripture may fight against it, humankind seems to be incurably syncretic; there is no major religion that has not absorbed some of the traditions of others. The visible expression of the syncretic *Din Ilahi* of the Mughal Emperor Akbar can be seen in much of the architecture of Akbar's time, and above all in the *Diwan-i Khas* or Hall of Private Audience in Akbar's city of Fatehpur Sikri. A great column stands isolated in the centre of the vaulted hall, supporting a platform and four railed catwalks leading to the four corners of the gallery. On this throne sat the Emperor, as regent of God; but it was also a Cosmic Tree set in the centre of the cosmic cross.

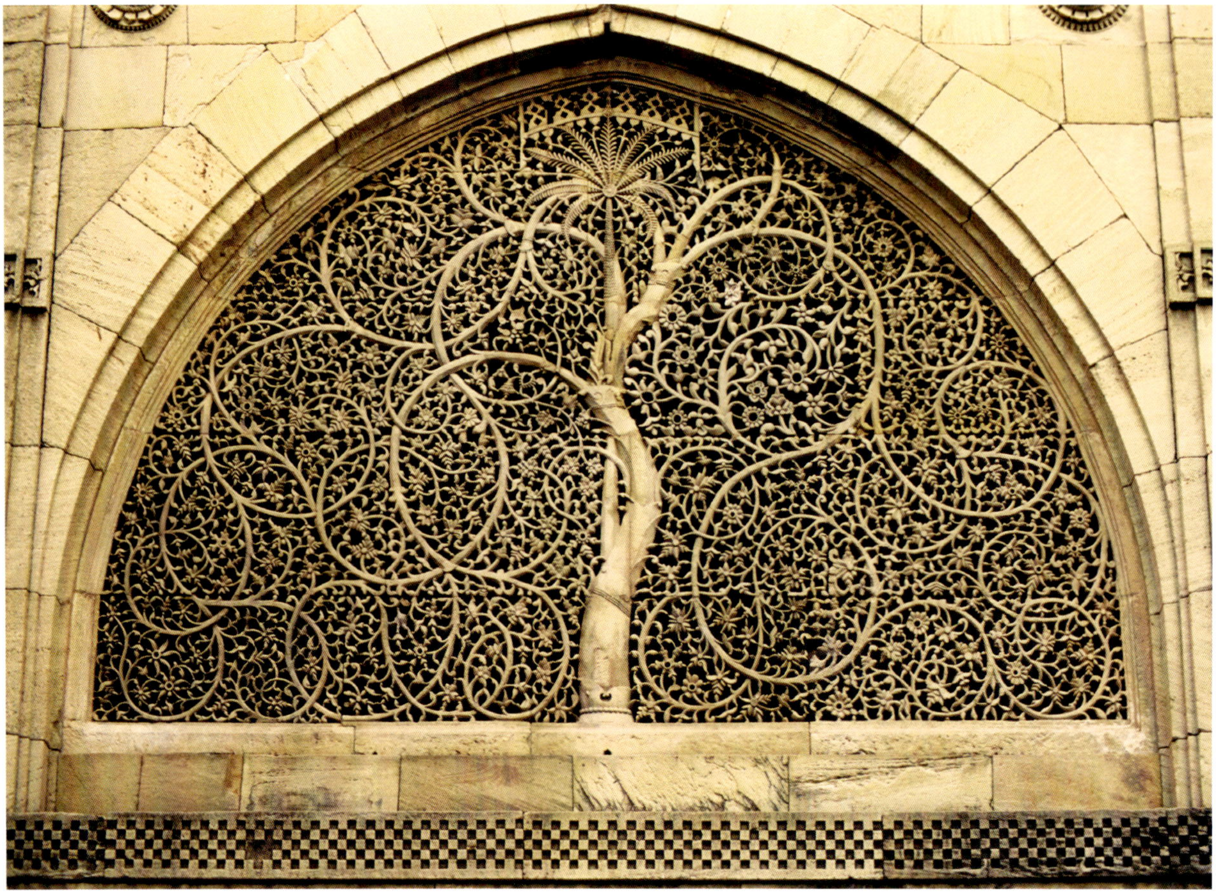

Illus. 38 *Stone carving of the tree of life, Ahmedabad.*

The symbol of the Cosmic Tree is one that appears again and again in different traditions, representing not only the cosmos itself, the *axis mundi*, the centre, the access to the highest heaven, but also life, immortality, and wisdom.[50] It is found in the cold north, with the Yggdrasil of Scandinavian mythology, and in the Mediterranean, with the tree that bore the golden apples of the Hesperides and the apple that is sacred to Aphrodite (see Chapter I). From the Middle East come the Biblical Tree of Life and the Tree of Knowledge of Good and Evil. The representation of the Sefirot (attributes of God) in Kabbalistic wisdom is a Tree of Divine Power of which En-Sof, the absolute reality, is both the hidden root and the life-giving sap. In Jewish esotericism, the tree is sometimes inverted: the *Zohar* tells us that "the Tree of Life extends from above downward." The symbol of the inverted tree appears also in Islam, with the Tuba tree in Paradise. In Sura 13, which also refers to the gardens of Paradise, the Qur'an promises "tuba," bliss, to those who believe and do good deeds. Later this became concretized as the Tuba tree of bliss in the gardens of Paradise – which is said to grow downwards, its roots attached to the underside of the *kursi* or pedestal supporting the Divine Throne (the *'Arsh*). The Lote tree of the Qur'an is the symbol of the boundaries between the created and the next world.

> *And indeed he saw him a second time by the lote-tree of the furthest limit, near unto the garden of promise, with the lote-tree veiled in a veil of nameless splendour . . . [And withal] the eye did not waver, nor yet did it stray: truly did he see some of the most profound of his Sustainer's symbols.*[51]

A painting from an early nineteenth century Shi'a divination album depicts the Prophet Muhammad seated beside Kausar tank from which four channels branch out, above which is the Lote-tree of the Boundary. Birds are perched in the tree, probably in reference to the hadith that the souls of the virtuous will be transformed into birds in paradise.[52]

The inverted tree appears in Indian traditions, too. The Rg Veda says "the branches grow towards what is low, the roots are on high." In the Katha-Upanishad we read:

This eternal Ashvattha, whose roots rise on high, and whose branches grow low, is the pure, is the Brahman, is what we call the Non-Death. All the worlds rest in it.

And the Bhagavad Gita tells us:

There is a tree, the tree of Transmigration, the Ashvattha tree everlasting. Its roots are above in the Highest, and its branches are here below. Its leaves are sacred songs.

India also has the jambu or rose-apple tree which grew at the centre of the Indian continent and gave it its ancient name of Jambudvipa, rose-apple island. Parijata was the tree of paradise – the delight of the nymphs of heaven, with flowers so fragrant that they perfumed the whole earth – with which the efforts of the gods were rewarded when they churned the sea of milk in the time of Vishnu's avatar the Turtle. And India also has the Bo-tree or Bodhi tree in the ancient sacred forests of Uruvela, beneath which Prince Siddhartha Gautam, the Buddha, achieved the awakening.

Sacred trees are often accompanied by a serpent or dragon, guardian of the source of life, symbol of wisdom. The garden of the Hesperides is guarded by the dragon Ladon. Water snakes coil themselves around the sacred trees of Indian tradition; the Naga or snake king Mucalinda protects the Buddha as he meditates beneath the Bodhi tree. Not all serpents are beneficent: in the Nordic myths, the immense tree Yggdrasil is threatened by the serpent Nidhogg which lives among its roots. In the Judaeo-Christian tradition the serpent is transformed from the symbol of wisdom to that of evil, tempting Eve to eat of the forbidden fruit which would make mankind "as gods" in wisdom.

In Eden grew "every tree that is pleasant to the sight, and good for food," providing Adam and Eve with blessed shade: and shade has its own meaning of particular force to desert peoples. The Tree of Life that stood "in the midst of the garden," the forbidden tree of the knowledge of good and evil, is the precursor of other symbolic trees. Indeed, the Tree of Life was for long believed to be the source of the wood that formed the Cross on which Christ was crucified, and the legend told that the Cross stood on the very site where the Forbidden Tree grew. Just before his death, John Donne (1572-1631) wrote his *Hymne to God my God, in my sicknesse*:

We thinke that Paradise and Calvarie,
Christs Crosse, and Adams tree, stood in one place

The Gardin, by Joseph Beaumont (1616-1699), is a poem permeated with the sense of "bitter loss" of the "Heav'n-planted Gardin, where felicitie/ flourishd on every Tree." The image of the tree recurs repeatedly throughout the poem, symbolizing not loss but paradise regained through the Crucifixion:

And thou, alas, hast locked up Lifes Tree.
O Miserable Me.
What held were left, had JESUS'S Pity not
Shewd me another Tree, which can
Enliven dying Man.
That Tree, made Fertile by his own dear blood;

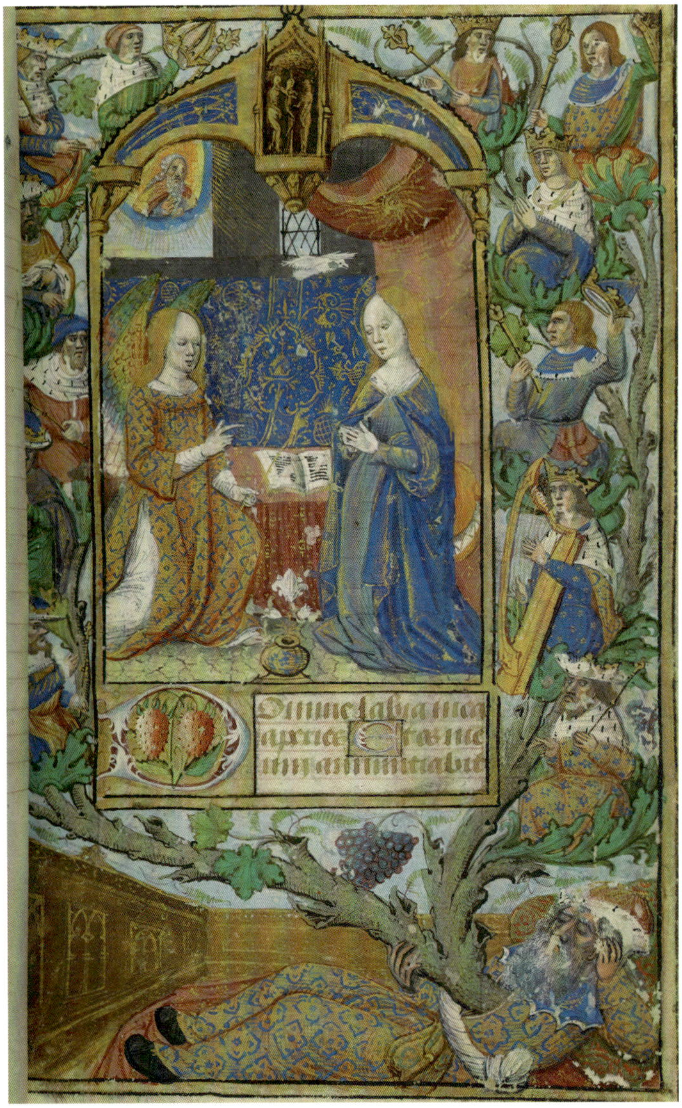

Illus. 39 *Annunciation, with the Tree of Jesse below. Book of Hours. Rouen, France, c. 1500.*

And by his Death with quickning virtue fraught.
I now dread not the thought
Of barracado'd Eden, since as good
A Paradise I planted see
On open Calvarie.

Yet another Tree image derives from Isaiah's prophesy of the coming of the Messiah: "And there shall come forth a rod out of the stem of Jesse, and a Branch shall grow out of his roots." By the tenth century, legend had come to associate the Tree of Jesse with the allegory of the enclosed garden of the Song of Solomon. By now this was seen as a symbol of the Virgin Mary, as in this early mediaeval hymn to the Virgin by John Audelay:

There is a flower sprung of a tree,
The root thereof is called Jesse:
A flower of price;
There is none such in Paradise![53]

The Tree of Jesse, through its association with the apple tree of the Song of Solomon, came to be connected with the Tree of Life in the Garden of Eden; and all three were linked to the tree of the Apocalypse:

In the midst of the street of it, and on either side of the river, was there the tree of life, which bare twelve manner of fruits, and yielded her fruit every month: and the leaves of the tree were for the healing of the nations. [54]

In the west, the Tree of Life was for long thought to be a vine; and some illustrations of the Tree of Jesse show it as heavy with grape-like clusters of the descendants of Jesse.

Water and the Four Quarters of the Universe

The symbols of the four rivers and of the four quarters of the universe, which have had such a profound influence on the design of gardens, are of great antiquity, and are widespread in both eastern and western traditions. The Tree of Life stood in the middle of Eden, from which "a river went out . . . to water the garden; and from thence it was parted, and became into four heads." [55]

But where were these rivers? Ptolemy thought that the four rivers arose in Transoxiana, which the Greeks called Sogdiana. The great Indus River thus came to be identified with the Phison of the Bible, though some said Phison was the Ganges.[56] The Manichaeans thought that the four rivers were the Tigris and the Euphrates, the Nile and the Ganges. The four rivers also appear in the Vedas of ancient India, together with the cosmic mountain, Meru, the centre of the world. In one version of the ancient Vedic myth, the celestial waters that flow down upon the earth divide into four rivers at Mount Meru, to bestow their life-giving qualities upon lotus-petal continents. One of these streams became the river Ganges and, echoing this myth, many Aryan villages have two diagonal thoroughfares with a tree marking the intersection, denoting the Tree of Knowledge that grows from Mount Meru. The symbolism of the living waters and the tree is found in the Kaushitaki Upanishad, where an ageless river runs beside the miraculous tree. Buddhist stupas, themselves symbolic mounts, are topped by a *chhattri* that represents the sacred Bodhi tree.

The rivers of the City of God in the fourth century CE Apocalypse of Paul are no longer of water:

> *Then the angel said to me: "Follow me and I shall lead you into the city of Christ.". . And in the round of the city there were found twelve gates of great beauty, and four rivers which encircled it . . . And I asked the angel: "What are these rivers which encircle this city?" And he replied: "These are the four rivers whose abundant flow is for those who are in this land of promise; as for their names, the river of honey is called Phison; and the river of milk, Euphrates; and the river of oil, Gihon; and the river of wine, the Tigris . . ."*[57]

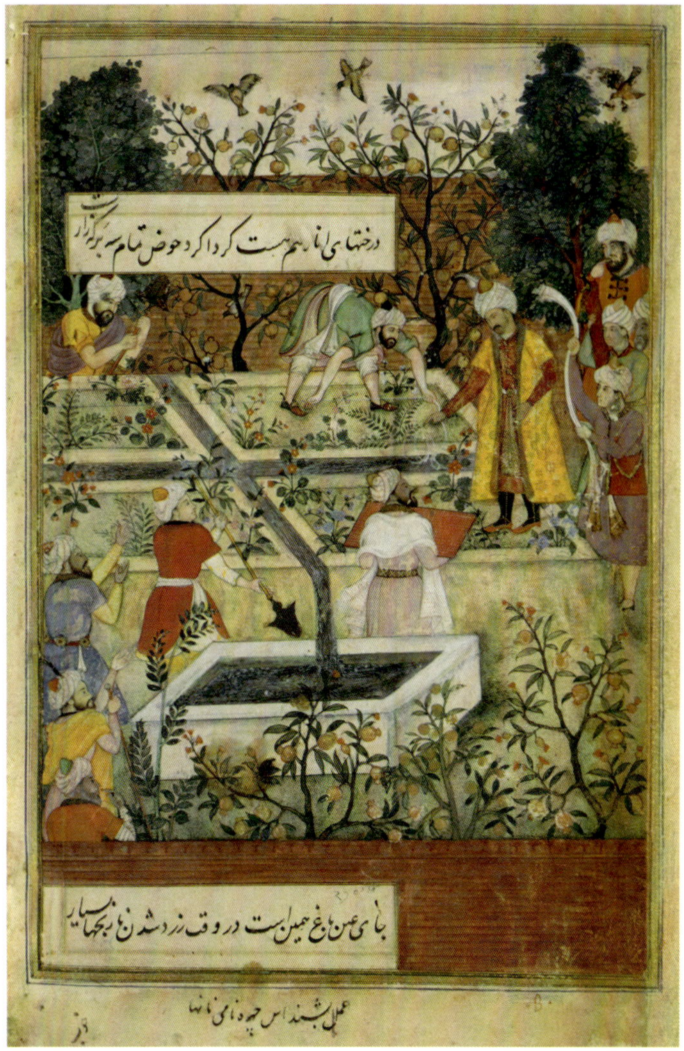

Illus. 40 *A pair of Mughal miniatures (c. 1590) by Nanha and Bishndas, showing Babur supervising the layout of his Bagh-i-Wafa (Garden of Fidelity), with intersecting channels, symbolizing the four rivers of Paradise, emptying into a pool.*

The imagery of four rivers runs throughout the Islamic world, always imagined as the rivers of Paradise, the garden that awaits the faithful. The Qur'anic rivers of *jannah*, which is Gan Eden, seem to echo the four rivers of the city of Christ:

> *This is the similitude of the Garden which the god-wary have been promised: Therein are rivers of water unstaling, rivers of milk unchanging in flavour, and rivers of wine – a delight to the drinkers – and rivers too of purified honey. . .*[58]

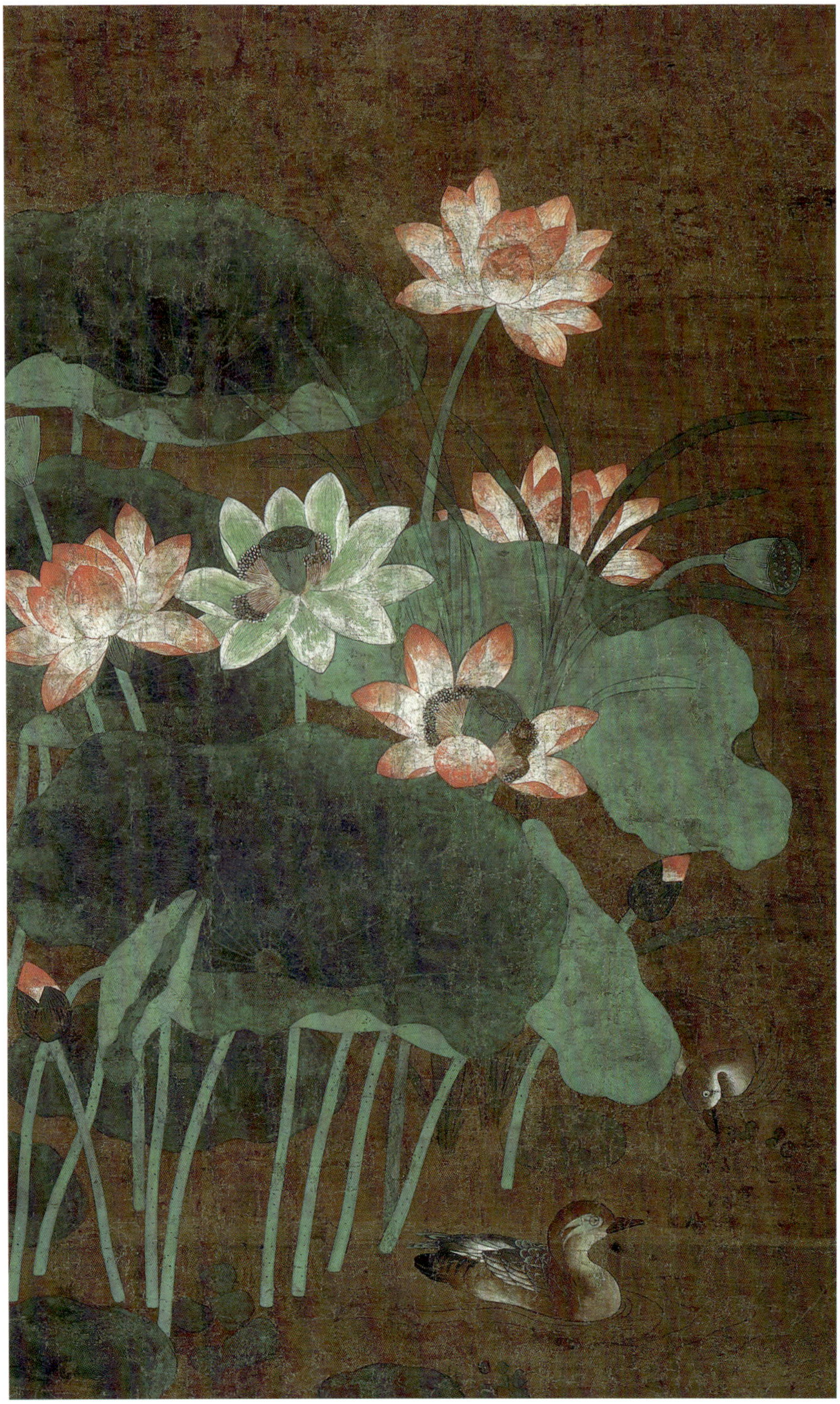

Illus. 41 *Sacred lotus, Nelumbo nucifera. Hanging scroll by an anonymous artist, probably P'i-ling, Kiangsu Province, 13th century. Museum of Far Eastern Art, Berlin.*

As we have seen, the age-old Persian garden design adopted by Islam was the wide cosmic cross formed by narrow, intersecting water channels, representing the centre of the world and the four cardinal points. The oft-repeated Qur'anic allusion to "gardens beneath which rivers flow"[59] becomes especially appropriate in the case of the tomb gardens such as that of the Emperor Humayun in Delhi, where the watercourses seem to run beneath the central mausoleum. The emperor thus has his foretaste of paradise while awaiting the Day of Resurrection in his tomb. The fourfold design *chahar-bagh* appears again in the tomb of the Persian Mirza Ghiyas Beg, Lord High Treasurer and father-in-law of the Emperor Jahangir. His mausoleum in Agra is unpretentious in size but exquisitely and elaborately decorated with inlaid marble work.

The garden surrounding Emperor Akbar's tomb at Sikandra, near Agra is also laid out as a cosmic cross. It has been interpreted as representing not only the Islamized *chahar-bagh* but also the Hindu mythologized geography of the world, with waters flowing from the cosmic mount at the centre to four cardinal points representing four the divine abodes or *char dham*.

In ancient Chinese mythology, the gods rule the four quarters of the universe. But in the idealized landscape of the Sino-Japanese garden style known as Shinden-Zukuir, developed in the Heian period (794 to 1185), water must flow from the east, the source of purity, to the west, washing away impurities.

The symbolism of water as the source of life, as the primal substance out of which comes all creation, seems near-universal. In the Iliad, Homer claims that Oceanus, who girdles the world, is the origin of all creation. The Bible begins with the words: "In the beginning God created the heaven and the earth. And the earth was without form, and void; and darkness was upon the face of the deep. And the Spirit of God moved upon the face of the waters." In the Qur'an, God "sends down" water as rain, just as He sends down His revelation; and from the rain God creates every plant,

the green leaf of it,
bringing forth from it
close-compounded grain,
and out of the palm-tree, from the spathe of it,
dates thick-clustered,
ready to the hand, and
gardens of vines,
olives, pomegranates. [60]

Water was one of the favourite symbols of the Daoists, washing away evil, and in stillness finding its own modest level, to mirror back images without distortion. It is the drink of the Immortals and the essence of woman, and was associated with the moon and with pearls. And from it grew the lotus that was so valued by the Chinese for its scented flowers; the great leaves, standing high above the water in summer, capture mist and rain in dewy pearls on their waxen, jade-green cupped surface. In the Vedic tradition, water is "the source of all things and of all existence." Out of this emerges the Vedic and Puranic symbolism of the lotus as the manifestation of the cosmos, as the created world arising above the primeval waters.

The Symbolism of Flowers

In Puranic tradition, the lotus from the centre of which Brahma is born corresponds to the cosmic tree emerging from the navel of Narayana/Vishnu. The rose-coloured lotus is the flower of the sunrise, and of Brahma's prayer, and the blue is sacred to Vishnu, who upholds the blue universe of day. The white lotus of evening is the flower of death and resurrection, the flower of Shiva, he who destroys and preserves. In post-Vedic tradition, Vishnu reigns in a heaven of gold and precious stones, seated upon white lotus flowers with his wife

Lakshmi at his side. In ancient Indian cosmology some accounts depict the continents as the petals of a lotus, with Mount Meru, the central axis of the world, as the carpel.

The lotus is also the flower of Buddha; indeed, it is the central symbol itself. At the moment of Buddha's conception, rivers stopped flowing, trees burst into bloom, and the waters of lakes were half-hidden by lotus flowers. When he was born, he began at once to walk, and wherever his foot seemed about to touch the earth a lotus appeared, to bear him. The Good Law, called the Saddharma-Pundarika, was borne on a lotus flower eastward and northward over the waters and the desert sands to Java, to China and Japan. The prayer of the Law is still known as the Lotus Sutra. As the lotus emerges unsullied from the slime beneath the life-giving water, it symbolizes the soul, seeking a path to out of the mire of this life. The eleventh century philosopher-cosmologist Zhou Dunyi wrote that the lotus is "to be regarded reverently from a distance, not profaned by familiar approach."

In ancient Egypt, the sun god was born as a lotus flower, and daily reborn out of the flower. The lotus was the flower of royal resurrection, and the ritual of embalming a dead king ensured his resuscitation (*Ounen-Nefer*) for eternity. Once the ceremonial processes were completed, the king, dead to the earth, would rise as a god, emerging from the lotus flower that dominates the waters of primeval chaos.

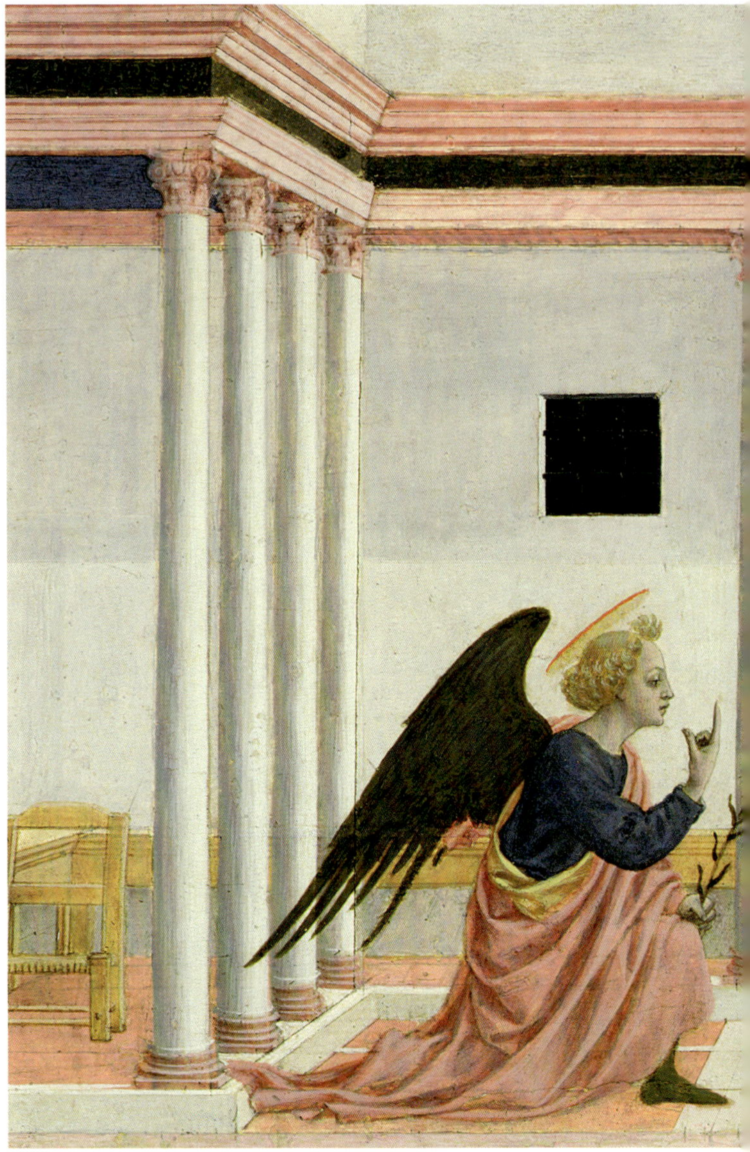

In the Abrahamic traditions the tulip, the iris and the rose have been endowed with religious significance. The tulip was much beloved, particularly in Persia and Ottoman Turkey, where it was known as *lale*. Often featuring on Iznik tiles and ceramic vessels, this is not the plump tulip of modern gardens, but the slender, elegant wild tulip of the steppes. It would seem that the Ottomans never quite lost their nostalgia for the nomadic life. Persians and Turks alike celebrated it in religious poetry, where it was the symbol of the martyr for the faith – in particular, the martyrdom of Hussein, whose bloodstained garments it symbolizes – and of the mystical, self-abnegating lover. For Muhammad Iqbal, the tulip is the flower of the manifestation of the divine fire, the symbol of the Burning Bush on Mount Sinai.

At the very origins of mythical time the mourning iris, *Iris susiana*, was among the flowers that Persephone was picking when Hades seized

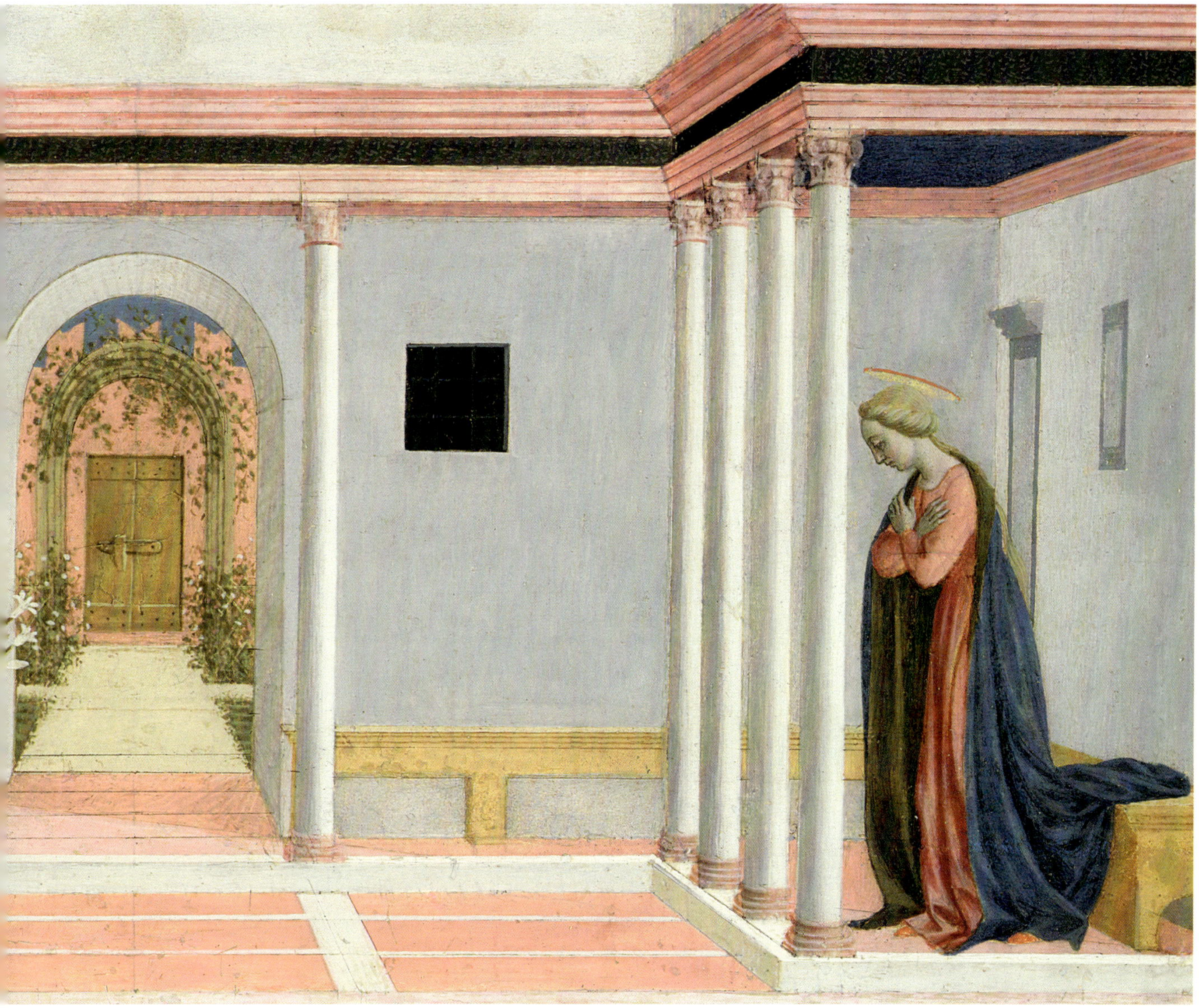

Illus. 42 *Domenico Veneziano (c.1400–61), The Annunciation, predella panel from the St. Lucy Altarpiece, c.1442–48, tempera on panel. Fitzwilliam Museum, University of Cambridge. The virgin receives the white lily that now bears her name, Madonna lily, Lilium candidum, the lily of purity, flowering at the time of the Feast of the Assumption (24 August); an Islamic-style chahar bagh beyond, with roses. Already at the turn of the 7th and 8th centuries, the Venerable Bede (673–735) described the Madonna lily as the emblem of the Virgin, its white petals symbolizing her purity, its golden anthers the glowing light of her soul.*

her and carried her off to the underworld. The iris is also the heraldic *fleur-de-lis* or flower de luce of the French royal coat of arms – in which the iris and the lily are conflated. The purple-blue *Iris germanica*, the *azul*, gave its name to the Moorish tiles of azure and sage green, turquoise and white, known as *azulejos*. The association of the iris with death passes into the Abrahamic traditions. The blue *azul* and, in particular, the ash-white *Iris florentina* are also the flower of Muslim graveyards, known as *gul-i mazar* in Urdu.

After the fall of Granada, many of the floral symbols of the Muslims were adopted as emblems of Christianity. The azure iris became a symbol of celestial contemplation, and the white iris and its counterpart the white lily became sacred to the Madonna. They feature in paintings of the Annunciation, and the three-fold outline of the iris also symbolizes the Trinity.

Throughout history, perhaps no plant has been invested with greater religious and mystical symbolism than the rose. It was already venerated in ancient times. In the twelfth century BCE, the delectably fragrant *Rosa gallica* was a religious emblem of the Medes and Persians.

Whether the rose of Isaiah's "The desert shall rejoice, and blossom as the rose" was in fact *Rosa* or the unrelated rose of Sharon scarcely matters; the seventeenth century translators of the King James Bible knew very well the power of such imagery. Though the rose was viewed with suspicion by Christians in the early, ascetic period because of its pagan, erotic associations, it later became established as a symbol of Christ's passion – the five petals representing the five wounds, its thorns the crown of thorns – and of the blood of the martyrs. As the ninth century Abbot Walafrid tells us in his *Hortulus*, the rose and the lily have for centuries been treasured, the rose in memory of the blood of the blessed martyrs, and the lily as "a shining sign of the faith."

The symbols recur in mediaeval alchemy, too. The *Rosarium Philosophorum*, one of the first synoptic texts on alchemy, dating from the mid fourteenth century, insists on the union of opposites, represented by the masculine and the feminine principles, form and matter, active and passive, spirit and body. The colour of the feminine element is white – the moon, the lily, the white rose; that of the masculine is red – the sun, the red rose.

Above all, however, the rose became the symbol of the Blessed Virgin Mary. Among Our Lady's titles in the breviary of the Roman rite are "first rose of the martyrs" and "the mystic rose," and there are a number of epithets for her as a white or a red rose. She was often depicted embowered in roses, and the five decades of prayer dedicated to her were counted on beads that came to be known as a rosary.

And the Blessed Virgin finds an honoured place, of course, in Dante's paradise, along with her lilies:

Here is the rose,
Wherein the word divine was made incarnate;
And here the lilies, by whose odour known
The way of life was follow'd. [61]

Early Christian mystics were entirely focused upon attaining paradise through prayer, contemplation and asceticism. Similar other-worldly impulses appear in early Muslim mysticism. But as Sufism developed in Islam, never so un-this-worldly a faith as Christianity, the natural world came increasingly to be seen as composed of signs of God's beneficence and symbols of His beauty. The Qur'an again and again calls upon the believers to observe nature, for "surely these are signs for those who understand."

The symbolic significance of the rose, the foremost flower of the poets of Islam, is wonderfully expressed in the poetry of Muslim mystics. The poetry of Maulana Jalaluddin Rumi (1207-1273), perhaps the greatest of the mystical poets of Persia, is permeated with garden imagery. He is one of the most fervent exponents of the belief that all of God's creation sings His praises, each in its own way, so that plants become symbols of the movements of ritual prayer. The whole garden and its every tree and flower, the seasons, the rain that refreshes it, remind Rumi of God, and the rose is the supreme manifestation of God. Repeatedly playing on the similarity of sound of *kull* (the All) and *gul* (rose), in the *Mathnawi* Rumi reminds his listeners that the rose brings a fragrant message from the rose garden of Unity, a foretaste of the splendours of paradise.[62]

Entire mystical poetical works are dedicated to the rose and rose gardens. Sa'di (1184-1291), a native of Shiraz, compiled a collection of stories, maxims, admonitions, advice, and poetry in Persian and Arabic, with quotations from the Qur'an, telling us that his aim was to "present a book of a Rose Garden, a Gulistan, whose leaves cannot be touched by the tyranny of autumnal blasts." In eight chapters, it is even designed like a two-fold *chahar-bagh*.

Of what use will be a dish of roses to thee?
Take a leaf from my rose-garden.
A flower endures but five or six days,
But this rose-garden is always delightful.[63]

Another Persian poet, Kamal Khojandi (d.1400), wrote a long poem about the rose, in which he likens the rose to Jesus, the Spirit of God. Muslims revere Jesus as one of the greatest of prophets; perhaps for this reason, the Prophet Muhammad is said to have loved roses. Ruzbihan Baqli of Shiraz (d.1209) relates a saying of the Prophet's that the red rose is part of the glory of God.

When the last rose of summer has withered, its fragrance lingers on in rose water and the precious attar of roses, the oil distilled from its petals. In this form, the rose holds a valued place in many religious ceremonies. The legendary general Saladin (1174-1194) had the walls and pavements of the Haram ash-Sharif washed with rose water when he entered Jerusalem, working alongside his men to clear the site of such abominations as the Templars' latrines. Later, Jewish legend tells us, Süleyman the Magnificent (1520-66) helped to clear the site for the new place of Jewish prayer at the foot of the Western Wall and to wash the Wall itself with rose water. To this day, rose water is used to wash the walls of the Masjid al Haram in Makkah for the

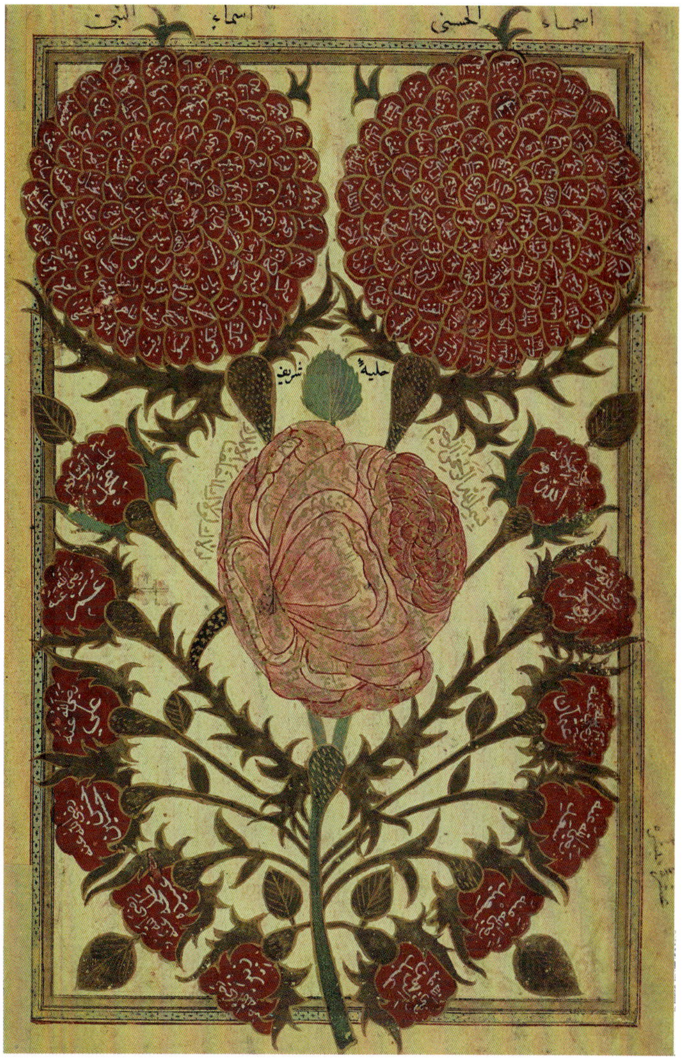

Illus. 43 *The Rose of Muhammad, from Turkish m/s Akhlaq-i Rasul Allah, Turkey, 1708. Staatsbibliothek, Berlin*

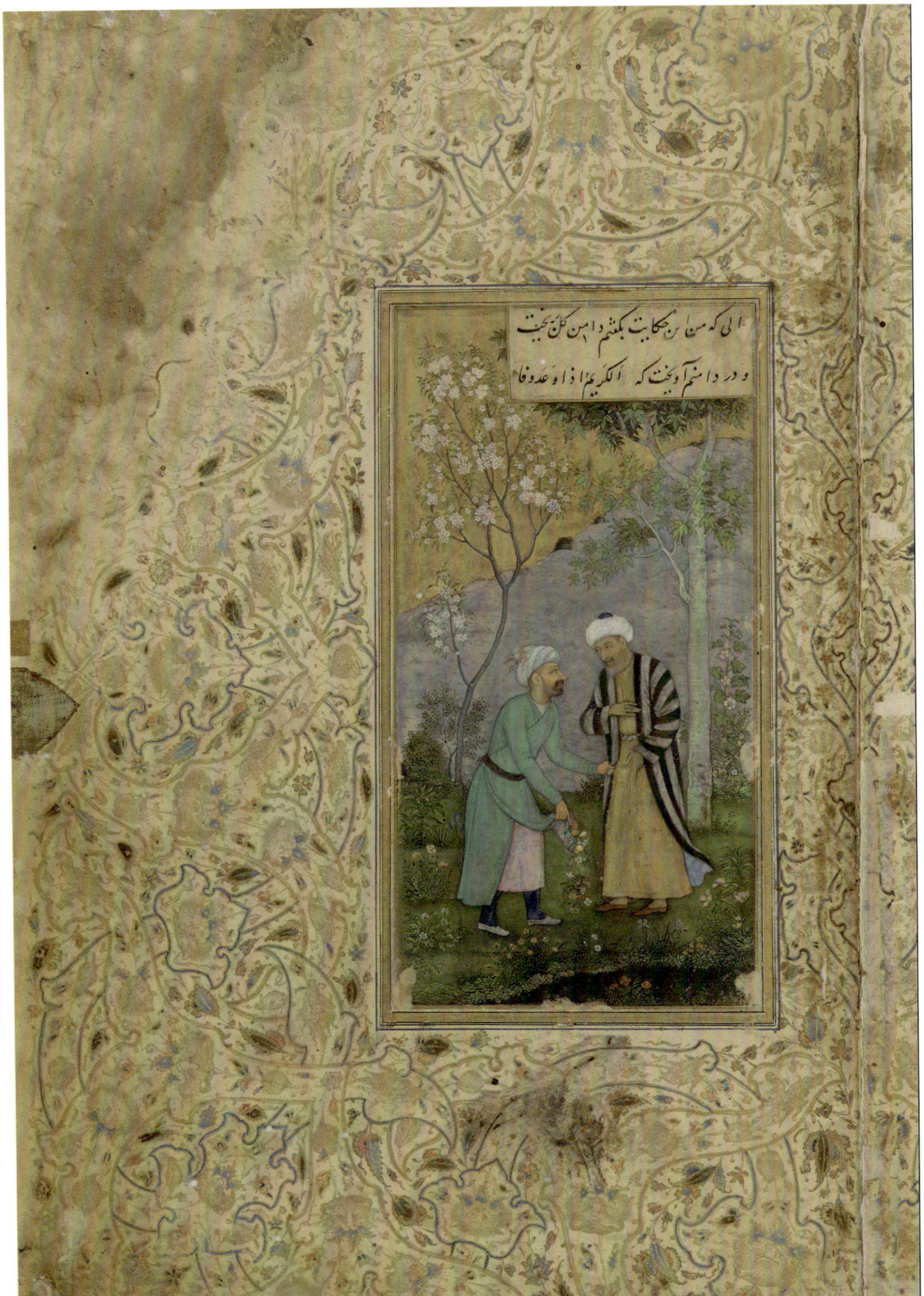
الی که من این حکایت بگفتم دامن گل بریخت
و در دامنم آویخت که الکریم اذا وعد وفا

annual Hajj. A phial of attar of roses, produced in nearby Taif, is bought by pilgrims who can afford it as a souvenir of their Hajj, or presented as a treasured gift to an honoured Hajji. Azizam Bibi, mother of the Empress Nur Jahan, is said to have invented a particular type of rose oil, prepared by distilling rose petals and passing the vapour through oil of sandalwood. Indian apothecaries in Makkah became the masters of this highly valued blend, which is still produced in India.

A selected form of the Damask rose, *Rosa* x *damascena trigintipetala*, is used to make attar of roses. The Damask rose was probably taken to Western Europe, together with attar of roses itself, by knights returning from the crusades. Ever since the crusaders returned with their precious phials, attar of roses has been one of the ingredients of the holy anointing oil used in the coronation of English monarchs. The original recipe dates back to the fifth century, when a phial of holy oil with miraculous healing properties is believed to have descended from heaven on the occasion of the baptism of King Clovis of France (481/482-511). In the eighth century, little more than a century after the death of the Prophet Muhammad, 30,000 bottles of attar of red roses were sent each year to the Caliph (who was both temporal and spiritual leader) in Baghdad from Fars, in Central Asia, one of four places described as earthly paradises.[64]

Even today, when the shops are filled with artificially scented products, the perfumes of nature herself hold sway over us. In all religions and at all times the senses have been one of the ways to partake of the sacred, to reach the divine, and it is the sense of smell that is the most powerfully evocative. The response to fragrance is often beyond ideas, and hence beyond words. The soul, quickening to the perfume of a rose or a lily, enters the realm of the inexpressible, as mystics through the centuries have recognized. The perfume of jasmine, narcissus or rose reminds mystics of God's beauty, to the point of intoxication, as Sa'di tells us in the introduction to his *Gulistan*. One of the devout, emerging from "the ocean of visions," was asked by his companions what gift he had brought from the garden where he had been. "He replied: 'I intended to fill the skirts of my robe with roses, when I reached the rose-tree, as presents for my friends, but the perfume of the flowers intoxicated me so much that I let go the hold of my skirts'."

Even if the mystical experience proves elusive, fragrance has the capacity to evoke memories and intangible impressions. Perhaps it is no coincidence that fragrant flowers are so greatly appreciated in societies that are still strongly traditional and rooted in their religious heritage; for paradise itself is a place of exquisite perfumes, and fragrant flowers in this world prefigure the bliss to come.

To this day, a gift of roses, and above all sweet-scented red roses, means "I love you," though the giver may not be aware that the rose was sacred to Aphrodite, the goddess of love.

Illus. 44 *Sa'di in the Rose Garden, folio from a Gulistan by Sa'di, text copied in Herat, 1468, illumination added early 16th century and repainted c. 1645 by Govardhan. Freer Gallery,*

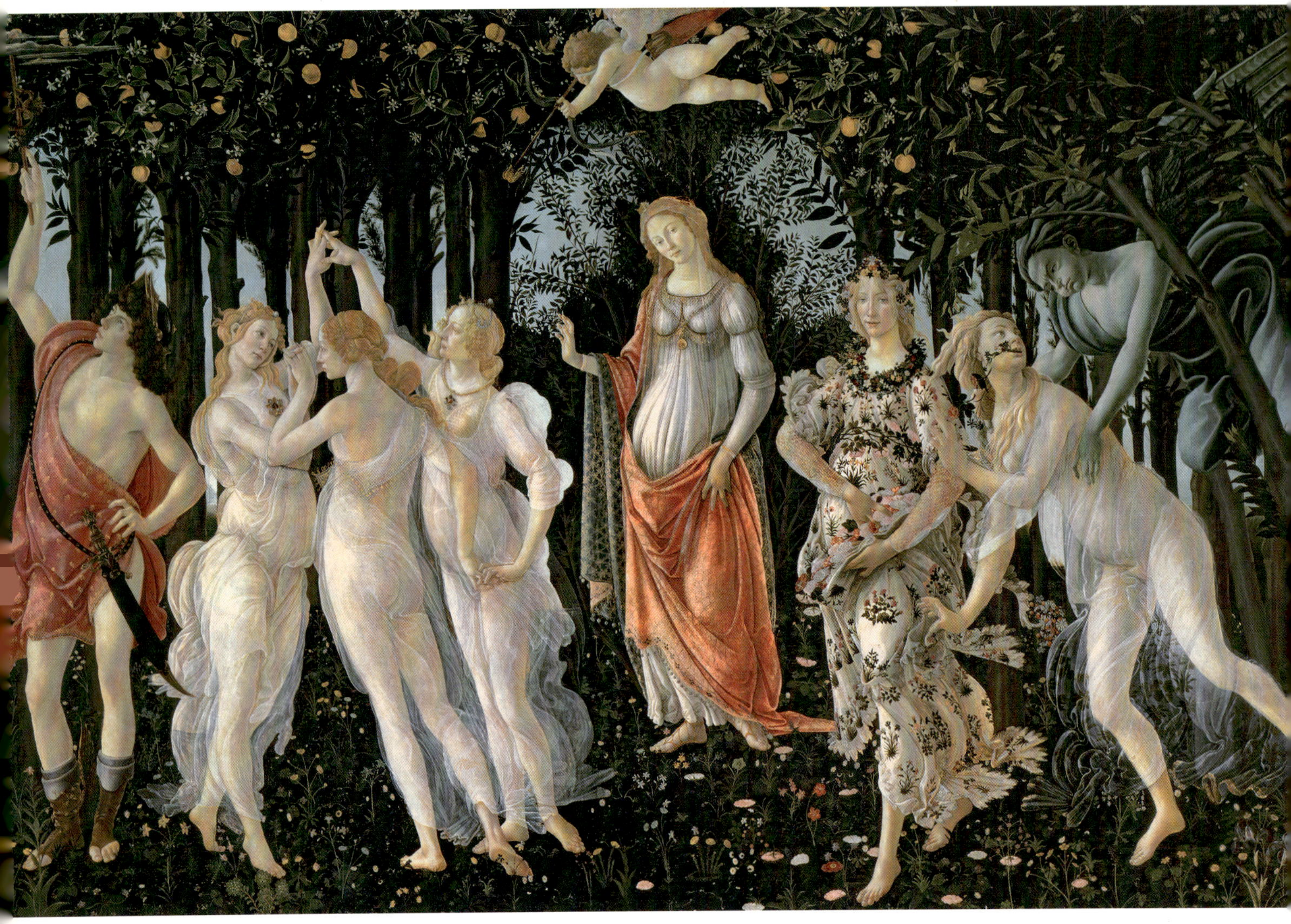

Illus. 45 *Sandro Botticelli (1444/5–1510), Primavera, 1478, tempera on panel. Galleria degli Uffizi, Florence. Venus (Aphrodite) is the modest figure in the centre, with a blindfolded Cupid above her, aiming his arrow at the three dancing Graces. To the left, Mercury points to the golden fruit in the trees, and to the right, Spring, flowers pouring from her mouth, flees from Winter's icy blast*

Aphrodite, Ishq and False Paradises

The rose and the lotus, the pre-eminent symbolic flowers of the Abrahamic and of the eastern religions, both have another potent association: they are the flowers of love. In the west, in this secular age, the rose is no doubt associated more with carnal love than with religion in most people's minds. And as it was in Eden before the Fall, so maybe even now, for some, the earthly paradise lies in erotic love, as Milton suggests:

These two
Imparadised in one another's arms,
The happier Eden, shall enjoy their fill
Of bliss on bliss. [65]

Pagan beliefs

Our pagan forebears would not have found this surprising. It is only in our modern, secular age, with its legacy of Christian guilt in the West, that love sacred and love profane have become so separate. For the ancients, the sexual act is not profane but in a very real sense holy, the union of two bodies a symbol of the primordial unity, the ecstasy of orgasm a cosmic fusion comparable to the ecstasy of religious experience. But sex also played another role: it is a defiance of death, the duel between Eros and Thanatos, between the life-giving libido and death. The great goddesses of the pre-Hellenic era, who survive in the triad of maiden, nymph and crone as Athene, Aphrodite and Hera, were procreators and destroyers, goddesses of life and of death. In choosing Aphrodite, the goddess of love, mankind triumphs over death, attains his immortality.

The poetess Sappho (d. c. 570 BCE) describes a sanctuary garden that evoked the erotic power of the goddess, with all the elements of a sacred space: the grove of apple trees, the altars fragrant with incense, the roses, where a rivulet "murmurs cold among the apple-tree boughs, and sleep streams down on the trembling leaves."[66]

The celebrated rose gardens of King Midas of Phrygia (2nd millennium BCE), mentioned by Herodotus, were almost certainly associated with the cult of Aphrodite. This was later introduced to Greece – whither the rose, according to Sappho, was brought from Macedonia. And Anacreon (570-488 BCE) described the rose as the breath of the gods, the delight of mortals and the plaything of Aphrodite.

In Virgil's *Georgics* (first century BCE), we read of the twice-flowering roses of Paestum, which were also grown in Pompeii. There they are figured in frescoes that survived the destruction of the city in 79 CE. Ausonius (c. 310-394 CE), the last of the pagan Latin poets, dedicates a charming poem to new-blown roses, "all my Paestum roses laughing at me, dew-drenched" in the rosy dawn under the morning star, "their lady Venus."

As the myths of love sung by Sappho and Anacreon modulated into philosophy, this direct apprehension of a reality beyond words was refined. In Plato's *Symposium*, Diotima, Socrates' guide to Love, maintains that love itself, in its highest expression, passes from the love of physical beauty to the love of knowledge, of the soul, of virtue, and finally to the Good itself.

Carnal versus Spiritual Love

In the Judaeo-Christian tradition, though innocent sex ended with the expulsion from the Garden of Eden, carnal and spiritual love were not immediately seen as separate and mutually exclusive. Some of the most potent mystical and religious imagery of gardens, rivers and fragrant plants, and their association with the beloved, is found in the *Song of Songs*:

A garden inclosed is my sister, my spouse; a spring
shut up, a fountain sealed.
Thy plants are an orchard of pomegranates,
with pleasant fruits; camphire, with spikenard.
Spikenard and saffron; calamus and cinnamon,
with all trees of frankincense: myrrh and aloes,
with all the chief spices:
A fountain of gardens, a well of living waters, and
streams from Lebanon.
Awake, O north wind; and come, thou south, blow
upon my garden, that the spices thereof may flow
out. Let my beloved come into his garden, and eat
his pleasant fruits.

The eroticism of the *Song of Songs* was transmuted, in early Christianity, into images of purity associated with the Virgin Mary. For despite the *Song of Songs*, Christians have often found *eros* difficult and painful. Western Christianity in particular was tormented by the sinfulness of sexuality, even within a licit relationship. The conventional view of the Fall was that it was brought about when Eve yielded to the serpent's blandishments and ate of the forbidden fruit. The Hermetic doctrine, however, held that the separation of the sexes was the result of sin, as St Ambrose, John Scotus, St Gregory of Nyssa and St John of Damascus all believed. St Augustine of Hippo developed a bleak doctrine of original sin which has left deep scars in the western psyche: mankind's sexuality is inherently sinful, and can only be repressed. At the same time, Augustine recognized that the erotic images of the *Song of Songs* could be understood in two ways. If regarded as sexual love, the eroticism of the *Song* became the symbol of concupiscence, but with Christ as its gardener, it symbolized charitable love. This dichotomy is carried to its extreme by St Bernard. In his view, the desire of the flesh sullies the soul, but the love of the soul for God, expressed in the identical language of eroticism, can lead to the moment of ecstatic union, a perfection attained in life only by the Virgin Mary. In religious poetry, she is the *hortus conclusus*, the *hortus deliciarum* or garden of delights, the reverse of Eve's transgression – in her, Eden is restored.

Christianity has been deeply affected by the Augustinian interpretation of the forbidden knowledge as carnal, and the Fall as primarily a sexual transgression which has left mankind irrevocably damaged by original sin. The Fall meant not only banishment and loss of innocence, but another kind of separation, which would add another strand to the yearning for the restoration of prelapsarian unity through the sexual act. Men and women became unable to understand each other's meaning, for they were divided by speech, as Milton knew:

Thus they in mutual accusation spent
The fruitless hours, but neither self-condemning:
And of their vain contest appear'd no end.[67]

This understanding of the Fall meant that the early Christian emphasis was on celibacy and virginity. Bishop Gregory of Nyssa (c. 331-395 CE) considered marriage "the last stage of our separation from the life that was led in Paradise." Virginity, for Gregory and others like him, was the way for sinful humanity to regain paradise.

Courtly Love

There was no more love poetry, no myths of love, in the West between the fall of the Roman Empire and the twelfth century. This was when *l'amour courtois*, a reinvention of the idea of love, came to Christendom. The old symbolism of the rose as

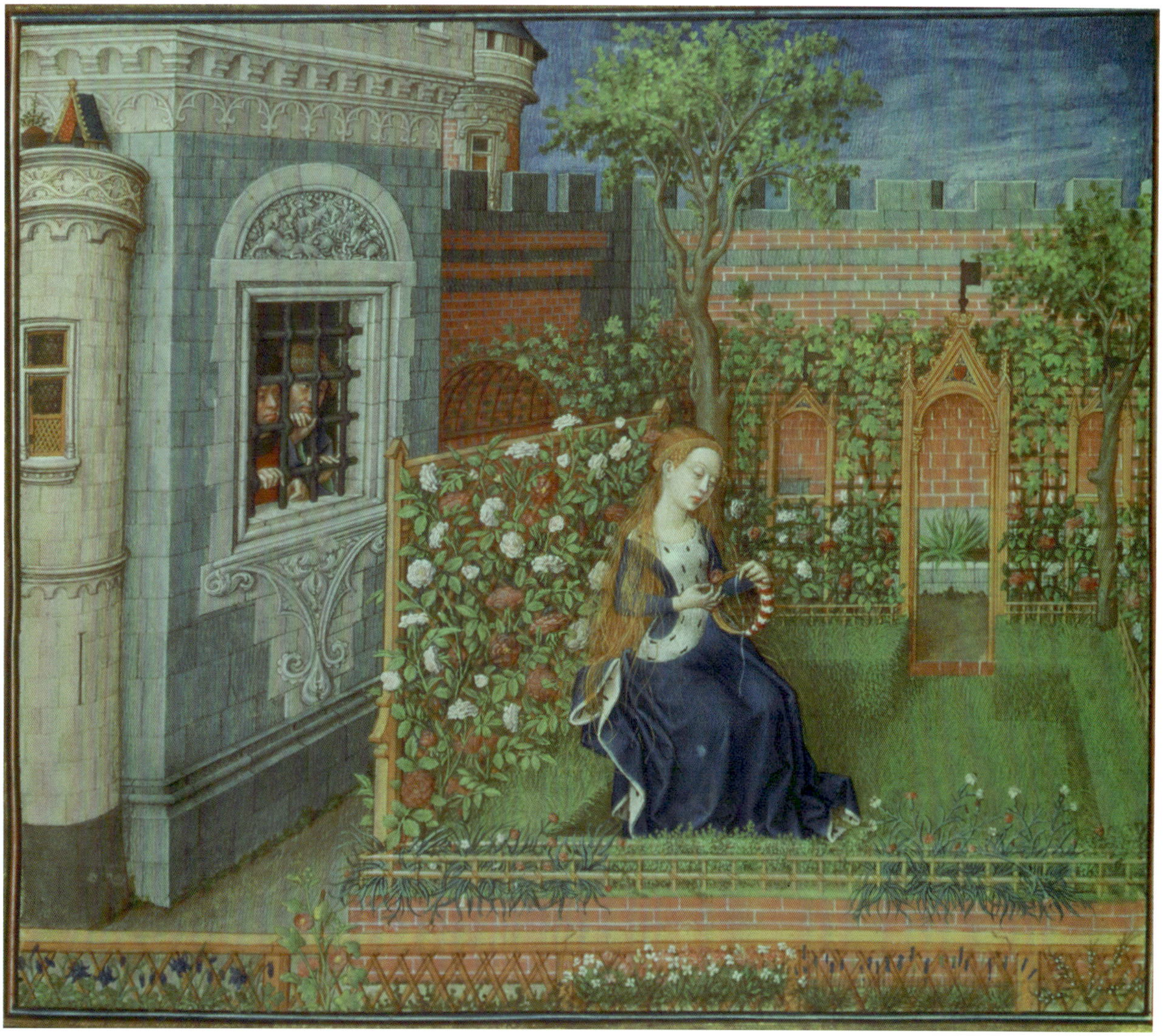

Illus. 46 *Emilia in the Garden, with the imprisoned knights Palamon and Arcite, from The Hours of the Duke of Burgundy, French school, 1454–55. Osterreichische Nationalbibliothek, Vienna*

the flower of love had survived, however, and the twin traditions of the *hortus conclusus* and the bower of Venus were ready to hand as the setting for the mediaeval gardens of love. In the first part of the allegorical thirteenth-century *Roman de la Rose*, the beloved is a rose, giving *l'amour courtois* a strongly mystical quality, symbolizing the love for a woman, real but inaccessible in her garden set about with thorns.

Unconsummated love, love for the unattainable *princesse lointaine*, was the very essence of *l'amour courtois* of the troubadours, for which the setting was almost always an enclosed paradise garden. The twelfth-century troubadours of Provence may have been inspired in part by the growing cult of the Virgin Mary. They exalted perfect love within the strict rules of chivalry, a transposition of divine love, mystical intoxication, and ardent sensuality. Islam,

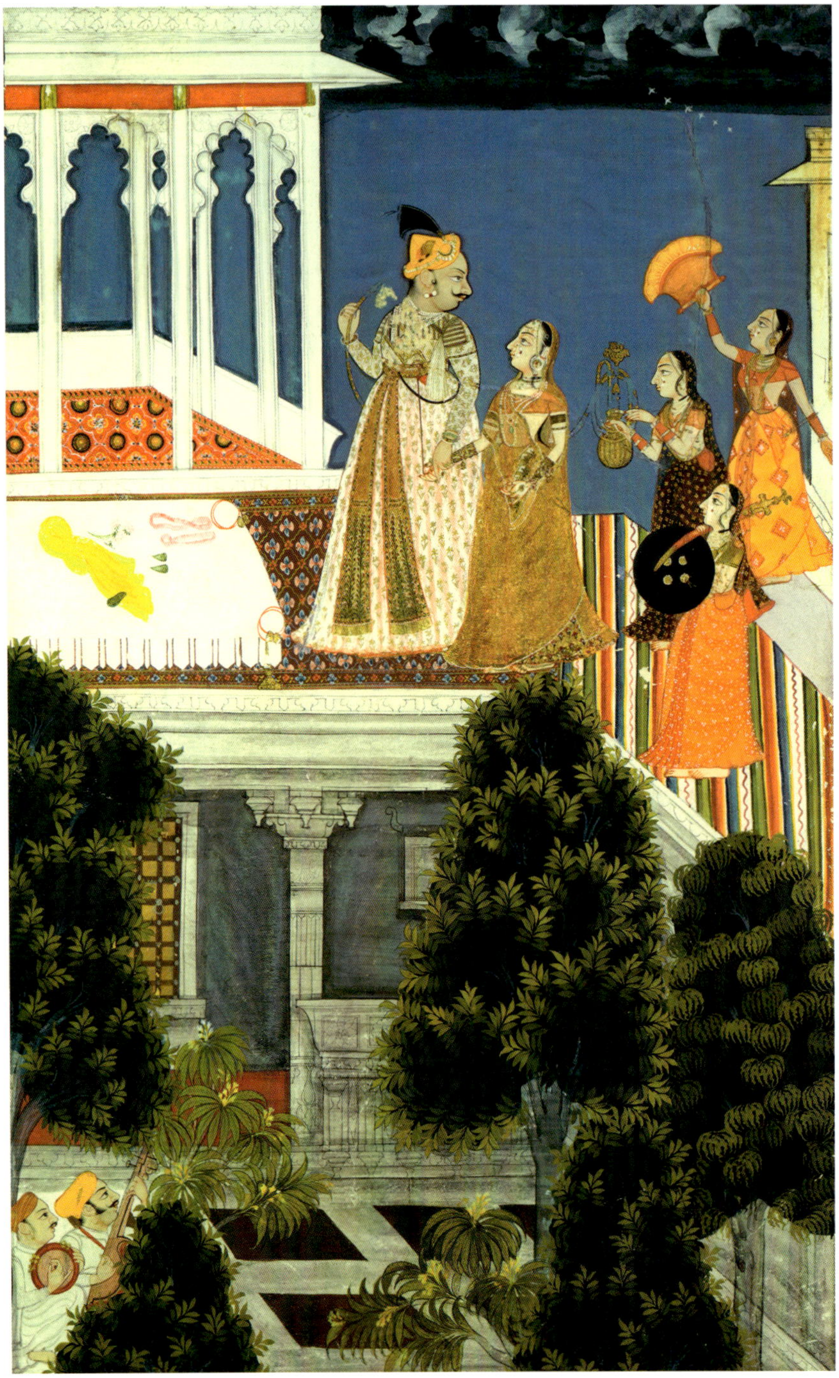

Illus. 47 *A maharana of Udaipur with ladies by a pavilion overlooking the garden atop the Zenana Mahal. Mewar, mid 18th century. Victoria and Albert Museum, London*

too, joined with Christianity in shaping the idea of *l'amour courtois*. Indeed, it is said that the art of the troubadours was brought to France by William IX of Aquitaine (1071-1126) from al Andalus or Moorish Spain. This, the westernmost outpost of Islam, was where Ibn Hazm (994-1063) wrote his *Tawq al hamama* (The Ring of the Dove) on courtly love. In the Islamic East, the Neoplatonist philosopher and physician Ibn Sina (known in the West as Avicenna) (980-1037) wrote his *Risala fi'-l 'ishq* (Treatise on Love). From the East, too, the crusaders brought to Europe not only the rose "from the land of the Saracens," but the very idea of a garden enclosed against the harsh world, where love both earthly and divine could safely find fulfilment.

Ishq, the Divine Bliss

As in the Bible, so in the Qur'an, there are scriptural warrants for regarding erotic love as an expression of divine bliss. The Qur'anic gardens of paradise are graced by "houris, cloistered in cool pavilions," "wide-eyed houris as the likeness of hidden pearls," and lovely boys or immortal youths.[68] Embroidering on these verses, the *qussas* or popular preachers of early Islam would describe paradise as a place where all the delights imaginable were to be enjoyed by the faithful: the very pleasures from which they were to abstain in this life. There they would drink wine that does not intoxicate, and enjoy the company of pure maidens or youths in a fragrant garden of surpassing beauty. Dressed in green silk and decked in precious gems, they would recline in the shade of trees amid the sound of cooling water. Caliphs and emperors, maharajas and nawabs, and their courtiers, made living gardens and palaces where they could enjoy the delights of paradise on this earth. It was for the poets, combining Qur'anic imagery and earthly joys, to elaborate these fancies into a sophisticated and subtle convention of symbols, where the imagery of gardens and wine and erotic mysticism can be read literally or metaphorically, as mundane or divine. In the Persian *ghazal*, and later in Urdu poetry of the same form, almost every line may be interpreted as *ishq-i majazi*, symbolic love, or *ishq-i haqiqi*, real love. *Ishq-i majazi* is earthly love, which – however all consuming it may seem to the *ashiq*, the lover – is only a symbol of *ishq-i haqiqi*, the real love which is the love of God.

Dante (1265-1321), heir to the troubadour tradition, does not doubt that the pure love of a man for a woman may lead him beyond the earthly paradise to heaven itself. As to Ibn Sina and Ibn Arabi before him, so to Dante too, desire was an expression of the yearning for the supreme Good. Seeing and loving Beatrice, he seemed to see the glory of God. Finally, in the great allegory of the Divine Comedy, she becomes a petal of the Mystical Rose itself, the revelation of the presence of God.

False Paradises

Dante would have been familiar not only with the erotic charge of the Song of Songs but also with the Qur'anic descriptions of paradise. He reflects both the troubadour tradition and also its rejection by those who saw the dangerous side of love, its capacity to sap the will and distract man from his higher Christian duty.

The false paradise was to become an important theme of the Renaissance. In Dante's *Commedia*, between the horrific landscapes of hell and the beauties of the earthly paradise lies Purgatory, with the Valley of the Princes. This was a *pairidaeza* of princes and rulers who were more concerned with worldly wealth than with the salvation of their immortal souls. It is an artificial paradise, though it resembles the true Eden in many ways, with the same brilliance of its flowers, the lushness of its grass, the sweetness of its mingled perfumes. It points to a revival of the rejection by Bishop Anselm and others of the garden as a sensual distraction from man's true duty. These illusory false paradises are inhabited by women who practise the black arts.

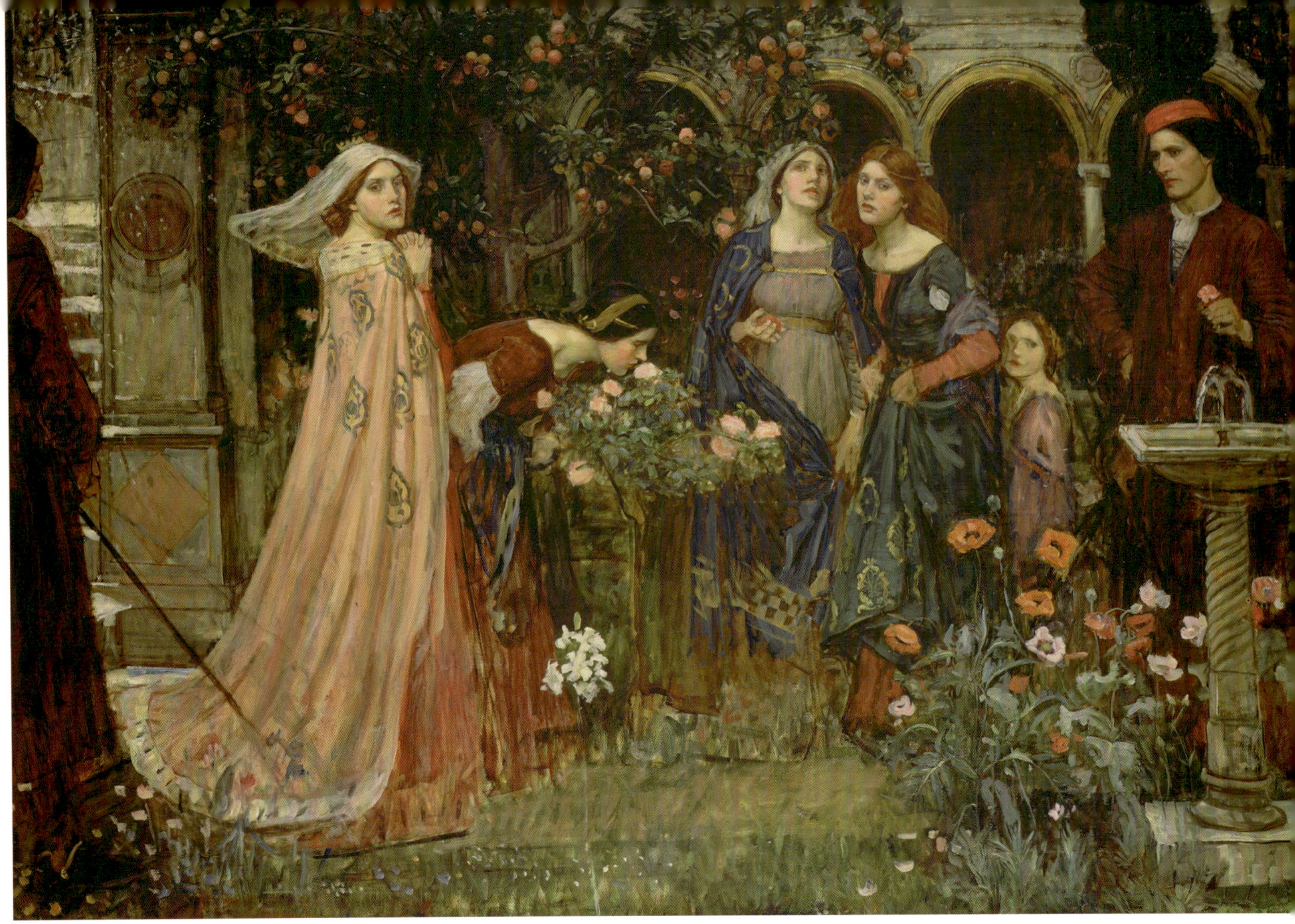

Illus.48 *John William Waterhouse (1849-1917), The Enchanted Garden, 1916-17. Lady Lever Art Gallery, National Museums Liverpool. One of the tales from the Decameron by Boccaccio, an admirer of Dante, concerns Ansaldo's pursuit of Dianora, who agrees to become his mistress if he can produce in January a garden with all the fruits and flowers of summer – which he does, with the help of a magician.*

Whereas Dante's Matilda is a descendant of Eve, Ariosto's Alcina, Tasso's Armida and Spenser's Acrasia are sorceresses, descendants of Homer's Circe, and, like their gardens, the more alluring they seem the more dangerous they are.[69] The garden of the enchantress Alcina, creator of illusion, is a conventionally beautiful place in a remote island, while the "paradiso" of the city is a Venus' bower. Both are revealed to be false paradises, and the lovely Alcina is in truth a foul hag.

Both the Renaissance epics of Dante, Ariosto and Tasso and the mediaeval allegorical poem, as well as classical sources, inspired *The Faerie Queen*, by Edmund Spenser (1552?-1599). Eclectic and allegorical, *The Faerie Queen* is a very Christian poem, with a strong note of world-weariness and of yearning for the peace of heaven. It too includes some notable false paradises, temptations to distract man from his duty. The garden of Proserpina in Book II, "goodly garnished/With hearbs and fruits. . . direfull deadly black," is a garden of Hell. It is a parody of the Garden of Eden, complete with a tree near Proserpina's bower decked with golden apples, a pagan perversion of the fruits of Eden. The culminating garden of Book II is the Bower of Bliss of Acrasia, an enchantress whose "blis is all in pleasure and delight,/Where with she makes her lovers dronken mad." This is an artificial paradise, beautiful but evil. The poet compares it with the glories of the ancient world, and claims that it even surpasses "Eden selfe, if ought with Eden mote compayre." Acrasia is not merely a witch but also a blasphemer, imitating the Earthly Paradise for demonic ends. Here branches laden with grapes, both golden and real, bow down to the hand, recalling the fruits of St Peter Damian's true Paradise, or those of *jannah* in the Islamic tradition, that proffer themselves to the hand of the righteous in the afterlife.

Book III of *The Faerie Queen* contains another garden, the Garden of Venus and Adonis; this, like the Bower of Bliss, is twice described as "paradise." Indeed, as a landscape the Garden is a traditional earthly paradise, with a mountain-top grove. Unlike Acrasia's Bower, which claims to halt time and natural decay, the Garden is a place where Time has its proper function, even though "There is continuall spring, and harvest there/Continuall, both meeting at one tyme." This is a place where man can live at peace even in his post-lapsarian condition. Spenser saw the falseness of sexual indulgence, but also believes that the senses and the spirit can coexist harmoniously; true pleasure is not incompatible with duty. In this he was close to the Neo-Platonism of the Renaissance in Italy, which, like the "good" magic of that period, was an earnest attempt to transcend the mediaeval distinction between the physical and the spiritual. The idea of love was also affected by this philosophy. Since the senses were not separate from, but part of, man's entire nature, they were an echo of the soul's response to earthly beauty, which became the symbol and image of divine beauty.

Roses for Love

The dreamy Ronsard (1524-1585), like every other poet of the Pléiade, was both influenced by Renaissance Neo-Platonism and fascinated by Petrarch. But Petrarch's love for Laura was an idealized love, and he ultimately turned from her to the Virgin Mary. Ronsard's loves in his delicate sonnets and odes, the *Amours de Cassandre*, *Amours de Marie*, and *Sonnets pour Hélène*, were more carnal than spiritual. For Ronsard, too, the rose is the symbolic flower par excellence; he was an admirer of the *Roman de la Rose*. His famous ode which begins *Mignonne, allons voir si la rose . . .*, ends with the words:

Cueillez, cueillez vostre jeunesse: Gather, gather you your youth:
Comme à ceste fleur la vieillesse As for this flower, so for you
Fera ternir vostre beauté.
Age will make your beauty fade.
A devoté of the Greeks and the Latins, he must surely have known Ausonius's poem on the roses of Paestum, which ends with the couplet:
O maid, while youth is with the rose and thee,
Pluck thou the rose: life is as swift for thee.
It was a favourite theme; thus Ronsard's younger contemporary Edmund Spenser in The Faerie Queen. Here is how he describes the Bower of Bliss:
Ah see the Virgin Rose, how sweetly shee
Doth first peepe forth with bashfull modestee . . .
Loe see soone after, how she fades, and falles away.
So passeth, in the passing of a day,
Of mortall life the leafe, the bud, the flowre,
Ne more doth flourish after first decay,
That earst was sought to decke both bed and bowre,
Of many a Ladie, and many a Paramowre;
Gather therefore the Rose, whilest yet is prime,
For soone comes age, that will her pride deflowre:
Gather the Rose of love, whilest yet is time,
Whilest loving thou mayst loved be with equall crime.

Robert Herrick (1591-1674) is more succinct in his "Counsel to Girls"

Gather ye rose-buds while ye may,
Old Time is still a-flying:
And this same flower that smiles today
Tomorrow will be dying.

The Metaphysical Poets

Herrick was a contemporary of the so-called metaphysical poets – John Donne, George Herbert, Francis Quarles, Richard Crashaw, Henry Vaughan, Thomas Traherne, Andrew Marvell (1621-1678) and others. The eroticism of the *Song of Songs*, and its imagery of the enclosed garden, lie behind many of their finest poems. Even when they were writing of divine love, they often used the language of erotic love. Love, for them, was not intrinsically evil; but like the earlier poets of the Renaissance epic, though they expressed it in very different terms, they believed that love could be pure or corrupt according as it lusted for the objects of the spirit or of the flesh.

The choice of object is a matter of will; for mankind can strive to transcend the base carnal self. Andrew Marvell's complex and subtle poem *The Garden* lies within the tradition of the *hortus conclusus*. Indeed, behind the entire poem is the imagery of the *Song of Songs*, where the erotic mirrors the spiritual life. In particular, the reposeful shade of the enclosed garden is contrasted in the opening stanza with the "short and narrow verged Shade" of the rewards – "the Palm, the Oke, or Bayes" – of worldly honour. And the garden's fruit offers itself to the passive narrator, echoing the passivity of the Bride/soul in mystical union with the Beloved. The poem also refers to Greek myth, and draws on the Hermetic doctrine that it was the separation of the original human, who partook of the nature of both male and female, into two sexes that lay at the root of mankind's unhappiness.

What wond'rous Life is this I lead!
Ripe Apples drop about my head;
The Luscious Clusters of the Vine
Upon my Mouth do crush their Wine;
The Nectaren, and curious Peach,
Into my hands themselves do reach;
Stumbling on Melons, as I pass,
Insnar'd with Flow'rs, I fall on Grass.

Mean while the Mind, from pleasure less,
Withdraws into its happiness:
The Mind, that Ocean where each kind
Does streight
Its own resemblance find;
Yet it creates, transcending these,
Far other Worlds, and other Seas;
Annihilating all that's made
To a green Thought in a green Shade.
Here at the Fountains sliding foot,
Or at some Fruit-trees mossy root,
Casting the Bodies Vest aside,
My Soul into the boughs does glide:
There like a Bird it sits, and sings,
Then whets, and combs its silver Wings;
And, till prepar'd for longer flight,
Waves in its Plumes the various Light.
Such was that happy Garden-state,
While Man there walk'd without a Mate:
After a Place so pure, and sweet,
What other Help could yet be meet!
But 'twas beyond a Mortal's share
To wander solitary there:
Two Paradises 'twere in one
To live in Paradise alone.

Islamic Mysticism

The mystics of Islam, like the heirs to the *Song of Songs*, knew that sexual imagery may invoke the dissolution of self in God. Islamic mystical poetry developed a sophisticated language of paradisal symbols in which not only the Beloved's bodily parts, but also every flower, every tree, the whole garden had its meaning. The Beloved may be God, or an earthly beloved, or both. Thus *bihisht* and *jannat* (Persian and Arabic, respectively, for the gardens of paradise) were the beloved's face; as were *gulshan* and *gulzar* (garden) and *gulistan* (rose garden). The cypress represented not only eternity, but also the beloved's slender figure. So too, more daringly, did the Tuba tree of paradise.

Without doubt some, at least, of the earthly loves expressed in this poetry would have been consummated. But much of the poetry, like that of the troubadours, sings of the unattainable Beloved, of the poet's longing for union. And the rose and the nightingale, above all, are the symbols of this yearning love. The imagery of the fleeting rose is one that crosses cultural boundaries. The rose and nightingale of Persian and Urdu poetry combine with the sentiments of Ausonius, Ronsard and Herrick in this couplet from a *ghazal* by Mir (c.1722-c.1808), one of the greatest poets of love, who knew how fleeting are the joys of this life:

Bûe gul yâ navâe bulbul thi
Umr afsôs kya shitâb gayi
(The sweet scent of the rose, the bulbul's song,
Life too, alas, how swiftly is it gone.)

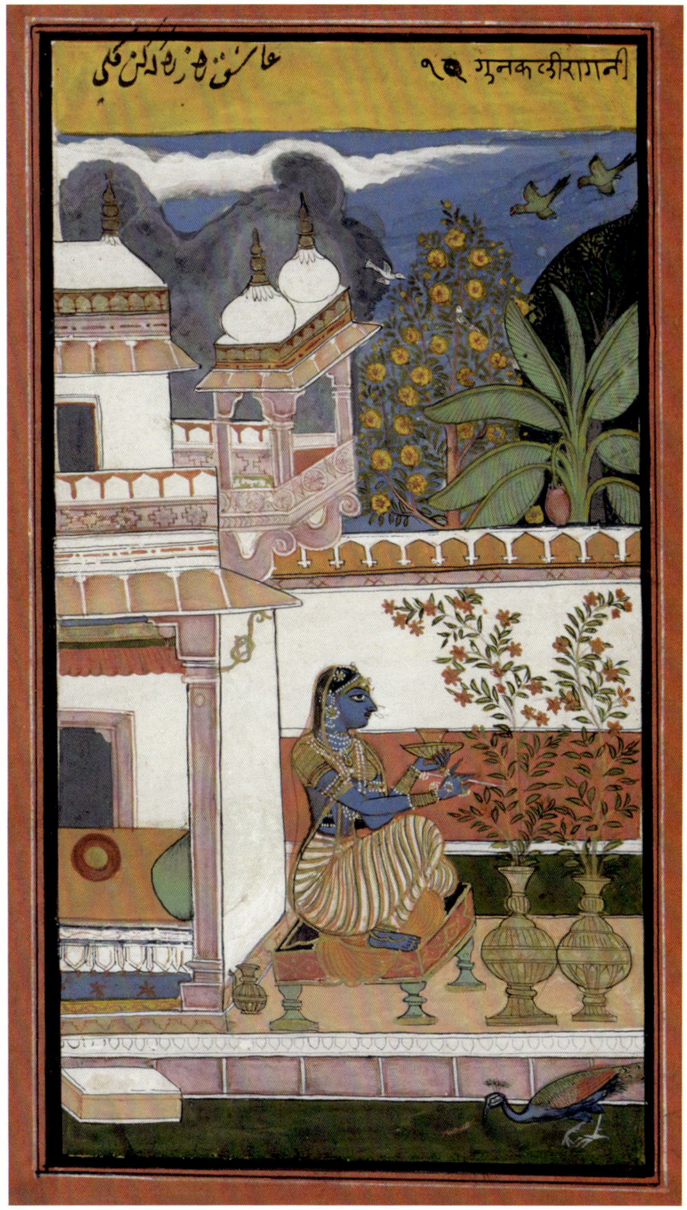

Illus. 49 *A lady tending her garden; behind the wall are a kadamba tree in flower and a banana plant. Bundi, c. 1680. Victoria & Albert Museum, London. The painting is part of a ragamala – a series of paintings that illustrate the musical modes of the ragas or raginis by depicting the activities of lovers. This scene, of a lady picking flowers in preparation for the arrival of her lover, is the traditional representation of Gunakali ragini.*

To western ears the constant repetition of the theme, the continual use of the same symbols, may seem superficial or tedious. To connoisseurs of Arabic, and above all of Persian and Urdu poetry – from poets such as Farid al-Din al Attar; the Persian poets Sa'di, Jami, Hafiz and Jalaluddin Rumi; and the Urdu poets Dard, Mir and Ghalib – the poetic and mystic power of symbols is the essence of the songs. The poet's skill in handling them draws cries of appreciation as the verses are recited. Thus Sa'di, in his *Gulistan*:

Not only the Nightingale in the Rose-bushes sings his hymn of praise,
But every Thorn itself is a voice of adoration to the Deity.

As every lover knows who ever gave or received a red rose, the association of roses with love was not broken in the Occident when men ceased to worship Aphrodite or Venus. The goddess is not so easily dismissed.

The Sacred in the Sexual

Other spiritual traditions seem quite explicitly to celebrate sexuality as one of the gifts of creation. A more refined understanding suggests that sacralized sexual relations, and in particular the technique of seminal retention, were a way to prolong life (to "gain immortality") and to transcend desire, drawing nearer to the longed-for annihilation of self. In the Daoist tradition sexual practices, combined with techniques of meditation, were seen as a way of harmonizing the energies of heaven and earth. In Indian traditions the frank images of temple architecture that so shocked some western colonists and missionaries also express the belief that the skills of love-making, properly learned and practised, act as a lightning conductor. They condense and direct the cosmic energy, represented by the two poles, the active masculine Purusha, symbolized by the *lingam* of Shiva, and the passive feminine Prakriti, its symbol the *yoni* of Shakti. The *Brihad Aranyaka Upanishad* describes the primordial Cosmic Being as "a woman and a man closely intertwined." Surely here is the origin of Plato's myth of the primordial Androgyne. It likens the ecstasy of union with the infinite Self to the sexual orgasm. With the development of tantra, sexual union was ritualized. Its ultimate objective was to achieve the beatitude of nirvana through *maithuna*, ceremonial union.

For those unwilling or unable to perfect themselves in such techniques, the garden is the ideal setting for ecstasy. The power of flowers and fragrance to create the perfect ambience for sexual activity is referred to in treatises such as the *Kama Sutra*. Young men entering society life are advised to take a house near water, surrounded by a garden. "In the garden there should be . . . a bower of creepers covered with flowers, in which a raised parterre should be made for sitting."

And wives who aim to run a harmonious household and please their husbands should grow both vegetables and sweet-scented flowers.

Clusters of various flowers such as
the trapa bispinosa, the jasmine,
the jasminum grandiflorum, the
yellow amaranth, the wild jasmine,
the tabernamontana coronaria, the
nadyaworta, the china rose and others,
should likewise be planted, together
with the fragrant grass andropogon
schaenanthus, and the fragrant root of the
plant andropogon miricatus. She should
also have seats and arbours made in the
garden, in the middle of which a well,
tank, or pool should be dug.[70]

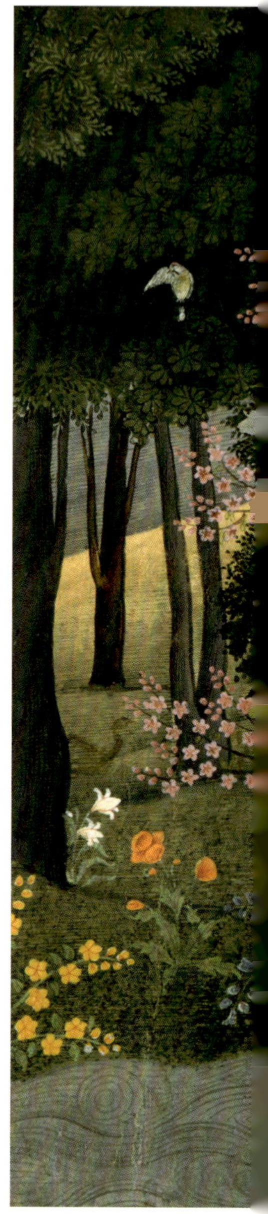

As the rose, in the western traditions, is associated with love as well as with the divine beauty, so in the Indian tradition is the lotus. Kama, the god of love, like Aphrodite's companion Eros (or Venus and Cupid, in the Roman pantheon), carries arrows – but his are tipped with lotus flowers. In *Gita Govinda*, an erotic mystic poem recounting the love affair of Krishna with Radha, his limbs are described as soft and dark as a garland of lotus flowers. The ideal of womanly beauty is the *padmini* or lotus woman, whose face is as the full moon, her limbs as fragrant as the lotus, her *yoni* like a newly-opened lotus bud.

It would be a long time before western cultures could be as frank as this about sex, and the legacy of Christian guilt ensured that that frankness, when it did emerge, was not accompanied by such reverence, or by a sense of the holiness of sexual union. Mankind cannot return to the happy state of unity, the condition of Adam before the creation of Eve – and the West remains profoundly exercised by the sense of loss this entails. The increasing

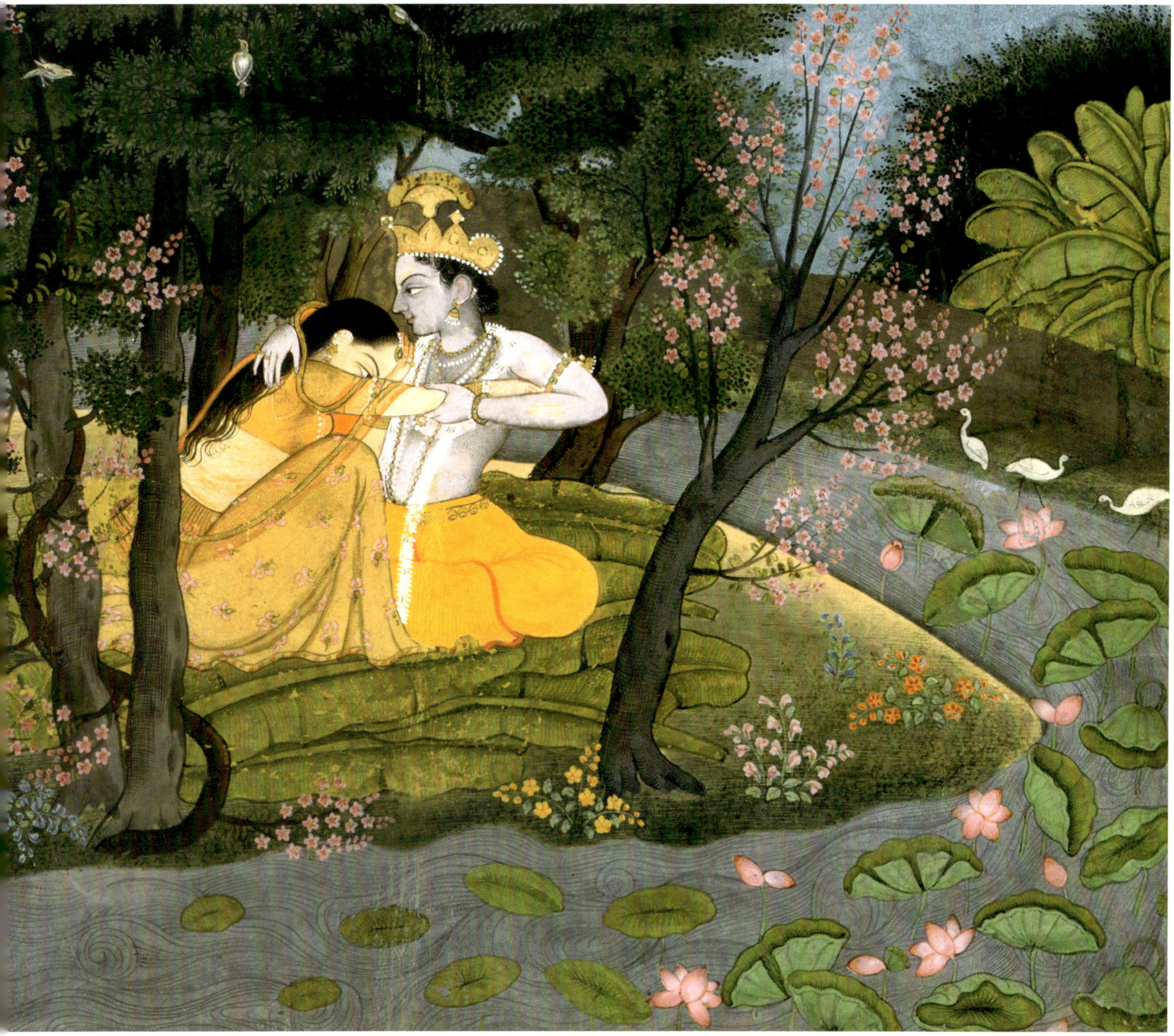

Illus. 50 *Radha and Krishna in the grove, Kangra, c. 1780. Victoria & Albert Museum, London*

dominance of Western culture, imposed or insidiously proffered and avidly embraced, over these more traditional societies, bodes ill for the future – or does it? Is the resurgence of religion that has been so often remarked on over the past few decades merely a feature of millennial ferment and *angst*\? Or – despite often taking extremist, nationalist, "fundamentalist" and anti-mystical forms – does it presage a healing, a restoration of broken links, in which the old symbols could again become invested with something of their former potency?

Epilogue

In the modern world, particularly in the West, the distant past has come to be seen as primitive. The present, almost axiomatically, is thought of as better, and the future as full of potential. With the loss of belief in a perfect and potentially recoverable past, the power of the paradise myth has been debased. The question before us is whether it is redeemable, or utterly beyond recall.

There is a growing reaction against the materialistic world view that was the background to the twentieth century, the bloodiest in world history. Increasingly, we are aware that our hubris threatens to lead us, not into a glorious future, but into disaster. Unlike the tribal myths, based on particularist readings of history, which lay behind so much of the past century's violence, the paradise myth, like all stories that embody aspects of universal human experience, is an archetypal one. The loss of its potency, its power to console and to instil hope, is the more tragic as a result. What now is our access to paradise; to that which is no longer conceived as "out there," but – as mystics have always known – lies within ourselves? For millennia these yearnings of the spirit, the dream of paradise lost, the hope of paradise to come, led men to seek to recreate on earth their image of paradise. Now, we seem lost in a void between the paradise of our origins and the paradise of the world to come.

Anatole France (1844-1924) saw the desolation that followed loss of faith, and used the language of the old symbols to express it: "We have eaten the fruits of the tree of knowledge, and are left with the taste of ashes in our mouths . . . It was sweet to believe, even in hell." But Carl G Jung (1875-1961) understood very well that faith alone, without the power of symbol, still leaves us bereft. In *The Symbolic Life*, he writes "We have no symbolic life, although we all have the greatest need for it. Only the symbolic life can express the needs of the soul." It is not easy to live without the symbols of heaven and hell, especially when we see all around us the manifest inequity of life on this earth, the suffering of the innocent and the apparent impunity of the wicked. More than ever, we need a way of recreating heaven on earth; but instead, it seems that increasingly we are replacing the Hell of the Bible or Qur'an, in which many no longer believe, with hell on earth. And the most extreme manifestation of earthly hell is the concentration camp – the death camps of World War II, the Soviet gulags, the rape and torture camps of Bosnia and Herzegovina in the 1990s. In a grotesque perversion of the idea of the enclosed garden as paradise, the unscalable barbed wire fence becomes the enclosure of a living hell.

Modern science, too, has turned many of our old certainties on their head. Einstein proved that time and space are relative, different for each of us, by demonstrating that only the speed of light is always the same. And sub-atomic physics has taught us what the mystics have always known, that there is no absolute knowledge accessible to the human mind: in the quantum revolution, physics becomes metaphysics. When dealing with the infinitely small, as with the infinitely vast, the senses fail us and only the poetic imagination will serve.

The old theologies and metaphysical speculations about the origins of the universe – was it eternal, or was it created by God at some specific past time – seem redundant, even as scientists continue to search for its origins. Orthodox, literalist religious beliefs in paradise and hell as "places" where we go after death begin to appear merely the imaginings of simple minds, when the very concepts of space and time are so radically undermined. And new research into the way the human brain works, strongly suggesting that there is no "ghost in the machine," undermines our belief in the self, the soul, as a separate entity that can survive the death of the brain.

Whether we see our passage through time as a descent from lost perfection to ever-increasing disorder, or as progress from the primitive to the ever-more advanced, change is a fundamental characteristic of our lives on this earth. Like our ancestors before us, we are on a journey of which we do not know the destination. But unlike so many of our forebears, who lived within a conceptual framework that gave them an answer, right or wrong, we now know that we do not know. How then are we to read the signposts? Can the twin notions of paradise lost and paradise to be gained, expressed through so many centuries and cultures through the prism of the garden, again serve us on our way?

Footnotes

1 Genesis Chapter II v. 8
2 Diodorus Siculus, active c. 60-30 BCE, perhaps drawing on the writings of Ctesius of Cnidus, early fourth century BCE
3 From an inscription in the temple at Karnak, in James Henry Breastead, *Ancient Records of Egypt*, 1906
4 Breasted, op.cit.
5 From the dedicatory inscription on the temple, Breastead, op.cit.
6 Harris Papyrus, from J.H. Breasted, *Ancient Records of Egypt*, Part Four, 1906
7 *Oeconomicus*, trans. H. G. Dakyns, Macmillan, 1897
8 Hesiod, *Works and Days*, translated by Hugh G. Evelyn-White, 1914
9 Ovid, *Metamorphoses* I, trans. Sir Samuel Garth, John Dryden, et al, 1717
10 Virgil, *Aeneid*, Book VI, translated by J W MacKail, 1885
11 Pindar, fr. 129 Maehler, from Francis Turner Palgrave, *Landscape in Poetry from Homer to Tennyson*, 1897
12 Robert Graves, *The Common Asphodel: collected essays on poetry, 1922-1949*, Ardent Media, 1949, 328
13 Pindar (518/517-438? BCE), *Olympian Odes*, ii.72-3, in *The Extant Odes of Pindar*, trans. Ernest Myers, 1904
14 Alexander Pope, 1688-1744: from Homer's *Odyssey*, Book VII
15 Loeb classical library, *Lyra Graeca* II, ed. and trans. J. M. Edmonds, 1927, 85
16 *Plutarch's Lives*, translated by John Langhorne D.D. and William Langhorne M.A., London, 1770
17 Plato, *Phaedo*
18 The text of Theophrastus' will is given in Diogenes Laertius' *Lives of the Philosophers*, V, 51-57
19 Horace, *Satires*, ii.6:1-4, trans. Theodore Martin (1816-1909)
20 *Purgatorio*, Canto XXVIII, 139-141, trans. H. F. Cary, 1814
21 Genesis 2, 8-10
22 Genesis 2.15-17
23 Genesis 3.24
24 Isaiah 2.2, 4
25 Isaiah 2.2, 4
26 Ezekiel 47.12
27 1 Enoch (Ethiopic Enoch), 61:12, trans. Robert Henry Charles, 1912
28 The Book of the Secrets of Enoch, Chapter 8, trans. Robert Henry Charles, 1896
29 Philo, *On the Allegory of Laws*, 1.57-58, trans. C. D. Yonge, 1854-1890
30 Revelation 22.2-3
31 Quoted in William Holden Hutton, *The Church of the Sixth Century*, 1897, 279
32 Genesis 3, 19
33 Isaiah 35.1
34 Qur'an, Sura 56, *al-Waq'ia*, the Event, 15-23 and 28-33, trans. A J Arberry
35 Genesis 1:29
36 Evelyn drafted a chapter on the history of gardens for his *Elysium Britannicum*, which he began with the Garden of Eden and the Elysian Fields.
37 *Spectator*, No. 414, 25 June 1712
38 Horace Walpole, *History of the Modern Taste in Gardening*, 1780
39 in a letter to William Mason, 10 February 1783
40 First published in Walpole's *Anecdotes of painting in England Volume 4* (1780), but written some years earlier.
41 James Thomson (1700-1748), *The Seasons (Autumn)*
42 Sima Sharma (formerly a member of the

editorial board of the quarterly journal of the India International Centre, Delhi), personal communication.

43 see Christopher Tadgell, *The History of Architecture in India: From the Dawn of Civilization to the End of the Raj*, 1990, p. 17.

44 John Watson McCrindle, *Ancient India as Described in Classical Literature*, 1901, quoted in Ray Desmond, *The European Discovery of the Indian Flora*, Oxford: 1992, p. 258. See also J W McCrindle, *Ancient India as Described by Megasthenes and Arrian*, 1877, which includes a translation of fragments of the *Indica* of Megasthenês collected by Dr Schwanbeck, 1846

45 H A Giles, *The Travels of Fa Hsien, Cambridge*: 1923; Thomas Walters (ed.) *On Yuan Chwang's Travels in India*, London: 1904-5; S. Beal, *Life of Hsuen Tsiang by the Shaman Hwvi Li*, London: 1911 – quoted in Patrick Bowe, "The Indian Gardening Tradition and the Sajjan Niwas Bagh, Udaipur," *Garden History* (Journal of the Garden History Society) Vol. 27 no.2, Winter 1999, pp. 189-205; *The Record of Buddhistic Kingdoms by Chinese Monk, Fa-Hsien*, translated and annotated by James Legge, 1886. According to Rev. H. Heras, S.J., M.A. (*Journal of the Bihar and Orissa Research Society*, Part I. Vol. XIV, 1928), the Kie-ni or Kanaka referred to by Hwui Li in his *Life of Hsuan Tsiang* was a red-flowered *Datura* or moonflower.

46 Isaiah 2, 2, 12 and 14

47 See Isaiah 2, 2, 12 and 14, 65, 2-3, 1,29; II Kings17.10-11, 16; I Kings 14.23

48 Luke, 22.39

49 Sura XCV, *At Tin*, the Fig

50 Even the Christmas tree of western Christianity may be a distant and debased echo of this primordial myth

51 Qur'an 53.13-14 trans. Muhammad Asad.

52 Wayne E Begley, "The Garden of the Taj Mahal: A Case Study of Mughal Architectural Planning and Symbolism," in James L Wescoat and Joachim Wolschker-Buhlmahn, *Mughal Gardens: Sources, Places, Representations and Prospects*, 1996, pp. 227-228.

53 Quoted in Stanley Stewart, *The Enclosed Garden: The Tradition and the Image in Seventeenth-Century Poetry*, 1966, p. 81, from *Spiritual Songs from English MSS of Fourteenth to Sixteenth Centuries*, ed. Frances M. M. Comper (London: 1936)

54 Revelations, 22:2.

55 Genesis 2:10

56 The sixth century Cosmas Indicopleustes, author of *Christian Topography*, was unsure whether the Phison was the Ganges or the Indus. Isidore of Seville (c. 560-636) wrote that "the River Ganges, which the Holy Scripture calls Phison, flows from Paradise to the realms of India."

57 From *The Apocryphal New Testament*, with translation and note by *M.R. James*, Oxford: Clarendon Press, 1924.

58 Qur'an 47:15

59 E.g. Qur'an 3:136.

60 Qur'an, Sura 6, *al An'am*, Cattle, 99, trans. A J Arberry

61 Dante, *Paradiso*, Canto XXIII, 73-5, trans. H. F. Cary, 1814

62 *Mathnawi*, I.2022

63 *Gulistan, or Rose Garden of Sa'di*, trans. E. Rehatsek, ed. M H Tasbihi, Tehran, 1988.

64 The other three were the gardens near Basra, the orchards of Damascus and the gap of Bavvan in Faris

65 Milton, *Paradise Lost*, 1.505

66 From Francis T Palgrave, *Landscape in Poetry from Homer to Tennyson*, 1897

67 Milton, *Paradise Lost*, 9.1187-89

68 See, e.g. Qur'an suras 55 and 56

69 Ludovico Ariosto's (1474-1533) *Orlando Furioso* is a fantastical and ironic poem in which one of the themes is the code of chivalry. The *Gerusalemme Liberata* of Torquato Tasso (1544-1595) pivots on the distinction between city and nature.

70 The *Kama Sutra of Vatsyayana*, trans. Richard Burton, 1883, from the chapter "On the Manner of Living of a Virtuous Woman."

Photo Credits

© The British Library Board (followed by the source/shelfmark)
illus. 13, 27, 29
illus. 15 All rights reserved

© The Trustees of the British Museum
illus. 5

© Victoria and Albert Museum, London.
illus. 40, 47, 49, 50

Photo by Frantisek Staud/www.photostaud.com
Illus.33 and 34

© The Morgan Library and Museum
illus. 39

Photo © The National Gallery, London
illus. 21

The Bridgeman Art Library
illus. 1, 2, 4, 6, 8, 9, 10, 11, 12, 15, 16, 17, 18, 20, 22, 23, 24, 25, 26, 36, 42, 45, 46, 48

Bildarchiv Preußischer Kulturbesitz
illus. 7 bpk / Alfredo Dagli Orti
illus. 41 bpk / Museum für Asiatische Kunst, SMB / Jürgen Liepe
illus. 43 bpk / SBB / Ruth Schacht

The Wellcome Library
illus. 19

Freer Gallery
illus. 30, 31, 32, 44
Freer Gallery of Art, Smithsonian Institution, Washington, D.C.: Gift of Charles Lang Freer, F1913.47, F1911.188, F1908.170
Freer Gallery of Art, Smithsonian Institution, Washington, D.C.: Gift of the Art and History Trust in honor of Ezzat-Malek Soudavar, F1998.5.6

Nelson-Atkins Museum of Art, Kansas City
illus. 3 The Nelson-Atkins Museum of Art, Kansas City, Missouri. Purchase: acquired through the Fortieth Anniversary Fund, F75-43. Photo credit: Robert Newcombe

Getty Images
illus. 35 Photo Jauder Ho / jauderho.com
illus. 38 Photo Dinodia Photos

National Museum, Delhi
illus. 28